Lecture Notes in Computer Science

Edited by G. Goos, J. Hartmanis, and J. van Leeuwen

Springer
Berlin
Heidelberg
New York
Barcelona
Hong Kong
London
Milan
Paris
Tokyo

Herwig Unger   Thomas Böhme
Armin Mikler (Eds.)

Innovative Internet Computing Systems

Second International Workshop, IICS 2002
Kühlungsborn, Germany, June 20-22, 2002
Proceedings

Springer

Series Editors

Gerhard Goos, Karlsruhe University, Germany
Juris Hartmanis, Cornell University, NY, USA
Jan van Leeuwen, Utrecht University, The Netherlands

Volume Editors

Herwig Unger
Universität Rostock, FB Informatik
18051 Rostock, Germany
E-mail: hunger@informatik.uni-rostock.de

Thomas Böhme
TU Illmenau, Institut für Mathematik
Postfach 10 05 65, 98684 Ilmenau, Germany
E-mail: tboehme@theoinfo.tu-ilmenau.de

Armin Mikler
University of North Texas
College of Art and Sciences, Department of Computer Science
76203 Denton, TX, USA
E-mail: mikler@cs.unt.edu

Cataloging-in-Publication Data applied for

Die Deutsche Bibliothek - CIP-Einheitsaufnahme

Innovative internet computing systems : second international workshop ;
proceedings / IICS 2002, Kühlungsborn, Germany, June 20 - 22, 2002. Herwig
Unger ... (ed.). - Berlin ; Heidelberg ; New York ; Barcelona ; Hong Kong ;
London ; Milan ; Paris ; Tokyo : Springer, 2002
    (Lecture notes in computer science ; Vol. 2346)
    ISBN 3-540-43790-8

CR Subject Classification (1998): C.2, D.2, F.3, H.3-4, I.2.11, K.4.3-4

ISSN 0302-9743
ISBN 3-540-43790-8 Springer-Verlag Berlin Heidelberg New York

Springer-Verlag Berlin Heidelberg New York
a member of BertelsmannSpringer Science+Business Media GmbH

http://www.springer.de

© Springer-Verlag Berlin Heidelberg 2002

Typesetting: Camera-ready by author, data conversion by Christian Grosche, Hamburg
Printed on acid-free paper   SPIN 10869985   06/3142   5 4 3 2 1 0

Preface

I²CS 2002 was the second workshop on Innovative Internet Computing Systems, a series of international workshops on system and information management for the Next Generation Internet (NGI). The workshop series commenced with I²CS 2001, which was held at the Technical University of Ilmenau. It brought together scientists whose research addressed different aspects of Internet-based and network-centric computing. This year's workshop was held in the inspiring atmosphere of the old Baltic Sea resort of Kühlungborn near Rostock (Germany).

The unprecedented pervasiveness of network access and the associated emergence of large distributed computing infrastructures have presented researchers with new challenges in Information and Web technology. The management and retrieval of web-based information, the classification of contents, and the management of web-based communities are some of the key areas addressed by some of this year's contributions. Other papers focus on the structure and retrieval of information from large distributed data bases as well as the representation of the distributed nature of information by the means of graph-theoretical models.

Like I²CS 2001, this year's workshop was organized by the Gesellschaft für Informatik (GI) in Germany to support the exchange of experiences, results, and technology in the field. The 21 papers (2 invited, 19 regular contributions) presented at the conference and in the present volume were selected from more than 30 submissions. Every submission was carefully reviewed by three members of the program committee.

We would like to thank all those who contributed to this book for their excellent work and their great cooperation. Roswitha Fengler and Katrin Erdmann deserve special gratitude for their great efforts and perfect work concerning all administrative matters of the workshop. We wish to acknowledge the substantial help provided by our sponsors: the University of Rostock and the TKK Techniker Krankenkasse Rostock.

We hope all participants enjoyed a successful workshop, made a lot of new contacts, held fruitful discussions helping to solve the actual research problems, and had a pleasant stay on the coast of the Baltic Sea. Last but not least we hope to see you again at the third I^2CS conference in 2003, which will be held in the Leipzig area in the heart of Germany.

June 2002

Herwig Unger (Chair)
Thomas Böhme (Co-chair)
Armin R. Mikler

Organization

I^2CS was organized by the Gesellschaft für Informatik (GI) in Germany.

Executive Committee

Roswitha Fengler
Katrin Erdmann

Steering Committee

Herwig Unger (Chair)
Thomas Böhme (Co-chair)
Armin R. Mikler

Program Committee

A. Brandstädt	G. Hipper	A. Pears
J. Brooke	N. Kalyaniwalla	M.A.R. Dantas
M. Bui	K. Kleese	D. Reschke
N. Deo	N. Krier	A. Ryjov
M. Dietzfelbinger	P. Kropf	M. Sommer
W. Fengler	M. Kunde	D. Tavangarian
T. Haupt	R. Liskowsky	D. Tutsch
G. Heyer	S. Lukosch	T. Ungerer

Sponsoring Institutions

University of Rostock
TKK Techniker Krankenkasse

Table of Contents

Workshop Innovative Internet Computing Systems

Invited Talk

Author Index

Living Hypertext — Web Retrieval Techniques

Ralf-Dieter Schimkat[1], Wolfgang Küchlin[1], and Frank Nestel[2]

[1] Wilhelm-Schickard Institute for Computer Science
http://www-sr.informatik.uni-tuebingen.de
Sand 13, 72074 Tübingen, Germany
{schimkat,kuechlin}@informatik.uni-tuebingen.de
[2] INA-Schaeffler KG
Industriestrasse 1–3, 91074 Herzogenaurach, Germany
Frank.Nestel@de.ina.com

Abstract. In this paper, we present a document metaphor called *Living Documents* for accessing and searching for digital documents in modern distributed information systems. Our approach is based upon a fine-grained document concept which glues computational services, data and meta data together. Viewing documents as micro servers is particularly well suited in environments where the document's content is changing continuously and frequently. Based on a case study of an existing state-of-the-art Web application, we show how to transform database-centric information systems into a hypertext of inter-linked *Living Documents*. We also discuss how to effectively use traditional as well as Web information retrieval techniques, namely topic distillation, in such hypertext environment. In particular, an extended version of Kleinberg's [11] algorithm is presented.

1 Introduction

It is generally agreed upon that the major task in information retrieval is to find relevant documents for a given query [9]. A document is a collection of digital information ranging from plain text files, data-related meta attributes to multi-media documents. Clearly a conceptual model of information retrieval dealing with text or multi-media documents should integrate different views on documents. Agosti et al. [1] point out that one of several differences in traditional information retrieval and information retrieval on the Web is the different kind of management of the collection of documents. In fact the web is a virtual collection since a real collection stored at one particular location such as one single database would be unmanageable.

In contrast to the Web, traditional information system design is about documents which are made persistent in a digital document archive, but their attributes (meta data) are kept in databases. Even virtual documents missing any digital content can be seen as an aggregation of their attributes. This leads to several potential drawbacks in classically designed information systems: (i) the specification of document attributes is bound to the database schema and is a priori determined at the time the database schema is set up. (ii) Furthermore,

H. Unger, T. Böhme, and A. Mikler (Eds.): I²CS 2002, LNCS 2346, pp. 1–14, 2002.

the static specification restricts a document's life cycle. For example, in most cases it is hard to add new kinds of meta data to the document's collection at run time.

Our goal is to provide a document metaphor and an implementation respectively which can be used in traditional as well as in Web information systems. Our approach is characterized by transforming documents into active containers managing their content and meta data in an uniform and extensible manner.

The main contributions of this paper are: (i) Introduction to a new document metaphor called *Living Documents*. (ii) Description of a complete implementation path of *Living Documents* based on a case study of a contemporary web information system. We centered our implementation around the concepts of mobile agents and general data description languages based on XML. (iii) We show how to deploy three different kinds of information retrieval techniques in *Living Documents*. In particular, we describe how to use state-of-the-art web information retrieval techniques as topic distillation within a web of inter-linked *Living Documents*. Finally, we present an extension of a well-known algorithm for the analysis of connectivity graphs in hypertext environments.

2   Living Documents

First, we give an introduction to the concept of *Living Documents*[3] from an abstract point of view neglecting any implementation details. In the next section we show an implementation path for *Living Documents*.

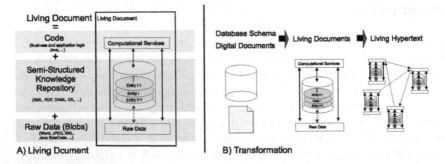

Fig. 1. A) Components of a *Living Document*. A *Living Document* is divided into three sections: *Raw Data* carries the document to manage, *Semi-Structured Data* contains all meta data about the managed documents, and the *Code* section keeps the computational services for accessing a *LD* and processing incoming requests (i.e. queries). B) Digital Documents are turned into *Living Documents*. *Living Documents* form a hypertext by keeping links similar to hypertext links to each other

---

[3] Home page of *Living Documents* at http://www.living-documents.org.

2.1   Towards a Micro Server Architecture

A *Living Document* (*LD*) is a logical and physical unit consisting of three parts, as depicted in Figure 1A:

1. code
2. semi-structured knowledge repository
3. raw data

CompServices are essentially *code* fragments which provide several facilities, such as access and query capabilities or general application services. The code fragments determine the degree of activities of a *LD* ranging from passive documents which are enriched with some arbitrary application logic to proactive documents. A proactive *LD* initiates complex tasks, discovers new services for instance and is more than just a reactive component. By deploying *LD*s the distinction between documents and applications blurs, because documents can contain application logic.

The *knowledge repository* of a *LD* provides facilities to store and retrieve information related to the document (raw data section) or to the whole *LD* itself. Each document has its own knowledge repository. Each knowledge repository is accessed through the code part. Basically a knowledge repository contains a set of *meta data* about the document itself. Each meta data is referred to as a document state information. A set of document state information builds a so-called document state report (DSR) which contains history-related information about who has accessed the document or when the document's attributes have been modified. In addition, it contains helpful links to other *LD*s which have some kind of relationship. Basically, a knowledge repository serves as an uniform access point for searching any kind of document-related meta data.

Each DSR is encoded as a semi-structured XML document according to the *SpectoML* [16]. Following an XML-based [21] implementation, the generation of a DSR is accomplished in an uniform way which favors neither a particular data format nor the use of special programming or scripting languages. The use of XML as the primary data format for document state information enables a DSR with query capabilities, such as the execution of structured queries to each document state information. Therefore, a DSR builds an XML-based knowledge repository which holds all relevant information about the entire document life cycle.

The *raw data* part can contain any information encoded as a digital document such as a word processing document, a music file or even serialized application code. Note that according to the definition given above, a *LD* does not need to have a real-world document contained in the raw data part. Thus, a *LD* solely consisting of computational logic and a knowledge repository is a well-defined *LD*.

Why is a *LD* called *living*? A *LD* is alive with respect to two key properties: First, implementing *LD*s as mobile agents they can move among nodes of a computer network, such as the Internet. That perfectly fits the notion of an autonomous and mobile entity pursuing its dedicated goals. Secondly, the ability to store and remove arbitrary artifacts into the knowledge repository changes the documents content naturally. It increases and decreases over time depending on the application domain and the environmental context the respective *LD* resides in. Even the raw data may evolve if reflected appropriately in the knowledge repository.

3   Case Study: Information Retrieval Using *Living Documents*

3.1   Case Study

The web-enabled n-tier client-server information system *Paperbase* serves as our motivating example. Its n-tier client-server architecture is typical for contemporary Web-enabled digital library and information systems. *Paperbase*[4] allows the creation of individual information workspaces using the Web. Users can easily create and manage their own workspace containing various media such as HTML, PDF, ASCII, or Office documents. The rationale behind *Paperbase* is to provide personal workspaces for users independent of their current physical location. Furthermore, they can easily share sub sets of their workspace among each other and collaborate.

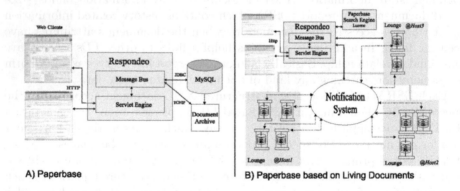

A) Paperbase   B) Paperbase based on Living Documents

Fig. 2. A) Overview of the n-tier client-server architecture of *Paperbase*. B) Architectural overview of *PaperbaseLD* based on *Living Documents*

As depicted in Figure 2A, users issue requests over the Web which are forwarded to the application server *Respondeo* introduced in [17]. *Respondeo*'s message bus mediates incoming user requests to the requested back end tier. In the case of *Paperbase* the back end tier solely consists of one database which stores all information about the documents' attributes based on a relational

---

[4] *Paperbase* is developed at the department of the University of Tübingen. It currently contains about 1500 documents. See http://www-sr.informatik.uni-tuebingen.de/~schimkat/pb for further information about *Paperbase*.

database schema. Note, that the document's content itself is stored separately in a so-called digital document archive. Only a link to the archive is kept in the relational database.

3.2 Implementing *Living Documents*

Based on the n-tier client-server Web information system *Paperbase* described in Section 3.1, we designed and implemented *Paperbase* differently (*PaperbaseLD*) using the concept of *Living Documents* which act as micro servers for documents, as described in Section 2.

Computational Services. As defined in Section 2.1 each *LD* contains a set of computational services. Within *PaperbaseLD* an agent is the key abstraction for managing various computational services for a *LD*. It provides services for

- accessing the *LD*'s knowledge repository and raw data part
- querying the *LD*'s knowledge repository
- viewing the content of knowledge repository encoded as an XML document
- viewing the content *LD*'s raw data part.

We enriched *LD*s with mobility capabilities to take their location actively into account as argued in [19]. Therefore, we integrated *LD*s into the mobile agent framework *Okeanos* [15,16]. *LD*s communicate and interact by exchanging messages in KQML (Knowledge Query Manipulation Language) [8]. In *PaperbaseLD* each "agentified" *LD* can dynamically reconfigure its computational services and add new services at run time. Each service and *LD*, respectively, is implemented in Java.

Knowledge Repository. As stated in Section 2.1, a knowledge repository contains a set of meta data or document state information which builds a DSR. In *PaperbaseLD* we encoded each DSR as a semi-structured XML document. Following an XML-based implementation, the generation of DSR is accomplished in an uniform way which neither does favor a particular data format nor the use of special programming or scripting languages.

Generally, each document state information belongs to a particular type of document descriptions. Within *PaperbaseLD* the meaning of a type is encoded as XML as well and kept separately from the document state information itself. Thus, a document state information contained in the *LD*'s knowledge repository is an instance of a particular type of a document description. The design rationale behind the separation of the actual document state information (syntax) and its meaning (semantic) is similar to the managing of semantically enriched XML documents in the semantic Web research community. However, from an implementation point of view we currently use a much simpler XML-based scheme to describe the meaning of document state information than the one proposed by the semantic web community - Resource Description Framework (RDF) [20]

In *PaperbaseLD* we currently defined several types of document state information, such as (i) access-related information about who is accessing the document with respect to time and location of the requesting document; (ii) history-related information about current and old locations of the mobile *LD*; (iii) the mapping of the relational database schema to document state information entries in the knowledge repository. This mapping is necessary due to the goal to provide at least similar retrieval facilities in *PaperbaseLD* as in *Paperbase*. We simply map each attribute in the relational schema which is directly related to the *LD* to a triple

$$DatabaseProperty = \langle type, name, value \rangle \,,$$

where *type* is an unique schema descriptor for *PaperbaseLD*, *name* is a string built from the table and column name of the relational database of *Paperbase*, and *value* is the value as contained in the relational database system of *Paperbase*.

Raw Data Part. As specified in Section 2.1 the *LD*'s raw data part (Blob) can contain any information encoded as a digital document. From an implementation point of view, we use in *PaperbaseLD* various kinds of documents such as Office documents, HTML pages, PDF documents, and several other data formats.

3.3   Distributed Information Retrieval Using *Living Documents*

Figure 2B gives an architectural overview of *PaperbaseLD* using *LD*s. The main application components of *PaperbaseLD* are the application server *Respondeo*, a notification system called *Siena*[5], and several distributed so-called *Okeanos Lounges*. Note that *PaperbaseLD* does not have any database system at the back end tier in contrast to the architecture of *Paperbase*. The relational schema is stored together with its instances in the *LD*s' knowledge repository, as described in Section 3.2. Within *PaperbaseLD Respondeo* neither holds any application logic nor manages any documents. It solely serves as a gateway for interfacing to the Web and users respectively. *Siena* is used as a global notification middleware system where each *LD* publishes information and subscribes for document-related notifications. *Siena* uses the publish/subscribe communication paradigm as opposed to the rigid client-server request/response style. By deploying publish/subscribe, sender and receiver of notifications are decoupled from each other which leads in the case of *PaperbaseLD* to a loosely coupled coordination of all *LD*s. Finally, a *Lounge* is the abstraction used in the *Okeanos* framework for an agent environment hosting several mobile agents. Inter-connected *Lounges* in *Okeanos* allow agents to move to remote destinations directly.

     Each document formerly stored in the document archive is – within *PaperbaseLD* – transformed into a *LD* which manages its knowledge repository

---

[5] For design and implementation details see the *Siena* home page at `http://www.cs.colorado.edu/~carzanig/siena/index.html`.

and raw data part. For illustration purposes in Figure 2B there are only three *Lounges* hosting 9 *LDs* altogether. If a user is requesting or searching for some *LDs* through the Web, it is up to each *LD* to respond to the request adequately.

In order to use *Living Documents* in a Web-like environment, each *LD* is able to generate dynamically an HTML view of its knowledge repository and document content. By this, we turned *LDs* into ordinary HTML pages. Furthermore, the generated HTML view depends on the actual content of and the query sent to the knowledge repository. Thus arbitrary HTML views of the same *LD* can be generated. By turning ordinary documents into *LDs* which are inter-linked with each other, a so-called *Living Hypertext* is established, as illustrated in Figure 1B. Generally, a *Living Hypertext* is a hypertext which consists of *LDs*.

Within *PaperbaseLD* each incoming request or notification is mediated through the computational services of a *LD*. Usually the handling of requests involves two different kinds of interactions between the services at the code part and the rest of a *LD*: First, the knowledge repository is contacted to determine if incoming requests can and should be handled. In addition, some accounting information is requested from the knowledge repository. Then, depending on the type of incoming request the services contact the raw data part for further and up-to-date information about the actual content of the document. For example, in order to perform a full-text search it is necessary not only to search for particular document state information stored in the knowledge repository, but also to search the content of the document itself.

In *PaperbaseLD* a request or search can be performed in two ways:

LD Compliant Searching. An incoming search request is forwarded by the message bus of *Respondeo* to a designated *Lounge* which serves as an entry point into the network of *LDs*, as shown in Figure 2 (*Lounge* at *host3*). Basically any *Lounge* can play this kind of role. Then the request is turned into a *LD*, a so-called *LDSearch*. A *LDSearch* is a special kind of *LD* which only contains some processing logic and document state information about the type and content of the search request including the query itself. Then *LDSearch* interacts with its environment and dynamically determines available *Lounges* and their hosted *LDs* respectively. Generally, a *LDSearch* is a mobile *LD* which moves among the network of *LDs* and interacts with them locally. After the search process is completed, the results are returned to *Respondeo* and the user. After the search results have been returned, a *LDSearch* turns into an ordinary *LD* which just behaves as a regular *LD*. The hit list of documents retrieved by the original *LDSearch* are now part of the transformed *LD*'s raw data part. The uniform handling of search requests and ordinary *LDs* opens up several interesting possibilities in the area of information retrieval. Using *LDSearch* as a cached version of document hit lists can contribute to an improved distributed search performance within *PaperbaseLD*. Additionally, users or other *LDs* can make use of the knowledge about the search process contained in a *LDSearch*'s knowledge repository and document hit list. For performance reasons a search request can either be accomplished by a single *LDSearch* traveling around the network of

*LD*s or by creating a number of *LDSearch* clones to build a swarm to interact with remote *LD*s faster.

Cooperative Searching. By using the cooperative searching approach each micro server (*LD*) publishes information about its managed document to the notification system *Siena*. Each micro server also subscribes for notifications which are related to its managed document. As far as there is related information in *Siena* available, the interested micro servers are notified asynchronously according to the publish/subscribe communication paradigm used in *Siena*.

*LD*s publish primarily subsets of their document state information contained in the knowledge repository. For example, information about the type and description of the managed document is published to the notification system. Incoming user requests are handled by *Respondeo* which simply publishes user requests into *Siena*.

The cooperative search approach in *PaperbaseLD* only loosely couples *LD*s. Thus the content-based routing of notifications in *Siena* provides a cooperation mechanism which takes the independent and self-sufficient nature of micro servers adequately into account.

4 Topic Distillation with *Living Documents*

According to [13] "end users want to achieve their goals with a minimum of cognitive load and a maximum of enjoyment". Generally, searching for information which is stored in databases assumes that the user is familiar with and knows about the semantics of the respective database schema: What kinds of attributes exist? What are the relationships and dependencies between them ? The two search approaches described in Section 3.3 follow this kind of traditional, database-centered information retrieval approach. Note that even the cooperative search approach to *Living Documents* assumes knowledge about the underlying meta data scheme. In this section, we describe a third information retrieval approach to *Living Documents* which is used in the Web research community to search for relevant information on the Web - topic distillation. Topic distillation is the process of finding quality documents on a query topic [2]. It addresses the problem to distill a small number of high-quality documents that are most representative to a given broad topic. The goal in topic distillation is not to index, search or classify all the documents that are possibly relevant to a topic, but only the most authoritative information on the requested subject. In hypertext environments such as the web, a topic of a query can be found not only by analyzing the keywords of the query and the content of the retrieved documents, but also by taking the hypertext link structure into account.

Another key observation in large and dynamically changing hypertext environments is that (i) the preprocessing of documents including its content and link structure is not feasible because the number of documents might be too high. (ii) Furthermore, the hypertext structure might change continuously.

Within *PaperbaseLD* we created a hypertext of inter-linked *Living Documents*. Generally, there are two types of links contained in a *Living Document*: (i) A link in the raw data part is a so-called *original link*. For example, an ordinary web page which is turned into a *Living Document* keeps all its web links in its original HTML source. In addition (ii) there are so-called *meta links* between *Living Documents* which are stored as an entry in the *Living Document*'s knowledge repository. For example, each *Living Document* publishes its database mapping scheme (see Section 3.2) into *Siena*. Then all related *Living Documents* which share the same database attributes keep a meta link to each other in their knowledge repositories. Each link type is an additional source of information which can improve the retrieval process to find high-quality documents.

In the following we describe how to deploy topic distillation in a dynamic environment such as a hypertext of inter-linked *Living Documents* to find high-quality documents. Note, by turning digital documents into *Living Documents* the conceptual border between traditional database-centric information systems and the Web vanishes: A *Living Document* can play several roles depending on its current environment and context. In a Web-like environment it provides a dynamically generated HTML representation of its managed digital documents which makes it possible to deploy all the Web infrastructure such as search engines (e.g. Google, AltaVista). However, in a traditional environmental setting, as described in Section 3.1, it provides the same retrieval facilities as ordinary Client-Server systems.

The search engine *Smider* [14] was originally derived for topic distillation on the internet. It has been inspired mainly by three different ideas: First, it explores hypertext link structures to identify topic-related communities on the internet which is inspired by Kleinberg's work [11]. Second, the idea of selective spidering to answer a specific query [5]. Third, *Smider* incorporated the concept of focused crawling [4]: crawling the "best" web pages first. The focused approach is currently most prominently used by Google.

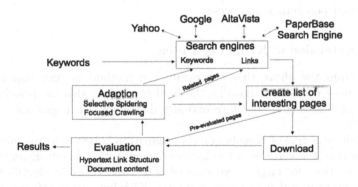

Fig. 3. Overview of *Smider*'s evaluation mechanism

4.1 *Smider* - The Principal Procedure

Smider is implemented in Java and is based on a multithreaded system architecture. While *Smider* is running it maintains a single priority queue of pages to be visited. The principal procedure of *Smider* to search for interesting documents related to given keywords, as depicted in Figure 3, is centered around an iterative evaluation process:

- *Smider* starts by queuing up few search engines as entry points to its search. This start set of documents contains either ordinary Web pages or *Living Documents* depending on the kind of search engine which has been contacted[6]. However, in our experiments we always used the *Paperbase* search engine as the primary search engine for *Living Documents*.
- Then it starts by spawning several spidering threads. From now on every spidering thread performs the following actions repeatedly: Get the most interesting page from the queue, retrieve it and feed links which have been found to *Smider*'s evaluation mechanism.
- After a certain number of documents (pages) have been retrieved, another thread starts which continuously evaluates all pages according to an algorithm which is an extension to Kleinbergs algorithm [11]. Our evaluation algorithm is described in detail in Section 4.2.

The concurrency of the evaluation and the spidering causes massive feedback within *Smider*: The actual priority of pages to be spidered is derived from their (preliminary) evaluation and of course the actual retrieval of pages changes the link structure which is known and changes the outcome of the next iteration of the evaluation process. This makes *Smider* fairly flexible, all kinds of *search engine pages* (e.g. ask Altavista for links, ask Google for next 10 links), *normal web pages* and *link resources* (e.g. Altavista *link : u* searches) are all held within that one queue and compete for getting retrieved next. There is no fixed schedule and the search for different topics might retrieve pages of above three types in fairly different percentage and order.

4.2 An Extension of Kleinberg's Idea

It follows from the above that the evaluation method is very important for *Smider*. It does not only determine the final result but also the priorization of pages during search and therefore actually decides which pages are visited in which order.

The basic principle of Kleinberg's [11] algorithm is based on the matrix representation H of the vertices of the hypertext connection graph. Essentially one performs iterations for large eigenvalues of HH^T and $H^T H$ to identify two special eigenvectors a and h of those matrices. Kleinberg demonstrates that the relative value of the entries of those eigenvectors yield good evaluation of the

---

[6] To be more precise, *Smider* uses the dynamically generated HTML representation of a *Living Document*.

quality as an authority or a hub of the corresponding page. Whereas authorities are pages considered relevant to the topic and hubs are pages which contain good links leading to a topic. Kleinberg's basic procedure has reasonable convergence and stability properties which is well-known in numerical mathematics.

On the other hand already Kleinberg and many others observed that the basic procedure is not perfect in practice. Therefore various modifications of the basic procedure already have been described in literature (e.g. [3]). Due to it's internal feedback *Smider* proved to be even more sensitive to its evaluation than Kleinberg's initial method, where the number of considered pages was found by a very statical method. For example, once a search run of *Smider* has been started investigating "blood fat", and somehow it surfed into "health and sports food", ending up with pages on "vitamin pills". Though this behavior somehow mimics an unconcentrated human server it is certainly not wanted. Therefore *Smider* uses some careful modifications to Kleinberg's basic principle.

A well known modification is to replace the matrix H by a weighted matrix to allow a notion of strong and weak links. *Smider* uses the type of link and the how often keywords appear in the text surrounding the link as a measure for the link strength[7].

Another problem due to *Smider*'s massive feedback is the "early valley", i.e. *Smider* can get stuck in a early good community not finding its way out. To help avoiding this *Smider* damps down the the eigenvalue iteration to slow down the convergence rate.

To help *Smider* to stay closer to its initial theme, it employs some statical analysis of the text found in pages, counting occurrences of keywords (that is what the first internet search engines used as their only criteria). These statical scores are added to the scores in every iteration step. Mathematically this turns the eigenvalue iteration into an iterative procedure to solve a certain linear system. Practically, the added score often creates only small disturbances of the eigenvalue problem.

More problems are due to wild anomalies of linking in the internet: There are pages with thousands of links which would receive a good Kleinberg score on a wide range of search topics. On the other hand sometimes links of pages go to sponsors, friends or colleagues and do not really represent a valuable thematic link. To cope with that *Smider* uses a non linear weighting to the summation in the iterative procedure. The weight for a link depends on a link's total contribution to the final value. The lowest contributing links are effectively weighted down to zero, while more contributing links are weighted higher, but the highest ones receive only medium weights.

From a pure mathematical point *Smider*'s search changes the dimension of the considered problem each time a new page has been found. Therefore every iteration step is done for a different mathematical problem. But fixing that is merely a notational inconvenience.

---

[7] Due to space limitations we omit the respective mathematical formulas and proofs.

4.3   Two Different Views on *Smider*

Aside from the technical motivations above, *Smider* can be looked at from a very different perspective. Consider someone who has to find information about a specific topic on the internet, what would he do?

- He would use his favorite search engines, if he is very careful he would use more than one search engine.
- While searching on engines he would most likely start to explore some of the better looking links he got only returning to the search engines, when he has read all the stuff on the followed links.
- In some cases he'd rather follow the most interesting links on found pages than look at more search engines and he would base that decision on his own (only partially conscious) evaluation of the worth of the resources he has already seen.

This is, *Smider* mimics a human surfer. Obviously it is not as smart as a human, but it can surf much faster than a human can. Although first designed for the World Wide Web, it turns out that *Smider* is a good tool in the environment of *Living Documents* for both generating high quality answers to user queries and structuring a repository into thematic categories. In both cases *Smider* profits from the highly linked structure of *Living Document*. A slight change to *Smider* could even allow it to become a *Living Document* itself: A *Living Document* which dynamically adapts it's evaluation to it's changing environment.

5   Related Work

Generally, database systems are characterized by the duality of managing meta data and content. Defining a data schema puts the documents content in direct relationship to the corresponding schema. One of the goals of *Living Documents* is to create dynamic documents without using predefined taxonomies and database schema. *Living Documents* provide a means to handle both meta data (schema) and content in an extensible and evolving manner. *Living Documents* do not provide any advanced database management facilities per se such as a distributed transaction management. However, they might be implemented on top of *Living Documents*. In this respect, they serve as a general middleware layer for information systems in decentralized computer networks as opposed to performance optimized digital document stores for distributed, but centralized, data-intensive applications.

Topic distillation [11,2,3] is an information retrieval technique which is primarily used in the Web to search for topic-related Web pages. Our approach of *Living Documents* tries to apply and extend this promising technique to a more general document metaphor than simple HTML pages.

Similar to the *Living Documents* approach, the *Placeless* [7,6] document model makes a strict separation between document content, document properties, and document storage. Document properties are directly assigned to documents, rather than with document locations. This means that documents retain their properties even when they are moved from one place to another. Properties can be specific to individual document consumers. Both *Placeless* and *Living Documents* provide uniform access to meta information of documents. Depending on the document consumer (provider) each document property can be viewed at differently. Therefore, the ability of generating different and complex views based on an uniform document properties model is a key factor in the design of *Placeless* and *Living Documents*.

Closely related to Living Hypertexts is the idea of so-called Intensional Hypertexts [18,12] which views documents as active entities embedded in living and continuously changing environmental contexts. Schraeffel et al. propose to extend the traditional, static document metaphor which sees documents primarily as passive containers for digital content. Instead a document itself should be able to provide several distinct versions of its own depending on the actual context an intensional document is currently used in. Intensional documents use so-called Context Memories to store and retrieve environmental contexts, as opposed to the knowledge repository approach deployed in *Living Documents*.

6 Conclusion

In this paper, we have presented the concept of Living Documents which act as self-sufficient and living micro servers for documents in document-centric information systems. *Living Documents* provide a basis for future information systems to effectively deploy traditional as well as Web information retrieval techniques uniformly. Our future work will focus on a thorough formalization of *Living Documents* and further improvements of our initial implementation. We will also incorporate information retrieval techniques based on logical inference mechanisms discussed in our previous work [10] into *Living Documents*.

References

1. M. Agosti and M. Melucci. Information retrieval on the web. In M. Agosti, F. Crestani, and G. Pasi, editors, *Lectures on Information Retrieval of the Third European Summer-School, ESSIR 2000, Revised Lectures*, volume 1980, pages 242–285, Varenna, Italy, September 2000. Springer LNCS.
2. K. Bharat and M.R. Henzinger. Improved algorithms for topic distillation in a hyperlinked environment. In *Proceedings of the 21st annual international ACM SIGIR conference Research and Development in Information Retrieval*, pages 104–111, Melbourne, Australia, 1998.
3. S. Chakrabarti, B. Dom, D. Gibson, J. Kleinberg, P. Raghavan, and S. Rajagopalan. Automatic resource list compilation by analyzing hyperlink structure and associated text. In *Proceedings of the 7th International World Wide Web Conference*, 1998.
4. S. Chakrabarti, M. van den Berg, and B. Dom. Focused crawling: A new approach to topic-specific web resource discovery. In *8th World Wide Web Conference*, Toronto, May 1999.
5. J. Cho, H. García-Molina, and L. Page. Efficient crawling through URL ordering. *Computer Networks and ISDN Systems*, 30(1–7):161–172, 1998.

6. P. Dourish, W.K. Edwards, A. LaMarca, and M. Salisbury. Using properties for uniform interaction in the Presto document system. In *Proceedings of the 12th annual ACM symposium on User interface software and technology*, Asheville, North Carolina, USA, 1999.
7. W.K. Edwards and A. LaMarca. Balancing generality and specificity in document management systems. In *Proceedings of the 7th IFIP Conference on Human-Computer Interaction (Interact'99)*, Edinburgh, Scotland, aug 1999.
8. T. Finn, Y. Labrou, and J. Mayfield. KQML as an Agent Communication Language. In J.M. Bradshaw, editor, *Software Agents*, pages 291–316. MIT Press, 1997.
9. N. Fuhr. Models in information retrieval. In M. Agosti, F. Crestani, and G. Pasi, editors, *Lectures on Information Retrieval of the Third European Summer-School, ESSIR 2000, Revised Lectures*, volume 1980, pages 21–50, Varenna, Italy, September 2000. Springer LNCS.
10. B.D. Heumesser and R.-D. Schimkat. Deduction on XML documents: A case study. In *Proceedings of the 14th International Conference of Applications of Prolog (INAP 2001)*, pages 20–29, Tokyo, Japan, November 2001.
11. J.M. Kleinberg. Authoritative sources in a hyperlinked environment. *Journal of the ACM*, 46(5):604–632, 1999.
12. P. Kropf and J. Plaice. Intensional objects. In M. Gergatsoulis and P. Rondogiannis, editors, *12th International Symposium on Languages for Intensional Programming*, pages 180–187, Athens, Greece, 1999.
13. G. Marchionini. Interfaces for end-user information seeking. *Journal of the American Society for Information Science*, 43(2):156–163, 1992.
14. F. Nestel. *Smider - Automatic resource compiling on the Web.* http://frank.spieleck.de/metasuch, February 2001.
15. R.-D. Schimkat, W. Blochinger, C. Sinz, M. Friedrich, and W. Küchlin. A service-based agent framework for distributed symbolic computation. In *Proceedings of the 8th International Conference on High Performance Computing and Networking Europe (HPCN 2000)*, volume 1823, pages 644–656, Amsterdam, Netherlands, May 2000. Springer LNCS.
16. R.-D. Schimkat, M. Friedrich, and W. Küchlin. Deploying distributed state information in mobile agents systems. In C. Batini, F. Giunchiglia, P. Giorgini, and M. Mecella, editors, *Proceedings 9th International Conference on Cooperative Information Systems (CoopIS 2001)*, volume 2172, pages 80–94, Trento, Italy, September 2001. Springer LNCS.
17. R.-D. Schimkat, S. Müller, W. Küchlin, and R. Krautter. A lightweight, message-oriented application server for the WWW. In J. Carroll, E. Damiani, H. Haddad, and D. Oppenheim, editors, *Proceedings of the 15th ACM Symposium on Applied Computing (SAC 2000)*, pages 934–941, Como, Italy, March 2000. ACM Press.
18. M.C. Schraefel, B. Mancilla, and J. Plaice. Intensional hypertext. In M. Gergatsoulis and P. Rondogiannis, editors, *Intensional Programming II*, pages 40–54, Singapore, 2000. World-Scientific.
19. J. Waldo, G. Wyant, A. Wollrath, and S. Kendall. A note on distributed computing. Technical Report TR-94-29, SUN Microsystems Laboratories, Nov 1994.
20. World Wide Web Consortium (W3C), http://www.w3.org/TR/REC-rdf-syntax/. *Resource Description Framework*, February 1999.
21. World Wide Web Consortium (W3C), http://www.w3.org/TR/REC-xml. *Extensible Markup Language (XML) 1.0*, 2001.

Automatic Analysis of Large Text Corpora - A Contribution to Structuring WEB Communities

Gerhard Heyer, Uwe Quasthoff, and Christian Wolff

Leipzig University
Computer Science Institute, Natural Language Processing Department
Augustusplatz 10 / 11, D-04109 Leipzig
{heyer,quasthoff,wolff}@informatik.uni-leipzig.de

Abstract. This paper describes a corpus linguistic analysis of large text corpora based on collocations with the aim of extracting semantic relations from unstructured text. We regard this approach as a viable method for generating and structuring information about WEB communities. Starting from a short description of our corpora as well as our language analysis tools, we discuss in depth the automatic generation of collocation sets. We further give examples of different types of relations that may be found in collocation sets for arbitrary terms. We conclude with a brief discussion of applying our approach to the analysis of a sample community.

1 Introduction

Searching the World Wide Web is a notoriously difficult task. As has been shown by Lawrence and Giles (1998), the coverage of any search engine is significantly limited, no single engine indexes more than about one-third of the "indexable Web". In view of the increasing efforts that need to be undertaken to keep up a search engine's index with the fast growing Web, alternative approaches start being investigated. One such approach is based on the "Small World"-Phenomenon - the principle that we are linked by short chains of acquaintances (cf. Milgram 1992) -, and aims to exploit the fact that users that share common interests tend to also share connected structures and services, thus forming a *community* (see Wulff and Unger 2000). Groups with a common interest often communicate with each other. In many cases, a sublanguage is created. This sublanguage typically contains technical terms which are only rarely used outside. Also, common terms are included in this sublanguage, sometimes in a very unique way.

This sublanguage analysis can be used to assign documents to communities or to estimate the benefit of a certain document for a community.

As a basis for gaining information about communities, very large amounts of text need to be processed. In the following we will present a corpus linguistic approach that might be suitable for this task based on a statistical analysis of co-occurring words. General characteristics of this approach are discussed in Ch. 2, Ch. 3 gives in-depth details of computing collocations. In Ch. 4 the results given by collocation

H.Unger, T.Böhme, and A.Mikler (Eds.): I²CS 2002, LNCS 2346, pp. 15–26, 2002.
© Springer-Verlag Berlin Heidelberg 2002

analysis are discussed and interpreted. Ch. 5 investigates the application of text corpus processing to community oriented distributed systems.

2   Analysis of Large Text Corpora

Corpus Linguistics is generally understood as a branch of computational linguistics dealing with large text corpora for the purpose of statistical processing of language data (cf. Armstrong 1993, Manning and Schütze 1999). With the availability of large text corpora and the success of robust corpus processing in the nineties, this approach has recently become increasingly popular among computational linguists (cf. Sinclair 1991, Svartvik 1992).

Text Corpus Infrastructure

Since 1995 a German text corpus of more than 300 million words has been collected at the department for automatic language processing at the University of Leipzig (cf. Quasthoff 1998B, Quasthoff and Wolff 2000), containing approx. 6 million different word forms in approx. 13 million sentences, which serves as input for the analysis methods described below. Similarly structured corpora have recently been set up for other European languages as well (English, French, Dutch), with more languages to follow in the near future (see Table 1).

Table 1. Basic Characteristics of the Corpora

	German	English	Dutch	French
Word tokens	300 m	250 m	22 m	15 m
sentences	13.4 m	13 m	1.5 m	860,000
Word types	6 m	1.2 m	600,000	230,000

Employing a simple data model tailored to large amounts of textual data and their efficient processing using a relational data base system at storage level, we employ a powerful technical infrastructure for processing texts to be included in the corpus. The automatic calculation of sentenced-based word collocations stands out as an especially valuable tool for our corpus-based language technology applications (see Quasthoff 1998A, Quasthoff and Wolff 2000). Furthermore, linguistic as well as general descriptive features of each language like information on usage or subject categories are collected and stored in the corpus database for further application (see Table 2).

Starting from this corpus analysis infrastructure, tools have been developed for various applications like

- search engine optimization (language plug-ins, client-side query expansion)
- automatic document classification
- electronic dictionaries
- indexing

- knowledge management, esp. Topic Map generation (see Heyer, Quasthoff, and Wolff 2000).

The corpora are available via a search interface on the WWW (*http://www.wortschatz.uni-leipzig.de*) and may be used as a large online dictionary.

Table 2. German Corpus Overview

Type of data	# of entries
Word forms	> 6 Million
Sentences	> 25 Million
Grammar	2.772.369
Pragmatics	33.948
Descriptions	135.914
Morphology	3.189.365
Subject areas	1.415.752
Relations	449.619
Collocations (Semantic Associations)	> 8 Million
Index	> 35 Million

System Architecture

Setup and analysis of text corpora are based on a common architecture which is used for the different types of application mentioned above. The text processing work flow can be divided into four major phases:

- Text collection, esp. by families web crawling agents and preprocessing (document format conversion etc.)
- Corpus build-up in the storage layer, using standard RDBMS technology
- Statistical as well as linguistic analysis, esp. computation of collocations (see Chs. 3 and 4 below) and
- The application layer applies data generated in steps 1 to 3 for various kinds of text-oriented tasks.

Figure 4 (see Appendix) illustrates this process.

3   Collocations

The calculation of significant collocations, or semantic associations, is a central component of our text analysis approach: Some words co-occur with certain other words with a significantly higher probability, and this co-occurrence is semantically indicative. We call the occurrence of two or more words within a well-defined unit of information (sentence, document) a *collocation*. For the selection of meaningful and significant collocations, an adequate collocation measure has to be defined. In the literature, quite a number of different collocation measures can be found; for an in-depth discussion of various collocation measures and their application cf. Smadja 1993, Lemnitzer 1998, Krenn 2000, Heyer et al. 2001.

The Collocation Measure

In the following, our approach towards measuring the significance of the joint occurrence of two words A and B in a sentence is discussed. Let

a, b be the number of sentences containing A and B,
k be the number of sentences containing both A and B,
n be the total number of sentences.

Our significance measure calculates the probability of joint occurrence of rare events. The results of this measure are similar to the *log-likelihood*-measure (cf. Krenn 2000):

Let $x = ab/n$ and define:

$$\text{sig}(A, B) = \frac{-\log\left(1 - e^{-x}\sum_{i=0}^{k-1}\frac{1}{i!} \cdot x^i\right)}{\log n}. \tag{1}$$

For $2x < k$, we get the following approximation which is much easier to calculate:

$$\text{sig}(A,B) = (x - k\log x + \log k!) / \log n \tag{2}$$

In the case of next neighbor collocations we replace the definition of the above variables by the following. Instead of a *sentence* we consider pairs (A, B) of words which are next neighbors in this sentence. Hence, instead of one sentence of n words we have $n-1$ pairs. For right neighbor collocations (A, B) let

a, b be the number of pairs of the type $(A, ?)$ and $(?, B)$ resp.,
k be the number of pairs (A, B),
n be the total number of pairs. This equals the total
    number of running words minus the number of sentences.

Given these variables, a significance measure is calculated as shown above. In general, this measure yields semantically acceptable collocation sets for values above an empirically determined positive threshold.

Comparison to the Log-Likelihood Measure

The most popular collocation measure is the log likelihood (Lgl) measure. Translating the formula given in Krenn 2000 into our notation and ignoring small terms we get

$$\text{Lgl}(A,B) = \frac{k \cdot (\log k - \log \lambda)}{n}. \tag{3}$$

Up to the difference in the normalization factor both formulae are very similar. Consequently, the collocations calculated do only differ slightly. This can be seen comparing the results described above with the collocations of *http://www.ids-mannheim.de/ kt/corpora.shtml*. While both the corpora and the calculation methods differ, the results are remarkably similar (see Tables 3 and 4).

Table 3. Comparison of Collocation Resources in Different Corpora

	IDS Cosmas I (W-PUB)	*Wortschatz (German)*
Corpus Size	374 Million	255 Million
Sources	Various, mainly Newspapers	Various, mainly Newspapers
Window size	Fixed size (here: ±5 words	Sentence
Collocation Measure	Log Likelihood	Poisson Distribution

Table 4. Most Significant collocations for *Bier*

Rank	*IDS Cosmas I*	*Cosmas Rating*	*Wortschatz (German)*	*Sig-Rating*
1	Wein	4351	trinken	1234
2	trinken	2745	Wein	648
3	getrunken	1715	getrunken	478
4	kühles	1627	Liter	460
5	Glas	1379	trinkt	428
6	Liter	1318	Glas	348
7	Faß	1236	Schnaps	318
8	Fass	1139	Hektoliter	300
9	Flasche	1071	Flaschen	272
10	Hektoliter	899	gebraut	269
11	Trinkt	881	Wein	244
12	Flaschen	873	Kaffee	242

Properties of the Collocation Measure

In order to describe basic properties of this measure, we write sig(n, k, a, b) instead of sig(A, B) where n, k, a, and b are defined as above.

Simple co-occurance: A and B occur only once, and they occur together:

$$\text{sig}(n,1,1,1) \rightarrow 1. \tag{4}$$

Independence: A and B occur statistically independent with probabilities p and q:

$$\text{sig}(n,npq,np,nq) \rightarrow 0. \tag{5}$$

Additivity: The unification of the words *B* and *B'* just adds the corresponding signifi-cances. For $k/b \approx k'/b'$ we have

$$\text{sig}(n,k,a,b) + \text{sig}(n,k',a,b') \approx \text{sig}(n,k+k',a,b+b') \quad (6)$$

Enlarging the corpus by a factor *m*:

$$\text{sig}(mn, mk, ma, mb) = m \, \text{sig}(n, k, a, b) \quad\quad (7)$$

Finding Collocations

For calculating the collocation measure for any reasonable pairs we first count the joint occurrences of each pair. This problem is complex both in time and storage. Nevertheless, we managed to calculate the collocation measure for any pair with total frequency of at least 3 for each component. Our approach is based on extensible ternary search trees (cf. Bentley and Sedgewick 1998) where a count can be associ-ated to a pair of word numbers. The memory overhead from the original implementa-tion could be reduced by allocating the space for chunks of 100,000 nodes at once. However, even when using this technique for processing the corpus data more than one run of the program may be necessary, taking care that every pair is only counted once. All pairs of words above threshold significance are put into a database where they can be accessed and grouped in many different ways. As collocations are calcu-lated for different language corpora, our examples will be taken from the English as well as the German database.

Visualization of Collocations

Beside textual output of collocation sets, visualizing them as graphs is an additional type of representation: We choose a word and arrange its collocates in the plane so that collocations between collocates are taken into account. This results in graphs that show homogeneity where words are interconnected and they show separation where collocates have little in common. Linguistically speaking, polysemy is made visible (see fig. 1 below).

• Technically speaking, we use *simulated annealing* to position the words (see Davidson and Harel 1996). In the first step, the collocations are randomly placed in a rectangle with the starting word in its center. All such points are uniformly charged to force repelling. Additionally an attracting force is inserted between collocations. Simulated annealing finds an equilibrium state which is displayed. Line thickness represents the significance of the collocation. The resulting pic-ture represents semantic connectedness surprisingly well. Unfortunately the rela-tions between the words are just presented, but not yet named. Figure 1 shows the collocation graph for *space*.

Three different meaning contexts can be recognized in the graph:
• real estate,
• computer hardware, and
• astronautics.

The connection between *address* and *memory* results from the fact that address is another polysemous concept. This kind of visualization technique has been successfully applied to knowledge management techniques, esp. for generating and visualizing Topic Maps.

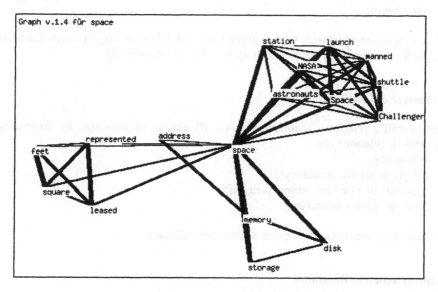

Fig. 1. Collocation Graph for *space*

4   Relations Represented by Collocations

If we fix one word and look at its set of collocates, then some semantic relations appear more often than others. The following example shows the most significant collocations for *king* ordered by significance:

> *queen (90), mackerel (83), hill (49), Milken (47), royal (44), monarch (33), King (30), crowned (30), migratory (30), rook (29), throne (29), Jordanian (26), junk-bond (26), Hussein (25), Saudi (25), monarchy (25), crab (23), Jordan (22), Lekhanya (21), Prince (21), Michael (20), Jordan's (19), palace (19), undisputed (18), Elvis (17), Shah (17), deposed (17), Panchayat (16), Zahir (16), fishery (16), former (16), junk (16), constitution (15), exiled (15), Bhattarai (14), Presley (14), Queen (14), crown (14), dethroned (14), him (14), Arab (13), Moshoeshoe (13), himself (13), pawns (13), reigning (13), Fahd (12), Nepali (12), Rome (12), Saddam (12), once (12), pawn (12), prince (12), reign (12), [...] government (10) [...]*

The following types of relations can be identified:
- Cohyponymy (e. g. *Shah, queen, rook, pawn*),
- top-level syntactic relations, which translate to semantic 'actor-verb' and often used properties of a noun (*reign; royal, crowned, dethroned*),

- category-name / instance-of (*Fahd, Hussein, Moshoeshoe*),
- special relations given by multiwords (*A* prep/det/conj *B*, e. g. *king of Jordan*), and
- unstructured set of words describing some subject area, e. g. *constitution, government*.

Note that synonymy rarely occurs in the lists. The relations may be classified according to the properties symmetry, anti-symmetry, and transitivity.

Symmetric Relations

Let us call a relation r symmetric if $r(A, B)$ always implies $r(A, B)$. Examples of symmetric relations are
- synonymy,
- cohyponomy (or similarity),
- elements of a certain subject area, and
- relations of unknown type.

Usually, sentence collocations express symmetric relations.

Anti-symmetric Relations

Let us call a relation r anti-symmetric if $r(A, B)$ only implies $r(A, B)$ for $A=B$. Examples of anti-symmetric relations are
- hyponymy
- relations between properties and its owners like action and actor or class and instance.

Usually, next neighbor collocations of two words express anti-symmetric relations. In the case of next neighbor collocations consisting of more than two words (like *A* prep/det/conj *B* e.g. *Samson and Delilah*), the relation might be symmetric, for instance in the case of conjunctions like *and* or *or* (cf. Läuter and Quasthoff 1999).

Transitivity

Transitivity of a relation means that $r(A, B)$ and $r(B, C)$ always implies $r(A, C)$. In general, a relation found experimentally will not be transitive, of course. But there may be a part where transitivity holds.

Some of the most prominent transitive relations are the *cohyponymy, hyponymy, synonymy, part-of* and *is-a* relations. Note that our graphical representation mainly shows transitive relations per construction.

5   Analyzing a Community

A collocational analysis of the characteristic text documents of a community as outlined above will yield:

1. A list of characteristic concepts based on a comparative frequency analysis (with respect to usage and frequency in general),
2. A list of characteristic collocations, and hence
3. A disambiguation of key concepts.

On the basis of the list of characteristic concepts and their collocations, a collocation profile for a community may be defined that can be used to compute degrees of similarity with new documents, neighboring communities, or search queries (cf. literature on search techniques based on vector space models, cf. Salton 1989).

For demonstration purposes, we have taken 150 MB of documentation on SAP's R/3 as a sample community, and have calculated the 30 most significant terms (assuming a frequency class of 8 or higher and a comparison factor of at least 16; the number following in parenthesis indicates the comparison factor, e.g. a term like *Abrechnungs-kostenart* in the domain analyzed is 23 times more frequent than in all other WEB documents):

etc (314), TCP (164), INDX (28), dsn (25), Nachfolgeposition (24), SHIFT (24), TRANSLATE (24), entreprise (24), Abrechnungskostenart (23), Alternativmengeneinheit (23), Anordnungsbeziehung (23), Anwendungssicht (23), Bandstation (23), Banf-Position (23), Berichtsspalte (23), Berichtszeile (23), CO-PC (23), DBSTATC (23), DSplit (23), Datumsart (23), ELSE (23), ENDDO (23), Entries (23), Freigabecodes (23), Hauptkondition (23), Leiterplanstelle (23), Merkmalswertekombination (23), Nachfolgematerial (23), Nettoberechnung (23), ...

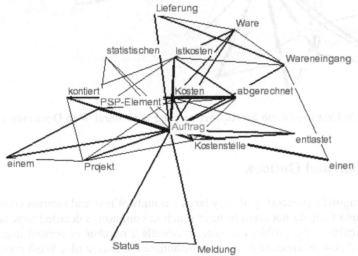

Fig. 2. Collocation Graph for *Auftrag* as computed from the SAP community

Note that a simple frequency analysis of the community documents is not very informative due to Zapf's law (cf. Manning and Schütze 1999):

die, Sie, der, und, in, werden, den, für, das, im, können, wird, zu, eine, auf, des, Die, ist, mit, ein, von, dem, the, oder, nicht, an, einer, aus, sind, In, einen, zur, als, über, System, kann, bei, einem, Wenn, Das, auch, nur, diesem, sich, eines, müssen, Daten, Der, daß, zum, to, haben, diese, alle, B, durch, z, R, wenn, nach, es, Feld, dann, of, wählen, Funktion, bzw, um, dieser, Wählen, Im, a, wie, is, Informationen, Diese, Bei, for, muß, and, vom, so, Für, Mit, unter, sein, keine, ob, soll, ...

For selected terms we can then calculate the list of collocations and again compare them with the available collocations in general; in the following example we have chosen the word "Auftrag":

In the following we depict the collocations for *Auftrag* in general. Apparently, the conceptual relation to PSP-elements is marginal. Instead, purely linguistic relations to dependant words like *erteilen* become very prominent. We also note that a new meaning appears, relating *Auftrag* to *Gutachten* (and not to *Ware*). Facts like these can be exploited for disambiguating search requests and identifying communities:

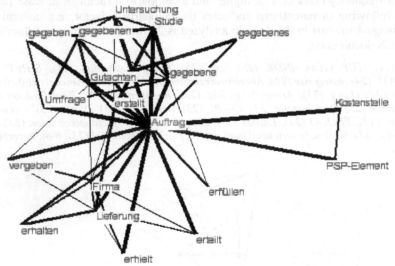

Fig. 3. Collocation Graph for *Auftrag* as used in General Web Documents

6   Discussion and Outlook

Although the linguistic processing of very large amounts of text and internet computing systems prima facie do not seem to have much in common, a detailed look at the matter, in particular at the problem of search, reveals a number of related interests and potentials of co-operation. In order to substantiate the notion of a WEB community, the corpus linguistic approach based on a collocational analysis of domain specific texts may help to classify communities and to recognize community specific documents.

References

Armstrong, S. (ed.) (1993). Using Large Corpora. Computational Linguistics 19(1/2) (1993) [Special Issue on Corpus Processing, repr. MIT Press 1994].

Bentley, J.; Sedgewick, R. (1998). "Ternary Search Trees." In: Dr. Dobbs Journal, April 1998.

Davidson, R., Harel, D. (1996). "Drawing Graphs Nicely Using Simulated Annealing." In: ACM Transactions on Graphics 15(4), 301-331.

Heyer, G.; Quasthoff, U.; Wolff, Ch. (2000). "Aiding Web Searches by Statistical Classification Tools." In: Knorz, G.; Kuhlen, R. (edd.) (2000). Informationskompetenz - Basiskompetenz in der Informationsgesellschaft. Proc. 7. Intern. Symposium f. Informationswissenschaft, ISI 2000, Darmstadt. Konstanz: UVK, 163-177.

Heyer, G.; Läuter, M.; Quasthoff, U.; Wittig, Th.; Wolff, Ch. (2001). „Learning Relations using Collocations." In: Maedche, Alexander; Staab, Steffen; Nedellec, C.; Hovy, E. (edd.). Proc. IJCAI Workshop on Ontology Learning, Seattle/WA, August 2001, 19-24.Krenn, B. (2000). "Distributional and Linguistic Implications of Collocation Identification." In: Proc. Collocations Workshop, DGfS Conference, Marburg, March 2000.

Krenn, B., 2000. Empirical Implications on Lexical Association Measures. Proceedings of the Ninth EURALEX International Congress. Stuttgart, Germany.

Läuter, M., Quasthoff, U. (1999). "Kollokationen und semantisches Clustering." In: Gippert, J. (ed.) (1999). Multilinguale Corpora. Codierung, Strukturierung, Analyse. Proc. 11. GLDV-Jahrestagung. Prague: Enigma Corporation, 34-41.

Lemnitzer, L. (1998). "Komplexe lexikalische Einheiten in Text und Lexikon." In: Heyer, G.; Wolff, Ch. (edd.). Linguistik und neue Medien. Wiesbaden: Dt. Universitätsverlag, 85-91.

Manning, Ch. D.; Schütze, H. (1999). Foundations of Statistical Language Processing. Cambridge/MA, London: The MIT Press.

Milgram, S. (1992^2). "The Small World Problem." In: Milgram, S.; Sabini, J.; Silver, M. (eds.). The Individual in a Social World: Essays and Experiments. New York/NY: McGraw Hill.

Quasthoff, U. (1998A). "Tools for Automatic Lexicon Maintenance: Acquisition, Error Correction, and the Generation of Missing Values." In: Proc. First International Conference on Language Resources and Evaluation [LREC], Granada, May 1998, Vol. II, 853-856.

Quasthoff, U. (1998B). "Projekt der deutsche Wortschatz." In: Heyer, G., Wolff, Ch. (eds.). Linguistik und neue Medien. Wiesbaden: Dt. Universitätsverlag, 93-99.

Quasthoff, U.; Wolff, Ch. (2000). "An Infrastructure for Corpus-Based Monolingual Dictionaries." In: Proc. LREC-2000. Second International Conference On Language Resources and Evaluation. Athens, May/June 2000, Vol. I, 241-246.

Salton, Gerard (1989). Automatic Text Processing. The Transformation, Analysis, and Retrieval of Information by Computer. Reading/MA: Addison-Wesley.Sinclair, J. (1991). Corpus Concordance Collocation. Oxford: Oxford University Press.

Smadja F. (1993). "Retrieving Collocations from Text: Xtract." In: Computational Linguistics 19(1) (1993), 143-177.

Svartvik, J. (ed.) (1992). Directions in Corpus Linguistics: Proc. Nobel Symposium 82, Stockholm, 4-8 August 1991. Berlin: Mouton de Gruyter [= Trends in Linguistics Vol. 65].

van der Vet, P. E.; Mars, N. J. I. (1998). "Bottom-Up Construction of Ontologies." In: IEEE Transactions on Knowledge and Data Engineering 10(4) (1998), 513-526.

Wulff, M.; Unger, H. (2000). "Message Chains as a new Form of Active Communication in the WOSNet." In: Proc. High Performance Computing (HPC) 2000.

Appendix: System Architecture Diagram

Figure 4 gives a simplified overview of our text corpus processing infrastructure as described in Ch. 2.2. It should be noted that this kind of text processing model can be applied to arbitrary text collections, thus making corpus comparisons possible, e.g. between domain specific texts and a general corpus database.

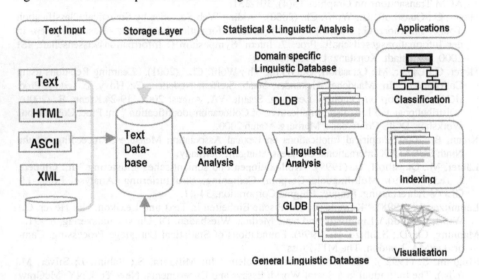

Fig. 4. *Common Text Corpus Processing Architecture*

A Data Mining Architecture for Distributed Environments

Mafruz Zaman Ashrafi, David Taniar, and Kate Smith

School of Business Systems, Monash University
PO BOX 63B, Clayton 3800, Australia
{Mafruz.Ashrafi,David.Taniar,Kate.Smith}@infotech.monash.edu.au

Abstract. Data mining offers tools for the discovery of relationship, patterns and knowledge from a massive database in order to guide decisions about future activities. Applications from various domains have adopted this technique to perform data analysis efficiently. Several issues need to be addressed when such techniques apply on data these are bulk at size and geographically distributed at various sites. In this paper we describe system architecture for a scalable and a portable distributed data mining application. The system contains modules for secure distributed communication, database connectivity, organized data management and efficient data analysis for generating a global mining model. Performance evaluation of the system is also carried out and presented.

1 Introduction

The widespread use of computers and the advance in database technology have provided huge amounts of data. The explosive growth of data in databases has generated an urgent need for efficient data mining techniques to discover useful information and knowledge. On the other hand, the emergence of network-based distributing computing such as the private intranet, internet, and wireless networks has created a natural demand for scalable techniques of data mining that can exploit the full benefit of such computing environments.

Distributed Data Mining (DDM) aims to discover knowledge from different data sources geographically distributed on multiple sites and to combine it to build a global data-mining model [3,4,8]. However, several issues emerge when data mining techniques are used on such systems. The distributing computing system has an additional level of complexity compared with centralized or host-based system. It may need to deal with heterogeneous platforms and multiple databases and possibly different schemas, with the design and implementation of scalable and effective protocol for communication among the nodes, and the selective and efficient use of the information that is gathered from several nodes [9].

A fundamental challenge for DDM is to develop mining techniques without having to communicate data unnecessarily. Such functionality is required for reasons of efficiency, accuracy and privacy. In addition, appropriate protocols, languages, and

H.Unger, T.Böhme, and A.Mikler (Eds.): I²CS 2002, LNCS 2346, pp. 27-38, 2002.

network services are required for mining distributed data to handle the required metadata and mapping.

In this paper, we present a system architecture for developing mining applications for distributed systems. The proposed architecture is not focused on any particular data mining algorithms, since our intention is not to propose new algorithms but to suggest a system infrastructure that makes it possible to plug in any mining algorithm and enable it to participate in a highly distributed real time system. The system is implemented in Java because it supports portable distribute programming on multiple platforms. Java thread, socket and data compression, JDBC techniques were utilized.

2   Related Work

In this section, we provide some background material and related work in this area. Several system including JAM, PADMA, Papyrus, BODHI, Kensington, PaDDMAS, and DMA have been developed/proposed for distributed data mining.

JAM [3] is distributed agent-based data mining system that uses meta-learning technique. It was develops local patterns of fraudulent activity by mining the local databases of several financial institutes. Than final patterns are generated by combining these local patterns. It assumes that each data site consists of a local database, learning agents, meta-learning agents and configuration modules which perform the major task of distributing computing by sending and receiving different requests from different sites.

PADMA [7] is an agent-based architecture for parallel /distributed data mining. It is a document analysis tool that works on a distributed environment based on cooperative agents. It aims to develop a flexible system that exploits data mining parallels. The data-mining agents in PADMA perform several parallel relational operations with the information extracted from the documents. The authors report on a PADMA implementation of unstructured text mining although the architecture is not domain specific.

The Papyrus [4] system is able to mine distributed data sources on a local and wide area cluster and a super cluster scenario. It uses meta-clusters to generate local models, which are exchanged to generate a global model. The originator reports that the system can support the moving of large volumes of mining data. The idea is founded on a theory similar to JAM system. Nevertheless they use a model representation language (PMML) and storage system called Osiris.

The BODHI [8] is a hierarchical agent based distributed learning system. The system was designed to create a communication system and run time environment for Collective Data Mining. It employs local learning techniques to build models at each distributed site and then moves these models to a centralized location. The models are then combed to build a meta-model whose inputs are the outputs of various models.

Kensington [13] Architecture is based on a distributed component environment located on different nodes on a generic network, like the Internet or Intranet. Kensington provides different components such as user oriented components, Application servers and Third level servers. It warps the analysis algorithm as Enterprise Java Bean components. PaDDMAS [8] is a Parallel and Distributed Data

Mining Application Suite, which uses a similar approach as the Kensington but has extended a few other features like, support for third party components, and a XML interface which able to hide component implementation.

The mining of association rules in distributed database has also been examined by David W.C. *et al.* They presented Distributed Mining of Association Rules (DMA) algorithm, which takes advantage of the inherent parallel environment of a distributed database. It uses the local counts of the large item-sets on each processor to decide whether a large item-set is heavy (both locally large in one database partition and globally large in the whole database), and then generates the candidates from the heavy large item-sets.

The proposed system was developed to support data mining in a distributed or parallel environment but has some significant differences from the abovementioned systems or architecture. In contrast with JAM, PADMA, and Papyrus, our model not only generated a global model from the homogeneous database but also from heterogeneous database. We also employ some secure communication techniques that are required in distributed environment. The Kensington and PaDDMAS systems are component-based. In BODHI system local models are gathered into a centralized site from the different remote sites and then they are combined to generate a global model. In our approach every individual site is capable of doing the same task as the centralized site of BODHI. It allows us to overcome the single point of failure. Moreover, we designed a repository for each site, which allows each site to do further analysis if needed. In contrast with DMA, in our system we analyze the association rule not only with support and confidence but we also consider the total number of record.

3   Design Rationale

The architecture of a data mining system plays a significant role in the efficiency with which data is mined. A typical DDM involves two tasks: local data compression and/or analysis for the minimization of network traffic, and the generation of global data models and analysis by combining various local data and models [12]. To perform these tasks successfully, a DDM system depends on various factors such as data source, security, multiple results etc. In the following paragraphs we evaluate our proposed architecture of distributed data mining on the basis of these factors:

3.1   Data Sources

The distributed data mining applications must run on multiple architectures and different operating systems (for example Windows, Unix). To achieve this, we use Java programming language and hence eliminate incompatibilities. Another challenge of distributed mining application is to find mining rules from different sources of formatted or unformatted data with diverse semantics. Because there are many kinds of data and databases used in different applications, and one may expect that distributed data mining system should be able to perform efficient data mining on different kinds of data [2]. In our module we used JDBC ODBC technology to handle different sources of RDBMS, which are distributed in different locations.

3.2   Multiple Results

In distributed data mining application, different kinds of knowledge can be elicited from large amounts of data including patterns which can be established by examining different mining algorithms (for example Decision Tree, Association rule, Sequential Patterns) in the same set of data. Because discovering knowledge from large database involves huge amounts of data processing cost, it is important to produce an organized way to devise rules, which can be used in the future. On the other hand, technology is evolving day by day, which makes us to think about the future communication between the distributed applications. Extensible Markup Language (XML) has become the standard for communication between applications. With XML, an application defines markup tags to represent the different elements of data in a text file so it can be read and handled by any application that uses XML. In this module, the data mining rule repository stores rules in XML format to achieve the abovementioned goal.

3.3   Technological Issues

As mentioned earlier we used Java technology for eliminating incompatibilities. Java allows us to achieve this by using several techniques: such as RMI and socket. The primary goal is for the RMI to enable programmers to develop distributed Java programs with the same syntax and semantics used for non-distributed programs. To do this, RMI allows Java classes and objects in different machines to communicate and work in a single Java Virtual Machine (JVM). As a result, Java RMI has some communication and implementation overheads. Java Socket level programming (a socket is a software endpoint that establishes bi-directional communication between a server program and one or more client programs) allows us start the server program with a specific hardware port on the machine where it runs so any client program anywhere in the network can be communicated with the server program. As a result Java Socket have less communication and implementation overheads.

3.4   Security

The security of network system is becoming increasingly important as more and more sensitive information is stored and manipulated online [11]. Distributed applications, which are guaranteed to be 'network friendly', pose a larger threat than usual. Whenever a request comes from outside the local environment, it poses a threat to security and privacy. Consequently special care must be taken to handle those kinds of attack. The system should support authentication and message security. In the proposed module we use one of the primitive approaches to resolve the authentication problem. And message level security implementation can be obtained by using the Java Secure Socket Extension API.

3.5   Cost Effectiveness

The volumes of data in databases are increasing day-by-day. Large-scale data sets are usually physically distributed. Current methods can handle data in the tens-of-gigabytes range. Association rule mining algorithms do not appear to be suitable for the terabyte range [10]. On the other hand, the Distributed Data Mining Application involves transferring huge amounts data through the networks. This requires implementing some kinds of compression technology. In our module we use Java ZIP compression technology for reducing the data traffic cost.

4   Distributed Data Mining Architecture

Our proposed mining architecture is a client/server-based system developed for performing knowledge discovery from large distributed sources of data. Due to the diversity of mining algorithms and the diversity of data sources, it is difficult to generate a mining model by combining mining rules on different sites. Our proposed system works independently to combine result from different sites. This section describes the abstract architecture model of the Distributed Data Mining and the interaction between its various subsystems. The architecture has the following subsystems: communication, mining, analyzing, and database. Figure 1 shows the architecture and the relationship between the different subsystems.

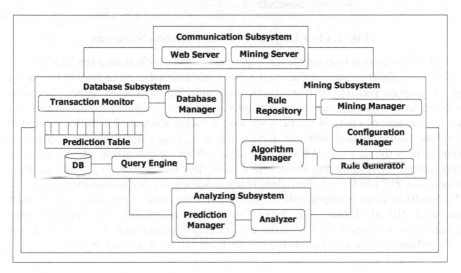

Fig. 1. Distributed Data Mining Architecture

4.1 Communication Subsystem

The communication subsystem is the heart of the network communication. It is responsible for sending and receiving requests to or from other sites registered with the local site. Because distributed systems are vulnerable, special care has been taken on this subsystem to handle unauthorized access. The following steps reduce vulnerability:

- Every time on the outside mining application wants to join with the local mining system, an object is generated which holds various information of that site and places that object in the active site table.
- Whenever any request arrives from that site a new object will be created and verify the active site table.

Sending mining rules to other sites is simple. It sends mining rules to those sites, which can be found on the active site table. Figure 2 shows the class diagram of the communication subsystem. The *MineServer* is an interface, which defines a certain set of functionality of the mining server. The *MineServerImpl* class implements the *MineServer* interfaces. It provides a coordinating facility between the other subsystems. The class *MineServerImpl* uses the Java thread model to concurrently handle multiple requests.

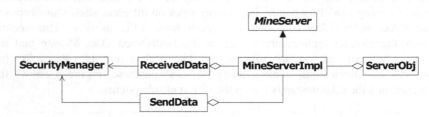

Fig. 2. Class Diagram of Communication Subsystem

The *Server* class is responsible for implements server sockets on a specified port. A socket is a software endpoint that establishes bi-directional communication between a server program and one or more client programs. The socket associates the server program with a specific hardware port on the machine on which it runs so that any client program anywhere in the network with a socket associated with that same port could be communicated with the server program. This class waits for requests to come in over the network. When it gets request from the authorized site, it opens the input stream for reading and saves it in a local file. The Server class reads the input stream as a ZIP file format. This class maintains a log file for management purposes. The *SendData* class is responsible for sending mining rules to the other sites. It sends data as a ZIP file format. The *ServerObj* class is responsible for registering new servers (that is wants to join with the data mining process) with the local sites. The *SecurityManager* class is responsible for verifying different security aspects.

4.2 Mining Subsystem

Figure 3 shows the class diagram of the Mining Subsystem. This is the core subsystem of the proposed distributed data mining system. It basically deals with the various data mining algorithms and manages the existing rules, in an organized way, into the repository.

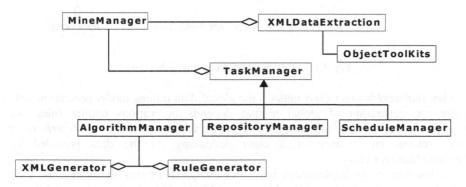

Fig. 3. Class Diagram of Mining Subsystem

The *MineManager* class is responsible for data processing and initiating different tasks. The *XMLDataExtraction* class deals with various incoming XML encoded data (received from the other sites), extracts them and saves them into a repository. The *XMLGenerator* class is responsible for encoding mining rules into the XML format. To define the legal building blocks of an XML document, we use a Document Type Definition (DTD). The DTD specification is actually part of the XML specification, which allows us to create a mining rule in a valid XML structure with a list of legal elements. This can be used it to ensure that the XML encoded data we read from the other site is indeed valid.

The *RuleGenerator* class is responsible for generating rules by using a specific mining algorithm on a particular data set. The *AlgorithmManager* class is responsible for implementing different mining algorithms that are part of the distributed data mining system. It generates rules based on those algorithms. The *RepositoryManager* class is responsible for maintaining the existing rules in an organized way. The *ScheduleManager* is responsible for performing different tasks on a routine basis.

4.3 Analyzing Subsystem

A successful DDM project involves several tasks including, examining and pruning the mining results and reporting the final result. Data mining results include classification, association, clustering, prediction, estimation, and deviation analysis. This subsystem is responsible for analyzing different data mining pattern gathered from multiple sites. It also generates a global model. Figure 4 shows the class diagram of this subsystem.

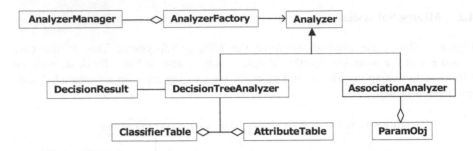

Fig. 4. Class Diagram of Analyzing Subsystem

The *AnalyzerManager* class initiates the global data-mining model generation task. Since the generation of global mining depends on various mining rules, we implemented a different rule analyzing class to achieve that. The *AnalyzerFactory* class returns an instance of a class depending on the data provided by *AnalyzerManager* class.

In this project we implemented two rules analyzed for two algorithms, the Rule Induction (Decision Tree) and the Association Mining. The former is a model that is both a predictive and a descriptive representation of a collection of rules. Rule induction is one of the most descriptive forms of knowledge discovery. It is a technique for discovering a set of "If / Then" rules from data in order to classify the different cases. Because it looks for all possible interesting patterns in a data set, the technique is powerful.

In the *DecisionTree* class we combined decision tree mining rules, each which has a classifier and a set of attributes. The classifier indicates the label or category to which the particular rule belongs. Attributes can be continuous that is, coming from an ordered domain, or categorical that is, coming from an unordered domain. We divided each rule on two parts, the classifier and the rule and represented them into two tables. The classifier table holds the classifier name and the corresponding rule number. The rule part is further divided into the attribute level and put into two different tables, the root and child, with the attribute name and rule number.

In a distributed computing environment, the database may fragment in different sites, as a result, can generate an overwhelming number of rules from several sites. To handle this kind of scenario we closely observed whether the attributes (root as well as child) of one rule fully or partly belongs to other rules or not and eliminated the fragmented rules. The rules in the rule induction form are independent and many may contradict each other. If we found any contradiction rule, we marked that rule as clash between the corresponding classifier. Human interaction is required to overcome such scenarios.

The association rule is used to find the set of all subsets of items or attributes that frequently occur in many database records or transactions, and additionally, to extract rules about how a subset of items influences the presence of another subset. The two important measures in the association rule are support and confidence.

The *AssociationAnalyzer* class analyzes different association mining rules received from the multiple sites and generates the global association-mining model. In a traditional (centralized-based) system, association rules are generated on the basis of local support and the confidence of the itemsets. In distributed environment the database may fragment, and the size of the database may vary from one site to another. This requires us to consider some additional parameter for generating a global model. This class generated global association mining model based is on four parameters: support, confidence, total support, and total confidence. The first two parameters provide the percentage of support and confidence of any particular itemset pattern. The parameter total support is measured by numbers of records present in the training set. Total confidence is measured by the numbers of times a particular item set with minimum confidence satisfies a particular pattern on it. In this class we implemented two different methods for generating a global model.

4.4   Database Subsystem

This subsystem is responsible for retrieving data from storage and saving it back to the database. To do this, it maintains a connection with a specific database. It has the capacity to generate a result by using SQL queries and stored-procedures within the context of a particular connection. Figure 5 shows the class diagram of this subsystem.

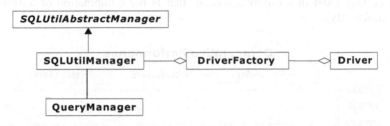

Fig. 5. Class Diagram of Database Subsystem

The *SQLUtilManager* class is the heart of this subsystem. It represents an individual session with the database and provides the methods necessary to save and retrieve objects it. It has the capability to support connections in various well-known databases and the *DriverFactory* class instantiate the corresponding driver for that database. The *QueryManager* class retrieves results from the database. The retrieve operation uses a simple SQL statement or calls a store procedure, which are, resides in the database.

5   Performance Evaluation

In this section we review the preliminary experiments of the proposed DDM architecture. We carried out a sensitivity analysis through a simulation. A sensitivity analysis is performed by varying performance parameters. The parameters were varied with different fragment schema, redundant rules, numbers of base classifier and total number of rules.

The experiments were run on a Windows 2000 server environment. The local rule model was generated from the data replicated and fragmented into three different sites. The local model consists of several thousand descriptive decision tree rules in If/Than format. We conducted this experiment by varying 5500 to 55500 of rules. The rule data contained a total number of 14 attributes. Some of the attributes are numeric, the rest categorical. The average length of each rule is 60 bytes. The experiment compared the total time of generating a global rule model by combining different local rules (that is generated each individual sites).

5.1   Result of Experiment

Figure 6 shows a comparative performance by varying the rules (received from three different sites) with a different base classifier. Each base classifier was equally distributed among the rules. In the first phase, each rule was scanned to identify the classifier of that rule and then to create the corresponding root and attribute table. The data are fragmented (both vertically and horizontally) and in a local rule model same rule may exist in a different format (that is the combination of attribute may appear differently).

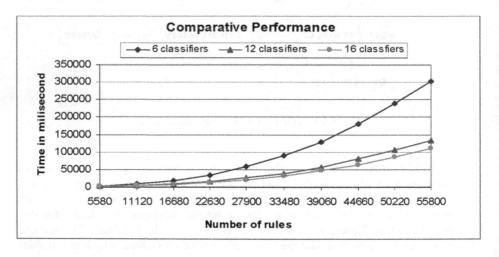

Fig. 6. Comparative Performance

The preliminary results indicate that the global rule model for the classifier set with 6 elements perform extensive data processing because its attribute table size increases with the proportion of rules. The major cost for scanning the data and finding rules with the same attributes. On the other hand, rules with elements of 12 and 16 classifier sets have smaller attribute tables compared with the classifier set of 6 elements. Hence, they scanned less data. On average, the classifier set with 16 elements is nearly two to three times faster then the classifier set with 6 elements.

6   Conclusions and Future Work

The distributed data mining uses communication networks to extract new knowledge from a large data set that exists in a distributed environment. It can enhance the computational time of knowledge extraction. In this paper we have defined and designed a system architecture for Distributing Data Mining, which allows us to combine local and remote patterns and to generate a global model for a different mining algorithm. The architecture is based on Java language. XML technique is used for data translation with support distributing computing. The secure socket layer is designed for communication between different sites. The Java thread is used to achieve parallelism.

Future work is being planned to investigate data security and privacy. It is important to consider when distributed knowledge discovery may lead to an invasion of privacy and what kind of security measures could be developed for preventing the disclosure of sensitive information.

References

1. David W. Cheung, Vincent T. Ng , Ada W. Fu, and Yongjian fu "Efficient Mining of Association rules in Distributed Databases". *IEEE Transaction on Knowledge and Data Mining*, Vol. 8, No 6, December 1996.
2. Chen M.S., Han J., and Yu P.S. "Data mining: An overview from a database perspective". *IEEE Transactions on Knowledge and Data Engineering*, Vol 8, No 6, pages 866-883, 1996.
3. Stolfo S.J., Prodromidis A.L., Tselepis S., Lee W., Fan D.W., and Chan P.K. "Jam: Java agents for meta-learning over distributed databases". *Proceedings of the 3rd International Conference on Knowledge Discovery and Data Mining*, pages 74-81, Newport Beach, CA, August 1997. AAAI Press.
4. Bailey S.M., Grossman R. L., Sivakumar H., and Turinsky A.L., "Papyrus: A System for Data Mining over Local and Wide Area Clusters and Super-Clusters". *Technical report*, University of Illinois at Chicago.
5. Rana O., Walker D., Li M., Lynden S., and Ward M., "PaDDMAS: Parallel and Distributed Data Mining Application Suit". *Proceedings of the Fourteenth International Parallel and Distributed Processing Symposium, pages 387-392.*
6. Kusiak A., "Decomposition in Data Mining: An Industrial Case Study". *IEEE Transaction on Electronics Packaging Manufacturing, Vol. 23 No 4 October 2000.*
7. Kargupta H., Hamzaoglu I., and Stafford B. "Scalable, Distributed Data Mining An Agent Based Application". *Proceedings of Knowledge Discovery And Data Mining, August, 1997.*
8. Kargupta, H., Park, B., Hershberger, D., and Johnson, E., (1999), "Collective Data Mining: A New Perspective Toward Distributed Data Mining". *Advances in Distributed and Parallel Knowledge Discovery*, 1999. MIT/AAAI Press.

9. Prodromidis, A., Chan, P., and Stolfo, S. (2000). "Meta-Learning in Distributed Data Mining Systems: Issues and Approaches". *Advances in Distributed and Parallel Knowledge Discovery*, AAAI/MITPress.

10. Zaki M. "Parallel and Distributed Association Mining: A survey". *IEEE Concurrency, special issue on Parallel Mechanisms for Data Mining, 7(4):14--25, December.*

11. Lee W., Salvatore J. S., Philip K. C., Eleazar E., Wei F., Matthew M., Shlomo H., and Junxin Z.. "Real Time Data Mining-based Intrusion Detection." *Proceedings of DISCEX II. June 2001.*

12. Sally M., "Distributed Data Mining". *Proceeding of Intelligence in Industry,* Issue 3, 2001.

13. Chattratichat J., Darlington J, Guo Y., Hedvall S., Kohler M., and Syed J., "An Architecture for Distributed Enterprise Data Mining". *HPCN, Amsterdam, 1999.*

Collaborative Highlighting
for Real-Time Group Editors

Haifeng Shen and Chengzheng Sun

School of Computing and Information Technology
Griffith University, Qld 4111, Australia

Abstract. Highlighting text is a common feature in most single-user editors. It provides users with a mechanism of communication and collaboration between the author and readers by emphasizing some important text. This feature is also necessary and even more valuable for multi-user group editors in the Internet environment. However, it is non-trivial to extend this feature from single-user editors to multi-user group editors because of the following challenges: 1) the need to differentiate highlights by different users, 2) the need to tackle inconsistency problems caused by concurrent operations and nondeterministic communication latency in the Internet environment, and 3) the need to provide a flexible undo facility with the capability of undoing any highlighting operation at any time. We will systematically address these issues and offer our solutions accordingly in this paper. These solutions have been implemented in the *REDUCE* (REal-time Distributed Unconstrained Collaborative Editing) system.

1 Introduction

Highlighting text is a common feature in most single-user editors, such as Microsoft Word. It provides users with the capability of emphasizing important text in order to support non-real-time communication and collaboration between the author and readers. This feature is naturally necessary for multi-user group editors because features available in single-user applications must also be available in corresponding multi-user applications for encouraging users to learn, use and adopt new collaborative applications. Moreover, this feature is even more valuable in multi-user group editors for the following reasons.

Firstly, besides supporting non-real-time collaboration (similar to that in single-user editors), it can help real-time and unconstrained communication and collaboration, such as highlighting key points in brainstorming, discussing interesting topics, or debugging programs.

Secondly, it may be used for other purposes that have never been met in single-user editors. Highlighting can be used for providing awareness hints. For instance, when doing some crucial tasks in an area, one can highlight the area to warn others against updating this area. To avoid conflicts, warning can be used as a complementary method to preventing that is normally achieved by the technique of locking.

H. Unger, T. Böhme, and A. Mikler (Eds.): I²CS 2002, LNCS 2346, pp. 39–50, 2002.

Finally, highlighting can be used as a complementary tool to *telepointing* for supporting real-time discussion in the Internet environment. Telepointing [2,6,7] is a well-known and commonly accepted tool in real-time collaborative applications for indicating remote users' cursor or mouse locations [2]. It can serve as a mechanism of gesturing communication through which participants indicate relations between the artifacts on the display, draw attention to particular artifacts, show intentions about what they are about to do, suggest emotional reactions, and so on [7]. However, a telepointer can only emphasize a single point, not a region of the document. Moreover, a telepointer dynamically moves around the document and the user cannot see its history, so it is not capable of simultaneously indicating multiple points in the document. Highlighting can compensate for these drawbacks because highlighting is naturally to highlight a region rather than a point and multiple highlights can be simultaneously maintained in the document.

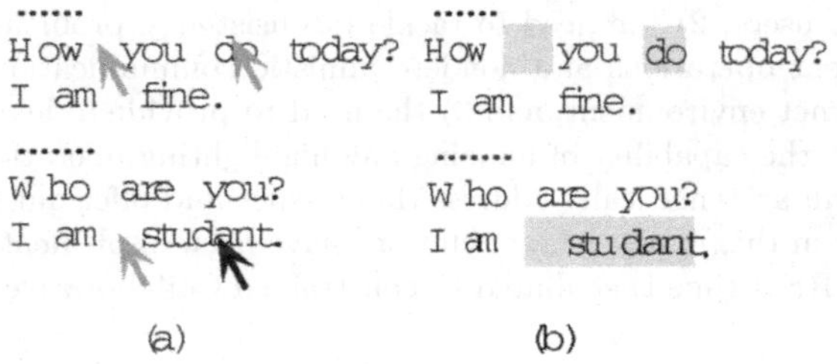

(a)   (b)

Fig. 1. Telepointing versus highlighting

To illustrate the above points, a concrete example is given in **Figure** 1. In this figure, a teacher continuously checks errors in a document and a student concurrently corrects the errors found by the teacher in the same document. In (a), the teacher's telepointer moves from one error to the other. The teacher has to wait for the student to correct the currently pointing error before moving to the next one because once his telepointer moves to the next error, the information on previous errors (shown as grey telepointers) will be definitely lost. In contrast, in (b), all found errors have been simultaneously kept as highlights and the last highlight particularly marks two errors (region emphasis), which have to be pointed out one by one by the teacher's telepointer in (a). The teacher and the student can therefore work in unconstrained collaboration mode. In other words, the teacher keeps checking and marking errors without waiting for the student to correct and the student keeps correcting the marked errors without catching up the teacher's pace.

However, it is non-trivial to extend highlighting text from single-user editors to multi-user group editors. Firstly, the user interface for highlights in multi-user collaborative editors should be carefully studied because it is necessary to distinguish different users' highlights in order to provide some sort of group awareness among collaborators [1,4]. User interface design has a fundamental impact on other issues, such as consistency maintenance, and undo.

Secondly, concurrent operations and nondeterministic communication latency may cause inconsistency problems [5,9] in the Internet environment. Consistency maintenance [9] is a general key issue in distributed collaborative applications.

Finally, collaborative undo of highlighting operations is needed. However, it is very challenging to do so because collaborative undo is non-trivial in general. All existing solutions [3,8] are about undo of editing operations and no work has been done on the undo of highlighting operations.

Collaboratively highlighting text is an important extension to collaboratively editing text [9]. It lays a foundation for handling other properties similar in nature to collaborative highlighting, such as collaborative underlining, collaborative overlining, collaborative font changing, and collaborative locking.

The paper is organized as follows. After the introduction, the user interface design is discussed. Then consistency maintenance is presented. The following section gives a flexible undo solution with the capability of undoing any highlighting operation at any time. Finally the paper is summarized with our major contributions and future work.

2   User Interface Design

The user interface for highlights is a fundamental issue. In single-user editors, a highlight is represented by changing the background of a text area to a particular color. The color is randomly chosen. However, in multi-user collaborative applications, it is commonly used to differentiate operations performed by different users with different colors so as to provide some sort of group awareness [4]. The unique color for representing a user is called the user's *ID* color. The same approach can apply to highlighting operations. For example, as shown in **Figure 2**, when a user highlights a text area, the background of the text area can be the user's *ID* color instead of a randomly chosen one.

It is important that a multi-user collaborative application emulates the user interface of the corresponding single-user application in order to encourage users who are used to the single-user application to learn, use and adopt the multi-user collaborative version. When a user performs a highlighting operation, the highlight is represented as a text background in his *ID* color.

Before presenting the solutions to other addressed issues, we would like to give the internal representation of a highlighting operation and some other notations. A highlighting operation can be simply denoted as HLT[P, N, OHS], which means highlighting N characters starting from position P. The data structure **OHS**(Original Highlighting Set) stores original highlighting status in order to support undo. Each element in an *OHS* is called **OHR** (Original Highlighting Region) = ⟨S, L, C⟩ where S is the starting position, L is the length, and C is the highlighting color. So an operation highlighting N characters starting from position P including m *OHR*s would be denoted as H=HLT[P, N, OHS] where OHS=$\bigcup_{i=0}^{m-1}\langle S_i, L_i, C_i\rangle$. Apparently $S_i=S_{i-1}+L_{i-1}$ ($0\leq i\leq m-1$), P=S_0, and N=$\sum_{i=0}^{m-1} L_i$.

H's inverse operation $\overline{H}$ can be denoted as UNHLT[P, N, OHS], which means recovering the highlighting status of N characters starting from the position P in the document. A highlighting operation H=HLT[P, N, OHS] can be also used to represent a de-highlighting operation, which removes the highlights of N characters starting from position P in the document if the default document background color instead of the user's ID color is used as the highlighting color. Therefore we will not differentiate highlighting and de-highlighting operations in presenting our solutions in the paper.

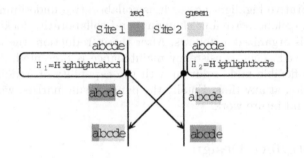

Fig. 2. Highlights represented as backgrounds

An editing operation is denoted as INS/DEL[P, N, S] to represent inserting/deleting string S whose size is N at position P. For any editing operation E, P(E) is the position parameter of E, N(E) is the size parameter of E, S(E) is the text parameter of E. Apparently N(E)=Len(S(E)). For a highlighting operation H=HLT[P, N, OHS], P(H) is H's position parameter, N(H) is H's size parameter, and OHS(H) is H's OHS parameter. For any editing or highlighting operation O, C(O) is the ID color of the user who performs O.

3   Consistency Maintenance

3.1   Divergence

Figure 2 reveals two problems. One is the latterly performed highlighting operation would overshadow the effect of the formerly performed one if they are overlapping. The other is different execution orders would produce different overshadowing results at different sites, leading to divergence.

The root of these two problems is the most recent operation has the final impact on the overlapping part, causing the effect of previously executed operations overshadowed. We propose the **DR** (Display Rotation) approach to solve these problems. In this approach, all versions of overlapping parts are stored in a data structure called **RT** (Rotating Table) in which each element is referred to as a **RE** (Rotating Element), which has the same representation of an *OHR*. Then the appearance of each overlapping part alternates according to the relevant *REs* in the *RT*. As a result, all operations' effect can be maintained and presented to the users and all sites can be considered convergent in terms of the dynamic visual effect.

For example, in **Figure** 2, when H_2 arrives and is executed at *Site 1*, the character *a* remains to be highlighted in red and the string *bcde* is highlighted in green. Then in terms of OHS(H_2), *Site 1*'s *RT*=[$\langle 1, 3, \text{red} \rangle$, $\langle 1, 3, \text{green} \rangle$] and therefore the string *bcd* will be highlighted in red and green rotatively. Similarly, *Site 2*'s *RT*=[$\langle 1, 3, \text{green} \rangle$, $\langle 1, 3, \text{red} \rangle$] and the string *bcd* will be highlighted in green and red rotatively. Therefore, the effect of both H_1 and H_2 is maintained and presented on the user interface in a dynamic way, and the two sites can be considered convergent because the two sites see the same dynamic visual effect on the user interface. One thing we must clarify is display rotation is only an external visual effect on the user interface and the internal representation of the string *bcd* is still in green at *Site 1* and red at *Site 2*.

3.2   Intention Violation

Consider a document contains the string *abcde*, replicated at two sites as shown in **Figure** 3. *Site 1* generates a deleting operation E=DEL[1, 1, a] to delete the character *a* and concurrently *Site 2* generates a highlighting operation H=HLT[1, 3, {$\langle 1, 3, \text{null} \rangle$}] to highlight the string *bcd* in green . At *Site 1*, after the execution of E, the document content is changed to *bcde*. When H arrives and is executed, the string *cde* is highlighted in green. This result apparently violates H's intention, which is to highlight the string *bcd*.

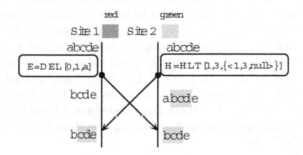

Fig. 3. An example of intention violation

Highlighting operations have no impact on the document content, therefore they have no impact on editing operations. However, editing operations make changes to the document content, therefore they may have impact on highlighting operations. The root of the problem in **Figure** 3 is the deleting operation E has changed the document content on which the highlighting operation H was originally defined. Concurrent editing operations may prevent a highlighting operation from preserving its intention.

In sum, an editing operation may affect a highlighting operation in the following ways:

- When the editing operation is an inserting operation,
  1. if it is performed at the left side of a highlighting area covered by a highlighting operation, the highlighting area shifts to the right;
  2. if it is performed within a highlighting area covered by a highlighting operation, the highlighting area expands;
  3. if it is performed at the right side of a highlighting area covered by a highlighting operation, it has no impact on the highlighting operation.
- When the editing operation is a deletion operation,
  1. if it is performed at the left side of a highlighting area covered by a highlighting operation,
     - if the deleting area covered by the deletion operation does not overlap with the highlighting area, the highlighting area shifts to the left;
     - otherwise the highlighting area trims off from the left;
  2. if it is performed within a highlighting area covered by a highlighting operation,
     - if the deleting area totally falls into the highlighting area, the highlighting area shrinks;
     - otherwise the highlighting area trims off from the right;
  3. if it is performed at the right side of a highlighting area covered by a highlighting operation, it has no impact on the highlighting operation.

We have further observed that even a subsequent editing operation has the same effect on a highlighting operation. Although the highlighting operation has already been executed, it should be correctly adjusted to include the impact of the subsequent editing operation in order to support undo. In conclusion, when a remote highlighting operation arrives at a site, it needs to be transformed against all executed concurrent editing operations at this site to include their impact. When an (local or remote) editing operation is executed, all highlighting operations executed at this site need to be transformed against this editing operation to include its impact. The transformation algorithms IT_HI(H, E) and IT_HD(H, E) are defined to inclusively transform a highlighting operation H against an inserting operation and a deleting operation E respectively.

```
Procedure IT_HI(H, E)
{ if P(E)<=P(H)
  { P(H)=P(H)+N(E);
     for (i=0; i<sizeof(OHS(H)); i++) OHS(H)[i].S+=N(E);
  }else if P(E)<P(H)+N(H)
  { N(H)=N(H)+N(E);
     for (i=0; i<sizeof(OHS(H)); i++)
        if P(E)<=OHS(H)[i].S OHS(H)[i].S+=N(E);
        else if P(E)<=OHS(H)[i].S+ OHS(H)[i].L OHS(H)[i].L=+N(E);
```

```
  }
}

Procedure IT_HD(H, E)
{ Adjust(P(H),N(H),E);
  for (i=0; i<sizeof(OHS(H)); i++)
    Adjust_HD(OHS(H)[i].S,OHS(H)[i].L,E);
}

Procedure Adjust_HD(Pos,Len,E)
{ if P(E)+N(E)<=Pos Pos-=N(E);
  else if P(E)<=Pos and P(E)+N(E)<=Pos+Len
    Len=(Pos+Len)-(P(E)+N(E));
  else if P(E)>=Pos and P(E)+N(E)<=Pos+Len Len-=N(E);
  else if P(E)<=Pos and P(E)+N(E)>=Pos+Len {Pos=P(E); Len=0;}
  else if P(E)>=Pos and P(E)+N(E)>=Pos+Len Len=P(E)-Pos;
}
```

In **Figure** 3, when H arrives at *Site 1*, it cannot be executed in its original form. Instead, its execution form should be achieved by IT_HD(H, E)=HLT[0, 3, {⟨0, 3, null⟩}]. After the execution of H's execution form, the string *bcd* is highlighted in green, which is correct.

4   Flexible Undo Solution

Most single-user editors have undo facilities to undo highlighting operations for recovering errors. In multi-user group editors, this facility is naturally needed and even more valuable because besides error recovering, undo is necessary for changing focuses during a discussion. To change the focus of a discussion, old highlights should be undone and new highlights need to be created.

Only chronological undo of highlighting operations is available in single-user editors. But it is too restrictive to be used in multi-user group editors because during a discussion, changing focus is not structured chronologically. The flow of changing focus is actually arbitrary subject to the nature of the discussion topic and the thinking style of every participant. Therefore we think selective undo [3,8] is most suitable for the undo of highlighting operations in multi-user group editors because it can support undo of any operation at any time.

Generally speaking, to achieve the correctness of undoing a highlighting operation, the effect of H (the operation to be undone) must be removed from the document while the effect of all other operations (executed before or after H) must be maintained. It is non-trivial to achieve selective undo of highlighting operations because the current highlighting status in the document could be different from the status when H was defined because there could be some operations executed after H. Simply executing H's inverse in the current context may not produce the correct result.

We propose the *SUCA* (Selective Undo Control Algorithm) algorithm that can support selective undo of any highlighting operation at any time. In this algorithm, each site maintains a data structure called **HT** (Highlighting Table) to keep all executed (local and remote) highlighting operations according to the execution order. Different sites may have different HTs because highlighting operations could have been executed in different orders at different sites.

To undo an operation H in the HT at a site, the following steps will be executed. Firstly, make H's inverse operation $\overline{H}$.

Secondly, $\overline{H}$ cannot be executed in its original form. Instead, it has to be transformed (with the proposed transformation algorithm IT_IH) against all operations placed after H in the HT to achieve its execution form $E\overline{H}$. On the other hand, those operations placed after H in the HT should be transformed (with the proposed transformation algorithms IT_HU or IT_HH) against $\overline{H}$ to include its impact. To make display rotation effect adjusted accordingly, if H is undone, all REs in the RT covered by H should be removed. Then new REs generated by IT_HU or IT_HH should be inserted.

Thirdly, by executing $E\overline{H}$ and the new RT, H's effect has been eliminated while the effect of all other operations have been preserved.

Finally, if the undo is initiated locally, the undo command carrying H's *ID* rather than $E\overline{H}$ itself is propagated to remote sites. There are two reasons for doing this. One is remote sites normally have different HTs, which may result in the $E\overline{H}$ derived in terms of the local HT not applicable to remote sites. The other is the direct execution of $E\overline{H}$ at remote sites could alter the effect of concurrent highlighting or undo of highlighting operations at remote sites because the derivation of $E\overline{H}$ has no knowledge of these concurrent operations at remote sites. Therefore we let remote sites derive H's execution forms in terms of their own context.

Suppose *Site k* has n highlighting operations stored in the $HT=[H_1, \cdots, H_i, \cdots, H_n]$ and an undo command is received to undo H_i, the algorithm $SUCA(H_i, \text{HT})$ will be invoked.

ALGORITHM $SUCA(H_i, \text{HT})$

1. Find H_i in the HT.
2. Make H_i's inverse $\overline{H_i}$. Concretely speaking, if to undo H_i, $\overline{H_i} = \text{UNHLT}[\text{P}(H_i), \text{N}(H_i), \text{OHS}(H_i)]$ and if to redo H_i, $\overline{H_i}=H_i$.
3. $\overline{H_i}$'s execution form $E\overline{H_i}$ should be determined by transforming $\overline{H_i}$ against a list of operations $[H_{i+1}, \cdots, H_n]$. On the other hand, the list of operations $[H_{i+1}, \cdots, H_n]$ need to be transformed against $\overline{H_i}$ to include its impact. Refer to the procedure **Transform**(i, HT).
4. Rearrange RT.
   - If to undo H_i, remove REs covered by H_i in the RT. That is to say, for $\forall RE=\langle S, L, C\rangle \in RT$, if $S \geq P(H_i)$ and $S+L \leq P(H_i)+ N(H_i)$, RE should be removed from the RT.
   - Insert new REs generated by IT_HU or IT_HH in Step 3 into the RT.
5. Execute $E\overline{H_i}$ and the new RT.
6. If the undo is initiated locally, the undo command carrying H_i's *ID* will be propagated to remote sites.

```
Procedure Transform(i, HT)
{//H=HT[i],HR: H's inverse,EHR: HR's execution form
  EHR=HR;
  for (j=i+1; j<=n; j++)
  { EHR'=IT_IH(EHR, HT[j]);
    if (H is not an inverse) HT[j]=IT_HU(HT[j], EHR); //To undo H
    else HT[j]=IT_HH(HT[j], EHR); //To redo H
    EHR=EHR';
  }
}
```

The transformation algorithm IT_IH(I, H) transforms an inverse operation I against a subsequent operation H to achieve I's execution form. Simply speaking, if the effect of I's original operation is overshadowed by H, I's execution form can be achieved by removing the overlapping part from I. The IT_IH transformation algorithm is described as follows.

```
Procedure IT_IH(I, H)
{ Adjust_IH(P(I), N(I), H);
  if N(I)==0 I=NULL;
  for (i=0; i<sizeof(OHS(I)); i++)
  { Adjust_IH(OHS(I)[i].S, OHS(I)[i].L, H);
    if OHS(I)[i].L==0 remove OHS(I)[i];
  }
}


Procedure Adjust_IH(Pos, Len, H)
{ if Pos<=P(H) and Pos+Len<=P(H)+N(H) Len=P(H)-Pos;
  else if Pos>=P(H) and Pos+Len<=P(H)+N(H) Len=0;
  else if Pos>=P(H) and Pos+Len>=P(H)+N(H)
  {Pos=P(H)+N(H); Len=Pos+Len-(P(H)+N(H));}
  else if Pos<=P(H) and Pos+Len>=P(H)+L(H)
  {Pos_Head=Pos; Len_Head=P(H)-Pos; Pos_Tail=P(H)+N(H);
   Len_Tail=Pos+Len-(P(H)+N(H));
   Pos={Pos_Head, Pos_Tail};Len={Len_head, Len_Tail};
  }
}
```

The transformation algorithms IT_HU and IT_HH transform an operation against the inverse of a previous operation to include the inverse's impact. Concretely speaking, if the inverse is an $UNHLT$ operation (i.e., to undo an operation), the IT_HU(H_2, H_1) transformation algorithm is to eliminate H_1's information from OHS(H_2) and to incorporate OHS(H_1) into OHS(H_2). If the inverse is a HLT operation (i.e., to redo an operation), the IT_HH(H_2, H_1) transformation algorithm is to reincorporate H_1's information into OHS(H_2). The IT_HU and IT_HH transformation algorithms are described as follows.

```
Procedure IT_HU(H2, H1)
{ for (i=0; i<sizeof(OHS(H2)); i++)
  { OHRi=OHS(H2)[i];
```

```
    if P(H1)<=OHRi.S and OHRi.S+OHRi.L<=P(H1)+N(H1) and
       OHRi.C==C(H1) { OHR=OHRi; break;}
  }
  for (j=0; j<sizeof(OHS(H1)); j++)
  { OHRj=OHS(H1)[j];
    if OHR.S<=OHRj.S and OHR.S+OHR.L<=OHRj.S+OHRj.L
    { OHRj.L=OHR.S+OHR.L-OHRj.S; OHRj.C=OHR.C;}
    else if OHR.S<=OHRj.S and OHR.S+OHR.L>=OHRj.S+OHRj.L
      OHRj.C=OHR.C;
    else if OHR.S>=OHRj.S and OHR.S+OHR.L>=OHRj.S+OHRj.L
    { OHRj.S=OHR.S; OHRj.L=OHRj.S+OHRj.L-OHR.S; OHRj.C=OHR.C;}
    else if OHR.S>=OHRj.S and OHR.S+OHR.L<=OHRj.S+OHRj.L
    { OHRj.S=OHR.S; OHRj.L=OHR.L; OHRj.C=OHR.C;}
  }
}


Procedure IT_HH(H2, H1)
{ for (i=0; i<sizeof(OHS(H2)), i++)
  { OHRi=OHS(H2)[i];
    if P(H1)<=OHRi.S and P(H1)+N(H1)<=OHRi.S+OHRi.L
    { Add a new OHR <OHRi.S,P(H1)+N(H1)-OHRi.S, C(H1)> to OHS(H2);
      OHRi.S=P(H1)+N(H1); OHRi.L=OHRi.S+OHRi.L-(P(H1)+N(H1));
    } else if P(H1)<=OHRi.S and P(H1)+N(H1)>=OHRi.S+OHRi.L
      OHRi.C=C(H1);
    else if P(H1)>=OHRi.S and P(H1)+N(H1)>=OHRi.S+OHRi.L
    { Add a new OHR <P(H1),OHRi.S+OHRi.L-P(H1),C(H1)> to OHS(H2);
      OHRi.L=P(H1)-OHRi.S;
    }else if P(H1)>=OHRi.S and P(H1)+N(H1)<=OHRi.S+OHRi.L
    { Add two new OHRs <P(H1),N(H1),C(H1) and
      <P(H1)+N(H1),OHRi.S+OHRi.L-(P(H1)+N(H1)),OHRi.C> to OHS(H2);
      OHRi.L=P(H1)-OHRi.S;
    }
  }
}
```

Let's take a concrete example to illustrate how the $SUCA$ algorithm works. Look at the example in **Figure** 2, a document contains the string *abcde*, replicated at two sites. *Site 1* performs the operation H_1 to highlight the string *abcd* in red and at the same time *Site 2* performs the operation H_2 to highlight the string *bcde* in green.

At *Site 1*, H_1=HLT[0, 4, {⟨0, 4, null⟩}], H_2=HLT[1, 4, {⟨1, 3, red⟩, ⟨4, 1, null⟩}], HT=[H_1, H_2], and RT=[⟨1, 3, red⟩, ⟨1, 3, green⟩]. At *Site 2*, H_2=HLT[1, 4, {⟨1, 4, null⟩}], H_1=HLT[0, 4, {⟨0, 1, null⟩, ⟨1, 3, green⟩}], HT=[H_2, H_1], and RT=[⟨1, 3, green⟩, ⟨1, 3, red⟩]. Then *Site 1* decides to undo H_1 and the $SUCA(H_1, HT)$ is invoked. Firstly, make H_1's inverse $\overline{H_1}$=UNHLT[0, 4, {⟨0, 4, null⟩}].

Secondly, $\overline{H_1}$ cannot be executed directly, otherwise, part of H_2's effect will be eliminated (i.e., besides the character a, the string bcd will be de-highlighted). Instead, $\overline{H_1}$'s execution form $E\overline{H_1}$=IT_IH($\overline{H_1}$, H_2)=UNHLT[0, 1, $\{\langle 0, 1, \text{null}\rangle\}$]. H_2 cannot remain its original form after H_1 has been undone, otherwise, when undoing H_2, the execution of $\overline{H_2}$=UNHLT[1, 4, $\{\langle 1, 3, \text{red}\rangle, \langle 4, 1, \text{null}\rangle\}$] would highlight the string bcd in red, which is obviously wrong because H_1 has already been undone. Therefore, H_2 should be transformed against $\overline{H_1}$ to exclude H_1's effect. That is, H_2=IT_HU(H_2, $\overline{H_1}$)=HLT[1, 4, $\{\langle 1, 4, \text{null}\rangle\}$]. Two REs in the RT should be removed because they are both covered by H_1. On the other hand, IT_HU(H_2, $\overline{H_1}$) does not produce any new RE, therefore RT=[].

Thirdly, by executing $E\overline{H_i}$ and the new RT, HT=[H^*_1, H_2], the character a is de-highlighted, and there is no display rotation effect any more. Finally, the undo command carrying H_1's ID is propagated to $Site$ 2. If $E\overline{H_1}$=UNHLT[0, 1, $\{\langle 0, 1, \text{null}\rangle\}$] itself rather than the undo command is propagated to $Site$ 2, after the execution of $E\overline{H_1}$ at $Site$ 2, only the character a would be de-highlighted, which is obviously wrong because part of H_1's effect still remains (i.e., the string bcd is still highlighted in red).

Therefore when $Site$ 2 receives the undo command, the $SUCA(H_1, HT)$ will be invoked at $Site$ 2 to undo H_1. Firstly, make H_1's inverse $\overline{H_1}$=UNHLT[0, 4, $\{\langle 0, 1, \text{null}\rangle, \langle 1, 3, \text{green}\rangle\}$].

Secondly, since there is no operation after H_1, $\overline{H_1}$'s execution form $E\overline{H_1}$=$\overline{H_1}$. Two REs in the RT should also be removed because they are both covered by H_1, therefore RT=[].

Thirdly, by executing $E\overline{H_1}$ and the new RT, HT=[H_2, H^*_1], the character a is de-highlighted and the string bcd remains highlighted in green, and of course there is no display rotation effect any more.

5   Conclusions

Highlighting text in multi-user real-time group editors is very useful and more challenging than doing that in single-user editors. The multi-user environment brings the necessity of differentiating highlighting operations performed by different users to support some sort of group awareness. The user interface for highlights in multi-user group editors is emulated as the one in single-user editors in order to attract user acceptance and highlights are differentiated by users' ID colors.

The distributed collaborative environment brings the issue of consistency maintenance because concurrent operations and nondeterministic communication latency may cause inconsistency problems. The proposed **DR** approach can solve the divergence problem caused by concurrent overlapping highlighting operations. To solve the intention violation problem caused by the mixture of concurrent editing and highlighting operations, we contribute transformation algorithms IT_HI and IT_HD.

We argue that selective undo is more suitable than chronological undo for the undo of highlighting operations in multi-user group editors. It is certainly non-trivial to achieve a selective undo facility for the undo of highlighting operations in multi-user group editors. We propose a flexible undo solution by contributing transformation algorithms IT_IH, IT_HH, IT_HU, and the *SUCA* control algorithm. Our solution has the capacity of selectively undoing any highlighting operation at any time.

All algorithms presented in the paper have been implemented in our *REDUCE* (REal-time Distributed Unconstrained Collaborative Editing) system. We are working to improve the *DR* approach and make the highlighting feature available for public demonstration.

Acknowledgment

The work reported in this paper has been partially supported by an ARC (Australia Research Council) Large Grant (00000711).

References

1. R.M. Baecker et al.: The user-centred iterative design of collaborative writing software. Proceedings of the conference on Human factors in computing systems (1993) 399-405
2. James Begole et al.: Flexible Collaboration Transparency: Supporting Worker Independence in Replicated Application-Sharing Systems. ACM Transaction on Computer Human Interaction, Volume 6(2) (1999) 95-132
3. Thomas Berlage: A selective undo mechanism for graphical user interfaces based on command objects. ACM Transaction on Computer Human Interaction, Volume 1(3) (1994) 269-294
4. Paul Dourish and Victoria Bellotti: Awareness and Coordination in Shared Workspaces. Proceedings of ACM Conference on Computer Supported Cooperative Work (1992) 107-114
5. C. A. Ellis and S. J. Gibbs: Concurrency control in groupware systems. Proceedings of the ACM SIGMOD international conference on Management of data (1989) 399-407
6. Kenneth J. Rodham and Dan R. Olsen, JR.: Smart Telepointers: Maintaining Telepointer consistency in the Presence of User Interface Customization. ACM Transaction. on Graphics Volume 13(3) (1994) 300-307
7. Mark Roseman and Saul Greenberg: Building Real-Time Groupware with GroupKit, A Groupware Toolkit. ACM Transaction on Computer Human Interaction, Volume 3(1) (1996) 66-106
8. C.Sun: Undo any operation at any time in group editors. Proceedings of ACM Conference on Computer Supported Cooperative Work (2000) 191-200
9. C. Sun et al.: Achieving convergence, causality-preservation, and intention-preservation in real-time cooperative editing systems. ACM Transaction on Computer Human Interaction, Volume 5(1) (1998) 63-108

Extending the Modeling Efficiency of the UML Activity Diagram for the Design of Distributed Systems

Olga Fengler, Wolfgang Fengler, and Veselka Duridanova

Ilmenau Technical University
Department of Computer Architectures
P.O. Box 100565, 98684 Ilmenau, Germany
{olga,wfengler}@theoinf.tu-ilmenau.de

Abstract. The design of complex distributed embedded systems often presents great challenges because of the large number and dimensions of their components. This research paper discusses some of the problems of designing such systems. The use of Colored Dynamic Activity Diagrams for modeling complex real-time systems is suggested as a possible solution. The Colored Activity Diagrams bridge a gap between modeling technique and description power of High Level Petri nets. By coloring Activity Diagrams the behavior of several objects or processes can be modeled in a single diagram. They also have additional mechanisms for mapping dependences and relationships between individual objects. The color is a property which supports the intended transformation into the High Level Petri Nets allowing further the formal verification of the whole system. The usability of the method is shown in a modeled reference example.

1 Introduction

As distributed systems become ever more complex because of the large number and dimensions of their components, the importance of modeling has increased. In parallel the modeling techniques shall be adapted to meet this increasing complexity.

This paper describes the development of a modeling technique, which can be used for describing complex concurrent processes and systems. This technique combines excellent engineering manageability with outstanding descriptive clarity.

Unified Modeling Language [1] is now seen as the standard language and notation for developing object-oriented systems. The UML is based on three methods, the Object Modeling Technique [2], the Object-Oriented Software Engineering [3] and the Booch Method [4] and provides a variety of graphic-oriented capabilities for specifying, constructing, visualizing, and documenting object-oriented Systems. Graphic-oriented methods gain in importance because of the general tendency to replace the textual and algebraic description languages by more expressive and understandable one.

The Activity Diagrams of the UML can successfully model the control flow in digital systems.

H.Unger, T.Böhme, and A.Mikler (Eds.): PCS 2002, LNCS 2346, pp. 51-62, 2002.

The UML offers a semantics for the Activity Diagrams, which defines the meaning of the graphical elements and the relation between the elements. In the present work, this semantics has been developed further to achieve the following aims:

- to make the representation of distributed functions serving automation less complex
- to adopt certain elements of High Level Petri nets, already an established concept into the Activity Diagrams
- to achieve compact representation of similar parallel processes or objects
- to transform the extended Activity Diagram into High Level Petri nets for the purpose of later verification.

The paper shows how the new feature, "color", was incorporated into the existing rules. Colored Activity Diagrams (CoAD) based on the standard Activity Diagrams of the UML are defined below and their applicability demonstrated.

2   The Activity Diagram of the UML

The Activity Diagrams of the UML are based on the Event Diagrams and are defined as a specialization of the State Diagrams. They include states and state transition. The states represent the activity of one or more objects, the state transitions are triggered by the end of such activity operations. Events are unusual in Activity Diagrams. The state transitions can depend on conditions. In that case the state transition will be executed if the pre-standing activity is completed and the condition is fulfilled. The transitions are divided into simple and complex ones as in State Diagrams. One subset of the complex transitions describes the splitting of the control flow into several concurrent processes. The second subset defines alternatives as a possible structure of the control flow.

An Activity Diagram is attached to a class, a method or an use case and describes the dynamic behavior of the corresponding elements. The aim of the Activity Diagram is the description of the control or work flows in a system.

3   Colored Activity Diagram

3.1   Semantics and Notation

The Standard Activity Diagrams are convenient for the specification of one process. Real systems and processes are often modeled by diagrams that are very similar in their elements and structure. Two such processes are described with the use of the standard UML by two diagrams: one for each control flow. This complicates the visual representation and the whole design and a complicated mechanism with intermediary state shall be used for showing the dependences and the connections between. In the range of information technology, telecommunication, control systems and also of business processes a method is required which allows the modeling of several processes within the same diagram.

The Colored Activity Diagrams have been developed for this purpose. CoAD does not change the semantics of UML. They are an extension of the Standard UML Activity Diagrams and represent "foldings" of several simple diagrams. "Folding" denotes overlaying activities and transitions with similar contents and structure. The CoAD has several control flows, the standard activity diagram has only one. The number of the control flows is equal to the number of the processes modeled within the same diagram.

Each process possesses an abstract equivalence - a color, which represents this process in the Colored Diagram. The color must be unique within a diagram It is modeling a type or a symbolic identifier of the process. Colors of tokens are therefore not necessary natural colors.

Tokens are included to mark the current state. A colored token describes the local state of the corresponding process. The flow of the colored token visualizes the control flow of the process. A red colored token in a action A means, that a action A for the process corresponding to the color red is executing at this time.

3.2   Colored Action

A *colored action state* is a folding of several simple actions, which are processed for various tokens. Each token is separately processed as in standard action states.

A case can occur in the flow, when a token cannot be processed in some action, or only limited number of tokens can possess an action simultaneously. A restriction of a action called *actions capacity* is provided for such situations. It is a Boolean expression, whose disjunctive normal form describes all possible combinations of tokens in a colored action. The composition of the expression is described in following examples:

- **gr&bl&rd** – the action can be processed for three tokens simultaneously, for green, blue and red (gr&bl&rd = green AND blue AND red). All other tokens cannot enter this action;
- **gr∨bl∨rd** – only one token of green, blue or red color can be processed in this colored action at the time (gr∨bl∨rd = green OR blue OR red);
- **gr&(bl∨rd)** – this action can be processed for two tokens simultaneously, the possible combinations appear from the expression: gr&(bl∨rd) = gr&bl∨gr&rd = (green AND blue) OR (green AND red). The total capacity equals two.

The colored action state is represented in the same way as the standard one with addition of the expression, that describes the action's capacity (Figure 1). The expression shall be written under the action's name (e.g. action A in Figure 1). Active colors are to write using bold or upper case letters.

When an action can be processed for all colors of the model simultaneously an alternative notation can be used: a black dot in the bottom left corner of the action can replace the expression and only the active colors are shown (e.g. action B in Figure 1).

In the case if the total capacity of an action is lower than the number of colors in model, but all colors can be processed in this action, the capacity in the bottom left corner replaces the expression and only the active colors are shown (e.g. action C in Figure 1).

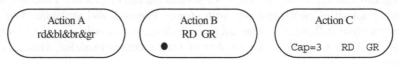

Fig.1. Colored actions

3.3   Transition

The transition in CoAD is a folding of standard transitions, each triggered only by one defined token. The transition can be triggered by all tokens independently or only by several tokens simultaneously – this depends on the *transition's function*. All other properties of transitions within the CoAD are the same as in standard UML diagrams.

The transition's function is a Boolean expression, which is attached to a transition and defines the triggering. The colors are used as arguments of this function. If the token is already processed by the source state, the value of the corresponding argument changes to true. If the value of the whole transition's function has been set to true, the transition fires for all these tokens.

A transition in CoAD is shown as a black arrow directed from source state to target state with the transition's function attached to it (Figure 2).

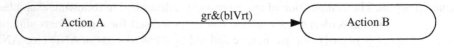

Fig.2. The transition in CoAD

If the transition's function represents a disjunction of all model's colors, the transition's function at the arrow can be omitted.

3.4   OR-Split

The CoAD offers the possibility to implement a conditional branch – for this purpose the element *OR-split* (a decision) is provided. The OR-split shall be used for a possible splitting of a token according to its color and guard conditions.

The OR-split (Figure 3) has one incoming and two or more outgoing transitions. The outgoing transitions can be split in groups: each group contains only the transitions with the same functions. All groups possess their own set of guard conditions, which are mutually exclusive within one group (the same rules apply to the guard conditions in standard activity diagrams). If a group consists of only one transition, no guard is attached to this transition, or this guard is always true.

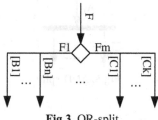

Fig.3. OR-split

The behavior of tokens can be described as follows: When a token enters the OR-split, the group has to be defined, whose function contains this color (there can be only one such group). The value of the guard conditions will be evaluated after that. There must be only one transition, whose guard equals true; this transition will be triggered by this token.

The OR-split can also be used for splitting one transition into several with more simple functions.

3.5   OR-Join

The *OR-Join* serves to merge the transitions that were split previously. In general case the OR-join (Figure 4) has several incoming and one outgoing transition, that possess functions F1..Fn and F respectively. The function F shall contain all colors of the F1..Fn functions, because the outgoing transition shall be triggered by all tokens that can enter this OR-join.

Fig.4. OR-join

3.6   AND-Split

The AND-split serves to split one token into several ones that flow in parallel branches. The AND-split has one incoming and several outgoing transitions (Figure 5).

The token entering the AND-split will be split and directed to all transitions, that can be triggered by this token. All transitions are triggered by one token simultaneously; if one of the outgoing transitions cannot be triggered, for example because the source state is occupied, no other can be triggered too.

All split tokens must be further merged in one AND-Join.

Fig.5. AND-split

3.7   AND-Join (Synchronization)

The *AND-Join* or Synchronization serves to merge the tokens that were split by the AND-split. The AND-join (Figure 6) has several incoming (functions F1..Fn) and one outgoing (function F) transitions.

All the incoming transitions can be assigned to one or more groups – each group corresponds to one color and consists of all transitions, whose functions contain this color. It is possible that one group consists of only one transition.

The outgoing transition will be triggered by the token only when this token has triggered all the incoming transitions of the corresponding group – the split tokens will be joined into one and it will enter the source activity. In all other cases the transition will not fire.

Fig.6. AND-join

3.8   Start and End States

Before executing the CoAD all tokens reside in the *start state.* The start state has one or more outgoing transitions whose functions do not contain idem arguments (c.f Figure 7). The tokens leave this state simultaneously, sequential or in any other order.

When a token reaches the end state, the execution of this process will be finished. The token can appear in the start state again and the process can be executed once again.

Sub activity states and swim lanes are also possible within CoADs. Their semantics does not differ from the standard and is specified in UML.

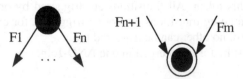

Fig.7. Start and End states

4   Time Intervals

Time intervals are implemented for a better observation of the model's behavior. The duration of action's execution can be defined depending on colors, i.e. the processing an action takes an explicit time.

The colored action possesses a new property – time interval. The time interval models the maximum and minimum duration of processing the action. This time interval can be the same for all colors, which can enter this action or each color can have its own time interval.

If the minimum processing duration is vanishing short, it can be set to zero.

The time interval can be expressed by constants, but also by variables. The variable time interval will be evaluated dynamically after the token enters this action; it can be different for various tokens.

The time interval is a parameter of a time event (see UML - state machine – time event); the expression must be attached to the outgoing transition. The following cases can occur:

- The time interval is the same for all colors: **after(Tmin, Tmax)**;

- The difference between **Tmin** and **Tmax** is vanishing short: **after(T)**;

- The time interval differs for some colors:
  after(Tmin1,Tmax1)/Color1,Color2; after(Tmin2,Tmax2)/Color3.

If there is no time interval attached, the action executes immediately.

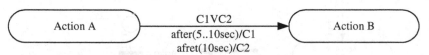

Fig.8. The notation of time interval

5   Transformation of Colored Activity Diagrams into High Level Petri Nets

A CoAD that is transformed into a Colored Petri-net [5] can be analyzed by formal and/or simulative methods that already exist.

The transformation of standard activity diagrams into Petri-nets was already developed [6]. The transformation algorithm especially for CoAD will be described here. This algorithm is specified in [7].

5.1   Transformation Rules

This transformation algorithm implements the following steps:
- Splitting the CoAD into separate elements;
- Replacing of the CoAD-elements by CPN-elements;
- Combining the CPN-elements to one colored Petri-net.

The net appearing after the transformation is a special class of CPN and has the following properties:
- All places have the capacity one for each color;
- All arcs have the multiplicity one for each color;
- The transition always reproduces the token color. The number of consumed and produced tokens depends on the specification of outgoing arcs;
- The outgoing arcs possess functions that include all the model's colors.

Step 1: Splitting CoAD to elements.
The CoAD is split into separate elements. Thereby the transitions are isolated and numbered.
Step 2: Replacing the CoAD-elements with CPN-elements.
In this step every CoAD-element must be replaced by the corresponding CPN-element.

The colored action state is replaced by a transition (Figure 9). The pre-place can adopt all the colors that are present in the incoming transition's function. The properties of post-place are defined by the pre-place of the following element.

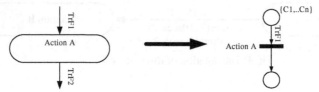

Fig.9. Transforming the action into CPN

The CPN-element that corresponds to the OR-split is shown on Figure 10. Each transition corresponds to one guard condition and fires when the condition is fulfilled.

The rules of composing the place capacities are equal to these in the previous section.

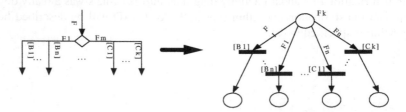

Fig.10. Transformation of OR-split into CPN

The CPN-element that corresponds to the OR-join is shown on Figure 11.

Fig.11. Transformation of OR-joint into CPN

The CPN-element that corresponds to the AND-split is shown on Figure 12.

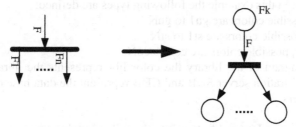

Fig.12. Transformation of AND-split ino CPN

The CPN-element that corresponds to the AND-join is shown on Figure 13. This construction implements the algorithm of synchronization.

The place capacities (Fc1..Fcn) are composed as shown in the previous sections.

CPN-transitions (T(C1)..T(Cm)) correspond to each group of incoming transitions (see 3.6). The number of the outgoing arcs from each pre-place is equivalent to the place's capacity.

From each pre-place exist as many outgoing arcs as the number of terms in this place's capacity: each arc corresponds to a color and is directed to the transition that represents this color (see Figure 13).

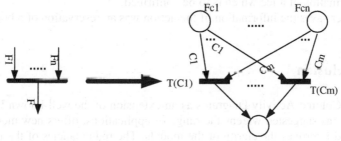

Fig.13. Transformation of AND-join into CPN

Step 3: Combining the CPN-elements into one colored Petri net.
By the last step the CPN-elements will be joined into one colored Petri-net. The places with the same identifiers shall be merged.

6   Example

In this chapter the possibility of modeling a system using CoADs is shown, as is the advantage of these diagrams in comparison to standard practice. The example describes the search algorithm in a library using internet connections and services. Each user of the library can operate from his (local) computer, the library has a server that belongs to a hierarchical system, e.g. university, which inspects the current status (user type) of the customer. This means that there are several user types with different authorization rights. In this example the following types are defined:

gu – guest, possible colors are gu1 to guN
st –student, possible colors are st1 to stN
co – coworker, possible colors are co1 to coN.

Within the diagram of the library the color libr represents the library server and within the administration server SDB and CDB represent the data base of the students resp. the coworkers.

The diagram shown on Figure 14, describes the following processes:

1. Each user has to login to the administration server with his name, birth day, status. (AuthorizationIdentification). The server confirms the login.
2. The library server verifies the data of the students and the coworkers by comparing with the data bases. This operation shall be omitted for the guests.

3. The user next chooses the service he needs: searching a book or renewing some one from his loan, coworker can operate with the data bases. (Further service "searching a book" has been followed by the diagram of fig. 14).
4. The server is now checking, if the desired book is available. In this case a student or a coworker can order the book immediately, a guest obtain the information of a fee which is to be confirmed.

The server saves the information, if the action was an reservation of a book.

7   Conclusion

The use of Colored Activity Diagrams as an extension of the well-known UML activity diagrams as suggested widens the range of applications, offers new modeling possibilities and improves the clarity of the models. The redundancies of the information are omitted. The practicability of the method was demonstrated on the model of a library server.

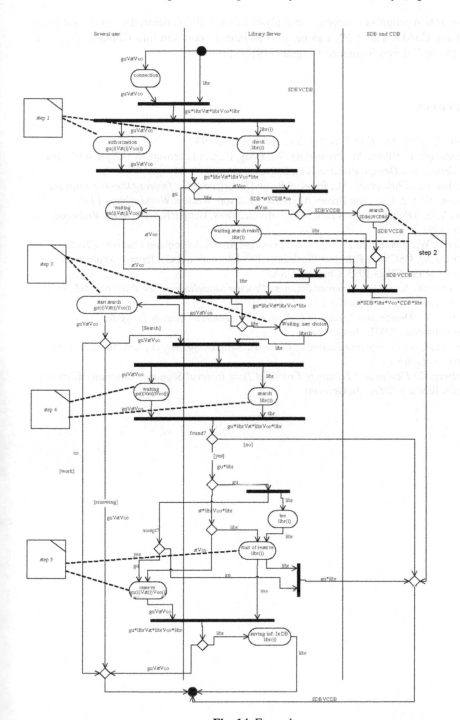

Fig. 14. Example

Research in progress concerns the analysis of the CPN generated by the transformation of the CoAD. This CPN can be used as interim notation into Colored State Diagrams [8] or Colored Sequence Diagrams [9] additionally.

References

1. OMG *Unified Modelling Specification*, ver. 1.3, June 1999.
2. Rumbaugh, J., Bllaha, M., Premerlani, W., Eddy, F., and Lorenson, W.: *Object-Oriented Modelling and Design*, Prentice-Hall, Englewood Cliffs, 1991
3. Jacobson, I., Christerson, M., Jonsson, P., and Övergaard, G.: *Object-Oriented Software Engineering*. A Use Case Driven Approach, Addison-Wesley, Workingham, 1992
4. Booch, G.: *Object-Oriented Design with Applications*, Benjamin/Cummings, Redwood City, 1991
5. Fengler, W.: *A coloured Petri Net Interpretation for Modelling and Control in Textile Processing*. CSCW & Petri Net Workshop, 14th International Conference Application and Theory of Petri Nets 1993, Chicago, USA
6. Mühlpfordt, A.: *Object-Oriented Business Process Modelling on the Basis of UML*, Ph.D. thesis, Ilmenau, 1998. (In German)
7. Riabov, Y.: *Design and Testing of Coloured Time Interval Activity Diagrams*, Diploma thesis, Ilmenau, 2001. (In German)
8. Slavianov, A.: *Design and Testing of Coloured State Diagrams*, Diploma thesis, Ilmenau, 2001. (In German)
9. Amberg, C.: *Design and Testing of Coloured Time Interval Sequence Diagrams*, Diploma thesis, Ilmenau, 2001. (In German)

An XML Knowledge Base System for Scheduling Problems

Leonilde Rocha Varela[1], Joaquim Nunes Aparício[2], and Sílvio Carmo Silva[1]

[1] University of Minho, School of Engineering
Dept. of Production and Systems Campus Azurém, 4800-058 Guimarães, Portugal
{leonilde,scarmo}@dps.uminho.pt
[2] New University of Lisbon, Faculty of Science and Technology
Dept. of Computer Science, Quinta da Torre, 2825-114 Monte de Caparica, Portugal
jna@di.fct.unl.pt

Abstract. Production Scheduling is an important function strongly contributing to the competitiveness of industrial and service companies. In this communication we make a contribution for XML based specification of scheduling concepts in order to allow for a standard representation of scheduling problems and related tasks. This information modeling is used in the development of a web based decision support system for the resolution of scheduling problems. An XML-based Knowledge Base System may be useful not only to facilitate the specification of scheduling problems but also in the search for the most suitable available algorithms and methods, which can then be used for finding good solutions to the problems. The existing algorithms, as well as their corresponding implementations, may either be local or remotely available, through the Internet.

1 Introduction

Production Scheduling may be defined as the activity, of allocating tasks to production resources, during a certain period of time. The result of this management activity is usually expressed as a production schedule. Such schedule can be more or less detailed, in accordance with the intended objectives and the period of the plan. In some cases we are only interested in obtaining a sequence in which the jobs should be processed by certain machines, and in other cases we may be interested, in knowing the planned start and finishing times of each operation of the jobs.

An effective and efficient resolution of a scheduling problem relies on the identification of suitable scheduling algorithms. When several methods and algorithms to solve the problem exist, it is important to make evaluation of solutions based on the alternatives available in accordance with some specified criteria and objectives to be achieved. Thus, we should be able to properly solve a problem, through the execution of one or more scheduling algorithms and, in this case, subsequently choose the best solution provided by them. These algorithms can be local or remotely available through the web. Thus, this work

H. Unger, T. Böhme, and A. Mikler (Eds.): I²CS 2002, LNCS 2346, pp. 63–74, 2002.
© Springer-Verlag Berlin Heidelberg 2002

intends to be a contribution for a better resolution process of scheduling problems, by means of web-based computation. The system is being developed by the cooperation of researcher from the Computer Science Department of the New University of Lisbon and the Department of Production and Systems of the University of Minho, in order to enable a better decision support for scheduling problems resolution. This requires identification of such problems, which can be classified by a set of factors, which, in turn, enable specifying a clear and objective problem categorization structure to which real problem instances belong. The existence of a great variety of scheduling problems demands for the adoption for a systematic notation for problem representation that serves as a basis for its classification[1]. This notation allows identifying, unequivocally and precisely, the underlying characteristics of the problem that we intend to solve. The nomenclature includes the manufacturing system identification, the definition of the performance measure to be considered and some additional constraints that may help to characterize a problem.

Here we propose a standard representation of scheduling problems and related concepts. According to this representation, the XML language is used as both a specification language for scheduling data modeling and solving scheduling on the Internet. This kind of data modeling allows, for instance, identifying scheduling problems and algorithms for its resolution. This identification process is achieved through a XML specification of scheduling problems and scheduling algorithms primitives. In order to make world wide collaboration of users, the proposed specification has to have a fundamental data structure and a basic framework of representation for scheduling problems and resolution algorithms as well as other related concepts.

This paper is organized as follows. The next section describes the nature of scheduling problems using a nomenclature for the classification of these problems and a brief description of the problem main characteristics and classification factors. Some algorithm references to common scheduling problem classes are also presented. Sections 3 and 4 illustrate the web based scheduling system architecture and its main functionalities. Section 4 also shows a sample XML specification of scheduling problem classes and other related modeling aspects and presents some advantages of using the XML language. The last section presents some concluding remarks as well as some additional discussion points related to the future developments of this work.

2 Problem Description

Scheduling problems belong to a much broader class of combinatorial optimization problems, which may either be easy or hard (NP-hard problems) to solve. Detailed information about complexity of scheduling can be found in [2],[3], [4] and [5]. In the presence of NP-hard problems we may try to relax some constraints imposed on the original problem and then solve the relaxed problem. The solution of the latter may be a good approximation to the solution of the original one. It is rather obvious that the time we often can devote for solving particular scheduling problems is usually short. Thus, the examination of the complexity of these problems should be a basis of any further analysis to problem solving. Fortunately, not all NP-hard problems are equally hard from a practical perspective. Some NP-hard problems can be solved pseudo-polynomially using approximation algorithms that generally provide only feasible solutions, which although normally sub-optimal are within a fixed percentage of the optimum. Examples of this kind of methods are dynamic programming or branch and bound techniques. Other approaches to obtain good or satisfactory solutions in acceptable time are based on the nowadays widely used local (or neighborhood) search techniques, such as Genetic Algorithms (GA), Simulated Annealing (SA), and Tabu Search (TS), which are also known as meta-heuristics and extended neighborhood search techniques. There are also other interesting types of scheduling approaches, which are also widely used, like simulation-based approaches and bottleneck methods, among many others. All these approaches tend to provide good results in the available time to take decisions, reasons why, in this work, we intend to incorporate them in the web scheduling system we are developing.

Good schedules strongly contribute to the increase companies success. This is achieved, among other ways, through deadlines satisfaction for the accepted orders, low flow times, few ongoing jobs in the system, low stock levels, high resource utilization and low production costs. All these objectives can be better satisfied through the execution of the most suitable scheduling algorithms available for the resolution of each particular problem. In order to execute the scheduling process it is necessary to clearly specify the problem to be solved. As mentioned above, scheduling problems have a set of characteristics that must be clearly and unequivocally defined. These characteristics include a class of factors related with the production environment, i.e. system and machines, and other classes that allow defining the characteristics of the jobs and resources and the performance measure or evaluation criterion. The first group of characteristics is related with the environment where the production is carried out. Thus, in a first instance it is necessary to specify the manufacturing environment, where the scheduling problem to solve occurs. The manufacturing environment specification is denoted by α and includes the production system type definition and, eventually, the indication of the number of machines that exist in that production system. Other characteristics associated with scheduling problems, important and necessary for an adequate characterization of problems, are the constraints imposed to the manufacturing environment and resources (β), e.g. machines and operators, and job processing conditions. Some important processing conditions are, for example, related with the existence of auxiliary resources, like robots and transportation devices and/or the existence of buffers, among others factors. All main scheduling problem factors are summarized in Tab. 1 that resumes a problem classification notation in the form of ($\alpha \mid \beta \mid \gamma$) [1], which serves as a basis for the XML-based problem specification model underlying to this work. This notation is based on notations proposed by Blazewics [2], Brucker [3] and Jordan [4], as well as on other information presented by Morton [6] and by other authors [5], [7], and [8].

Table 1. Scheduling problems characteristics

Class	Factor	Description	Value
α	α_1	Manufacturing system type	P, Q, R, X ,O, J, F, PMPM, ...
	α_2	Number of machines	O, k
	β_1	Job/operation preemption	$O, pmtn$
	β_2	Precedence constraints	prec, chain, tree, sp-graph
	β_3	Ready times	O, r_j
	β_4	Restrictions on processing times	$p_j = 1, p_{ji} = 1,$ $p_j = p, p_{inf} \leq p_j \leq p_{sup}, ...$
	β_5	Due dates (deadlines)	O, d_j
β	β_6	Batches/families processing	O,batch
	β_7	Number of jobs or tasks in a job (job shop case)	O, nj
	β_8	Job/task priorities	O, w_j
	β_9	Dynamic machine availability	O, avail
	β_{10}	Additional/auxiliary resources	O, aux
	β_{11}	Buffers	O, no-wait
	β_{12}	Setup (changeover)	O,setup*
γ	γ	Performance measure	$C_{max}, \sum C_j, \sum w_j C_j,$ $L_{max}, \sum T_j, ...$

The use of this notation can be illustrated by the example $F||C_{max}$ which reads as: "Scheduling of non-preemptable and independent tasks of arbitrary processing times (lengths), arriving to the system at time 0, on a (simple) flow shop, in order to minimize schedule length". Tab. 2 shows some typical examples of scheduling problems versus algorithms, based on information presented by Bruker [3], illustrating the close relationship between scheduling problem classes and correspondent resolution algorithms references. Information like this can be obtained through the web scheduling decision support system put forward in this work. The link between problems and algorithms is done using the information available in a knowledge base of scheduling algorithms. The system is able to quickly assign methods to problems that occur in real manufacturing environments. This is further explained in the next section.

The problems in Tab. 2 are a small sample of makespan flow shop scheduling problems among a vast universe of possible problems, which may appear in real world production systems. Table 1 resumes the scheduling problem classification nomenclature used, and includes a wide range of problem classification factors, which may be combined in many ways.

Some of those factors are related with constraints, such as precedence constraints. In presence of this kind of constraint and under forward scheduling, a job can be started only after all of its predecessor jobs have been completed. Another usual constraint is associated with processing times and affects job start and completion times. These scheduling problems in industry are concerned with solving the allocation of production tasks to production resources available in

Table 2. Scheduling algorithms attributed to problems

Problem classes	Algorithm reference	Observations
$F2\|\|C_{max}$	Johnson(1954)	Maximal polynomially solvable Without preemption
$F2\|rj\|C_{max}$	Lenstra et al (1977)	Minimal NP-hard without preemption
$F2\|rj; no-wait\|C_{max}$	Roeck (1984)	Maximal polynomially solvable with no wait
$F3\|pmtn\|C_{max}$	Gonzalez & Sahni (1978) Cho & Sahni (1981)	Maximal polynomially solvable with preemption
$F3\|\|C_{max}$	Garey et al (1976)	Minimal NP-hard without preemption
$F\|p_{ji}=1; prec\|C_{max}$	Leung et al (1984) Timkovsky (1998)	Minimal NP-hard without preemption
$FMPT\|n=3\|C_{max}$	Kraemer (1995)	Minimal NP-hard with multiprocessor task
$FMPM, 3\|\|C_{max}$	Garey et al (1976)	Minimal NP-hard with multipurpose machines
$FMPM, m\|r_j; p_{ji}=1\|C_{max}$	Brucker et al (1997)	Maximal polynomially solvable with multipurpose machines
$FMPM\|prec; p_{ji}=1\|C_{max}$	Ullman (1975)	Minimal NP-hard with multipurpose machines

different manufacturing systems. Typical such systems include several types of flow shops usually used in Product Oriented Manufacturing Systems (POMS) [9] and in cellular manufacturing systems. In spite of apparently simple, scheduling problems in flow shops can be quite complex. Complexity increases as flow shops become more complex, such as flow shops with multi-purpose machines (FMPM) [3]. This complexity increases still further due to additional constraints, related with availability of resources, time availability for scheduling decisions, and last not least, due to several dynamic sources of scheduling disturbances, often demanding for complex scheduling processes.

3   Web System Architecture and Functionalities

Since 1995 great happenings have changed the world of information technology, especially the emergence of new Internet technologies. The eXtensible Markup Language (XML) is one of those new technologies that has been having a wide acceptance and caused great impact on Internet real world applications, since its release by the World Wide Web Consortium (W3C) in 1998 [10]. XML enables to describe structures and meanings of data with a simple syntax and is an ideal candidate format for exchanging and processing data through the Internet. Other advantages of XML based representation are its openness, simplicity and scalability [11]. This is one of the main reasons why we have chosen XML to develop our application. For details about XML and related technologies (DTD, XSL, XML Schemas, Namespaces, etc.) see, for example [10], [11] or [12].

The Web applications can use XML for local data processing, for showing multiple views of the data and for representing more complex data structures. Therefore, XML may guarantee the future utilization of data formats and the exchange of data structures, so that the web documents and the platforms become more robust for systems integration [13]. There are many other web-based technologies available for data storage and transferring, but we think that it is more adequate and easier to develop a new system using these new techniques rather than using conventional techniques such as EDI (Electronic Data Interchange). XML based data exchange is becoming very popular in global manufacturing, and this will cause connectivity becoming more and more convenient and necessary. As it has been said before, the main purpose of this work consists on trying to improve the resolution of scheduling problems. Therefore, we decided to develop a web-based scheduling decision support system, based on XML modeling.

Figure 1 illustrates a general outline of the web technology necessary for XML applications development. XML documents, as well as related parts, may either be located on the server or on the client side. In this work the documents are stored on the server (e.g. XML and DTD documents) in order to achieve easily and efficient data transferring.

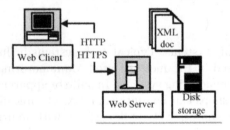

Fig. 1. Web technology for XML implementation

Some interesting XML applications, which are more or less related with this work, are PDML (Product Data Markup Language), RDF (Resource Description Format) and STEPml [14]. Other XML specifications devoted to manufacturing processes are JDF (Job Definition Format), PSL (Process Specification Language), PIX-ML (Product Information Exchange), PIF (Process Interchange Format) and XML-based workflow [12].

The system we are developing is schematized in Fig. 2. The main element of the system structure is an interface for introduction, validation, and transformation of manufacturing scheduling data. The interface is mainly controlled by DTD and XSL documents stored in a database. The system allows the execution of either local or remote scheduling algorithms. On remote executions, XML data is easily read and processed in every computer system since it is stored and sent as strings.

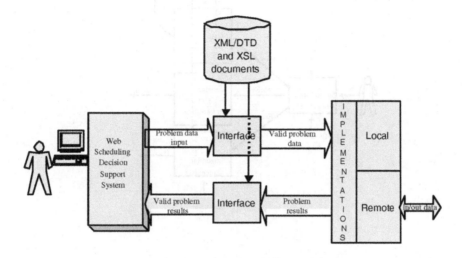

Fig. 2. Web-system architecture

Figure 3 presents an IDEF0 based diagram illustrating the Web-system functionalities. These include knowledge insertion, about scheduling problems and algorithms, and correspondent information searching. Another important functionality is the execution of scheduling algorithms, given the manufacturing scheduling problem definition. The selection of one or more specific algorithms is made through a searching process on the knowledge base of scheduling algorithms.

The main issues we want to address through fundamental system functionalities are closely related to information modeling, and are summarized as follows:

- Classification and identification of scheduling problems, by using a notation previously presented in Sect. 2.
- Classification and identification of scheduling methods and algorithms.
- Association of scheduling algorithms to scheduling problems for its resolution and, finally,
- Possibility of solving scheduling problems, through the selection of one or several algorithms, allowing results comparison and selection of the most suitable one.

The scheduling information is stored in XML documents. These documents are verified using DTDs, before being put in the XML database. Users can make requests for scheduling problem classes and algorithms information visualization, algorithms execution and scheduling problem results presentation and storage.

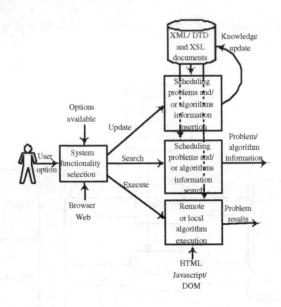

Fig. 3. Web-system funcionalities

The data can be shown in different views, using existing XSL documents, adequate for each specific visualization request.

The appropriate programs integrating the Web-based system enable the generation of XML data, and encoding programs read and process this data according to the existing rules.

XML is used as a standard to describe transmissive data on an open computer system network such as the Internet.

4   XML Specification Primitives

This section presents a general XML-based specification for production scheduling concepts modelling. In a narrow sense, the specification of scheduling concepts gives us syntax of data description for this kind of scheduling problems, but in a broader sense, it can be seen as a general modeling form of such problems.

The proposed specification framework provides a general model of scheduling problems and related concepts, and consequently a method of describing each particular problem and algorithm, by user information introduction.

With respect to the performance measurement parameters, we think that objectives cannot be put together into one parameter. In other words, the XML specification provides a set of important parameters necessary for the most common kind of scheduling decisions. Then a planner chooses his/her preferences according to the circumstances. However, the XML specification allows users to add their own domain specific performance measures to be considered.

In manufacturing, scheduling problems generally concern about jobs and resource availability for the processing of the jobs. Here, the primitive resource means workstations, machines, equipments, tools, labors, and so on. In these problems a job represents an action that has certain time duration. During that time, the job changes status of inventories of corresponding items, occupying or loading some particular resources. The jobs need some input materials and produce some outputs. In some cases, input or output are called parts, work-in-process inventories or products. In XML specification, these objects are referred as items. From the viewpoint of Scheduling Problems, objects in the shop floor can be classified as resource category or as item category. If the target objects are produced or consumed by the job, they are defined as items. Otherwise, if they are renewable after the job being completed, we define them as resources. In defining job release orders, many attributes have to be considered such as item, quantity, location or destination, due date, processing time, and so on.

One of the most critical success factors for implementation of shop floor scheduling systems is the possibility of dealing with various constraints in each kind of production process, as explained in Sec. 2.

When the designer deals with XML, he/she writes tags hierarchy as elements, and possible attributes. These structures are concerned as a kind of syntax for each application domain. According to that syntax, a XML parser for the particular application translates data for each problem.

Listing 1 shows a sample XML document, a partial knowledge about (scheduling) problem classes. In that specification the tag <problems> is the root element and can have several <problem> tags as second level tags. These tags, on the other hand, include tags such as <alpha>, <beta> and <gamma> which, in turn, can be subdivided in other third level tags, accordingly to the problem constrains under consideration that represent the real scheduling problem (c.f. Tab. 1).

List. 1 *Example of XML top-level description*

```
<?xml version="1.0"?>
<!DOCTYPE problems SYSTEM "problems.dtd">
<problems>
   <problem>
   <!--FMPM, m | rj; pji=1 | Cmax-->
      <alpha>
         <alpha1 system_type="FMPM"/>
         <alpha2 machines_quantity="m"/>
      </alpha>
      <beta>
         <beta3 ready_times="rj"/>
         <beta4 processing_times="pji=1"/>
      </beta>
      <gamma measure="Cmax"/>
   </problem>
</problems>
```

XML only models scheduling data. However, it is necessary to impose a process for controlling the data to be included in the XML documents, as well as its structure. Listing 2 shows DTD code, which describes the information that can be considered in the scheduling problem classes in the correspondent XML documents previously illustrated in List. 1.

List. 2 *Example of DTD specification*

```
<!-- Elements and attributes declaration -->
<!ELEMENT problems (problem+)>
<!ELEMENT problem (alpha?, beta?, gamma)>
<!-- Alpha elements -->
<!ELEMENT alpha (alpha1?, alpha2?)>
<!ELEMENT alpha1 EMPTY>
<!ATTLIST alpha1 production_system (O | P | Q | R | PMPM | ...) "O">
<!ELEMENT alpha2 EMPTY>
<!ATTLIST alpha2 machines (1 | 2 | 3 | m) "1">
<!-- Beta elements -->
<!ELEMENT beta (beta1?, beta2?, beta3?, ..., beta12?)>
<!ELEMENT beta1 EMPTY>
<!ATTLIST beta1 interruption (O | pmtn) "O">
...
<!ELEMENT beta12 EMPTY>
<!ATTLIST beta12 system_setup (O | setup) "O">
<!-- Gamma element -->
<!ELEMENT gamma EMPTY>
<!ATTLIST gamma measure (Cmax | ...) "O">
```

The DTD specifications and the XML documents are the main body that constitutes the specification framework underlying to this work.

With the addition of DTDs, XML can handle many more complex tasks. Besides the XML and DTD documents shown in List. 1 and 2, there are also other XML and DTD documents, corresponding to algorithms, algorithms implementations, and other lower-level documents, for instance, for detailed scheduling problems data and results storage, presentation and processing. The DTD code from List. 2 is also associated to the user interface illustrated in Fig. 4. In this case, the DTD enables validating the user data input, allowing only valid data introduction, according to the underlying scheduling problem characterization schema used.

It is still an open question how the Resource Description Format [14] can be used for describing resources in our system. It seam that the RDF is too general for our purposes but an adequate subset of the vocabulary may be used in the system.

5   Conclusions

In manufacturing enterprises, it is important nowadays, as a competitive strategy, to explore and use software applications, now becoming available through

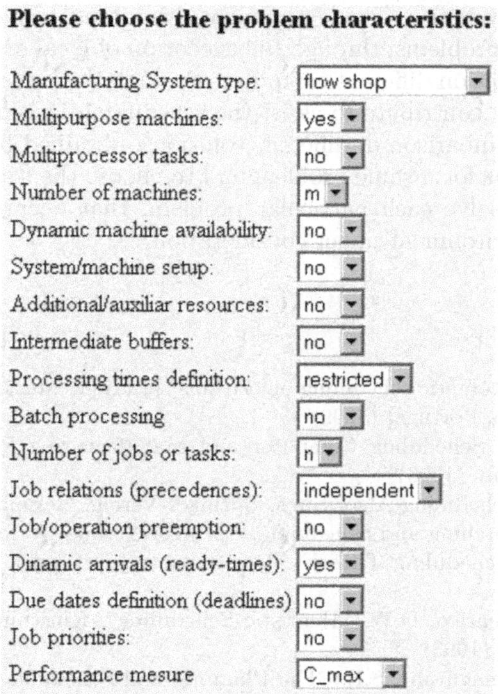

Please choose the problem characteristics:

Manufacturing System type:	flow shop
Multipurpose machines:	yes
Multiprocessor tasks:	no
Number of machines:	m
Dynamic machine availability:	no
System/machine setup:	no
Additional/auxiliar resources:	no
Intermediate buffers:	no
Processing times definition:	restricted
Batch processing	no
Number of jobs or tasks:	n
Job relations (precedences):	independent
Job/operation preemption:	no
Dinamic arrivals (ready-times):	yes
Due dates definition (deadlines)	no
Job priorities:	no
Performance mesure	C_max

Fig. 4. Submitting a problem characterization

the Internet and Intranets, for solving scheduling problems. This communication proposes an XML-based specification framework for production scheduling concepts modelling, in a web-based production scheduling decision support system. Some of the important functions include the ability to represent scheduling problems and the identification of appropriate available algorithms to solve them. In order to make possible flexible communication among different scheduling applications, it is used an XML-based data modelling. Therefore, an important aspect of the scheduling system is the XML-based scheduling data specification. This specification contributes to the improvement of the scheduling processes, by allowing an easy selection of several alternative available algorithms or methods for problem solving, as well as an easy maintenance of the knowledge base itself. This primarily includes both scheduling problems and algorithms, which are available through the Internet. It is also an adequate specification format for the exchange of scheduling data, since it enables to handle with loosely coupled systems and with complex hierarchical data. The XML based specification can be generated and visualized by computers in appropriate and different ways. An important issue is that the data representation model is general, accommodating a large variety of production scheduling problems, which may occur in different types of manufacturing environments. Furthermore, by using the web scheduling decision support system under development, we intend to facilitate the resolution of scheduling problems, through the execution of local or remote scheduling algorithms, available on different computers through the Internet. Therefore, the system will greatly contribute to assist the scheduling decision-making process, by allowing the comparison of different solutions, obtained by the execution of different algorithms for a same problem and to choose the solution which shows more suitable to solve each particular problem, that occurs in the identified manufacturing environment under consideration.

References

[1] Varela, L.: Automatic scheduling algorithms selection. Master's thesis, Universidade do Minho, Portugal (1999)
[2] Blazewics, J.: Scheduling Computer and Manufacturing Processes. Springer-Verlag, Germany (1996)
[3] Brucker, P.: Scheduling Algorithms. Springer-Verlag, Germany (1995)
[4] Jordan, C.: Batching and Scheduling. Springer-Verlag, Germany (1996)
[5] Pinedo, M.: Scheduling Theory, Algorithms and Systems. Prentice-Hall, USA (1995)
[6] Morton, T., Pentico, D.W.: Heuristic Scheduling Algorithms. John Wiley and Sons Inc, USA (1993)
[7] Artiba, A., Elmaghraby, S.E.: The Planning and Scheduling of Production Systems. Chapman and Hall, England (1997)
[8] Chrétienne, P.: Scheduling Theory and its Applications. John Wiley and Sons Inc, England (1995)
[9] Silva, S.C., Alves, A.C.: Spop – sistemas de produção orientados ao produto. In: TeamWork2001 Conference, Lisbon, Portugal (2001) 1–19
[10] Ceponkus, A., Hoodbhoy, F.: Applied XML. Wiley Computer Publishing, USA (1999)
[11] Abiteboul, S.S., Buneman, P., Suciu, D.: Data on the web: from relations to semistructured data and XML. Morgan Kaufmann Publishers, Los Altos, CA 94022, USA (1999)
[12] Harper, F.: XML Standards and Tools. eXcelon Corporation, USA (2001)
[13] Aparício, J.N.: Desenvolvimento de aplicações em XML. XML Course Notes - Portuguese (2002)
[14] Pardi, W.J.: XML: Enabling Next-generation Web Applications. Microsoft Press, USA (1999)

Compressibility as a Measure of Local Coherence in Web Graphs

Jeannette C.M. Janssen[1] and Nauzer Kalyaniwalla[2]

[1] Dept. of Mathematics and Statistics, Dalhousie University
Halifax B3H 3J5, NS, Canada
janssen@mscs.dal.ca
[2] Dept. of Engineering Mathematics, Dalhousie University
Halifax B3J 2X4, NS, Canada
nauzer@linear1.engmath.dal.ca

Abstract. A networked information space is a collection of information entities connected by links. In this paper, we propose a method to determine if a given subset of a networked information space is randomly chosen or thematically unified, based solely on the link structure of the subset. The proposed method uses compressibility as a measure of the link structure. The method is illustrated with an example.

1 Introduction

With the advent of the internet and especially the World Wide Web (WWW), networked information spaces have become very common. A networked information space is a collection of information bearing entities that are linked together. The canonical example of such a structure is the WWW, where web-pages are the information bearing entities and the hyperlinks form the directed links [4,12]. In digital libraries such as *ResearchIndex* [11], individual publications are the information bearing entities and the references in each publication form the directed links [2]. Other examples of networked information spaces are those that represent calling patterns or financial transactions, where information entities representing users are linked by the users' interactions. Distributed file sharing systems such as *Napster* follow similar principles of organisation.

One of the distinguishing features of a networked information space is that the link structure as well as the to the information bearing entities contain stored information. A fact recognised and exploited for the WWW by search-engines like *Google*, whose enormous success and popularity is largely due to a link-based page-ranking scheme. Understanding the link structure of networked information spaces would allow more effective mining of the enormous quantity of information present in a networked information space.

Research effort to understand the link structure of networked information spaces has taken two, related directions: (*i*) The experimental study of the statistics of the link structure of networked information spaces [8] of the WWW and that for the citation graph [2] and (*ii*) The creation of stochastic models that can generate a WWW-like link structure [4,12].

H. Unger, T. Böhme, and A. Mikler (Eds.): I²CS 2002, LNCS 2346, pp. 75–81, 2002.

Recently published experimental results for the WWW [13] strongly indicate a characteristic graph structure for networked information spaces. The experimental evidence in [13,8] indicates that the web has bipartite cores (two sets of nodes, where the nodes in one of the sets is linked to every node in the other set) far in excess of what would be expected of a comparable random graph. This is significant because bipartite cores are considered to be graph-theoretic signatures of community structure on the web. Other studies have shown remarkable consistency in the *in* and *out* degree-distributions of networked information spaces of several types [8,2], each of which show power-law distribution (*i.e.* for in- or out-degree d, $P(d) \sim d^{-\gamma}$ for some constant $\gamma > 0$). The question that arises out of these experimental results is:

How do we characterise the common link-structure properties, observed statistically, in a graph-theoretic manner?

From the experimental results published in [8], it is clear that the link structure of a thematically unified cluster (a cluster of web-pages that share a common trait - *viz.* content, web location, geographic location), mimics that of the entire network. Thematically unified clusters show in- and out-degree distributions, sizes of strongly connected components and distribution of bipartite cores that are statistically very similar to the network at large. Randomly chosen subgraphs do not show these statistical similarities. To this extent, we conclude that the thematically unified clusters mimic the statistical behaviour of the entire network while randomly chosen subsets do not. Hence, the above question can be rephrased as:

What graph-theoretic property distinguishes the link structure of a thematically unified cluster from that of a randomly chosen subset of a networked information space?

To address the above question, we examine the second distinguishing feature of networked information spaces: All such structures seem to have similar generative processes. In each case, a node and its edges are the result of the actions of an individual, independently acting player. Each player, possessing only limited information, arbitrarily determines how their node connects to rest of the network. Such evolutionary processes, driven solely by local interactions, tend to generate self-organising systems [3]. Hence, we name networks formed by the mechanisms described above as Self-Organising Networked Information Spaces (SONIS). The above idea and its consequences are discussed further in Section 2. A structure, consistent with a SONIS, emerges from the experiments described above; leading to a restatement of the central question addressed in this paper:

How can we recognise and measure the characteristic structure of graphs that represent a SONIS?

In section 3 we suggest just such a characterisation and measure: The compressibility of a graph as a measure of the coherence of the information contained at the nodes of the graph. Using the methods of [1] we apply it to an example in section 4. Examples of potential applications of our method are: *(i)* Incorporated into a search engine, it could refine the search by testing the obtained subset of web pages for thematic unity. *(ii)* It could allow authorities to locate unusual/thematically-related financial transactions in a sea of random transactions. *(iii)* It could provide the basis for a structural filter.

2 Local Coherence

To determine the graph property that characterises the link structure of a self-organising networked information space, we must examine the processes that create it. As mentioned in the introduction, a SONIS is the result of individual actions of a large number of independent players. The players form the link structure by determining how their information entities will be linked to the existing structure. It is therefore the overall behaviour of the players in creating links that will determine the characteristics of the link structure.

In itself, the fact that the links are the result of the actions of independent players is not enough to restrict their structure. If each player would connect at random, the resulting graph would be indistinguishable from a random graph. On the other hand, the assumptions we make about the behaviour of the players cannot be too specific, because common characteristics are observed in networked information spaces that contain information of very different natures (web pages, scientific papers, financial transactions, calling patterns).

However, there is a common element. Networked information spaces are generally vast. Therefore, it is unlikely that a player possesses any global knowledge about the general structure. Instead, players will base their links on knowledge about a very limited part of the network. For example, a player creating a web page will, in general, only include hyperlinks to web pages that are, in some way, part of a cyber community to which he or she belongs. Similarly, scientists writing a research paper will only be familiar with a small fraction of the papers in their discipline and hence *most* (not all) of the references in the paper will tend to be from a specific research community (it should be noted here that search engines and electronic indexing have increased the possibility for players to obtain global knowledge; however, we believe this still to be of minor importance, relative to the general trends described here). From this, we conclude that the players creating a SONIS mostly do so on the basis of "local" knowledge about the existing network. The principle described above is also the central idea underlying a stochastic model for the creation of the web graph as proposed by Kumar *et al.* in[12]. Their model has several variations; all variants departing from the premise that each new node created choses most of its neighbours from among a small number of existing nodes, and then adds a small number of random links.

Players determine the *out-neighbours* of the nodes they create. Hence, the graph structure that results from link creation with limited knowledge, is one where the out-neighbours of any node in the graph depend upon a very small portion of the graph. We call such graphs *locally coherent*. A locally coherent graph has the property that, for almost all of its nodes, the out-neighbourhood of the node can be inferred to a large extent from knowledge about a very small part of the graph. Casting this in slightly more technical terms, we obtain the following general definition:

A graph G is locally coherent if, for almost every node v of G, there exists a small subgraph g_v such that, if the structure of g_v is known, then only a small amount of additional information is needed to determine the exact neighbourhood of v.

3   Compressibility

The compressibility of a bit string is a measure of randomness of the bit sequence present. The more random a string the less compressible it is. For a discussion on randomness and compressibility see [6,7]. Compressibility, in the Lempel-Ziv sense [14], has been used to detect the presence of patterns in DNA and RNA strings (for example see [9]). In a similar manner, the compressibility of a graph can be used to identify the presence of a characteristic link-structure. This idea is explained below:

Suppose we want to recognise a *small* target set T, of graphs of characteristic structure, in a large set S, the set of all graphs with n nodes and m edges. For our case; T is the set of graphs characteristic of SONIS. The target set is very small compared with the set S. In general, an element of S would need at least $log|S|$ bits to encode, without any compression (Note: all logarithms are to the base 2). We now assume we can design a compression machine, to work near-optimally on T. The condition of near-optimality on T implies that elements of T are encoded by the machine using only $\log|T| + o(\log|T|)$ bits. Now, there are only $2^{[\log|T|+o(\log|T|)]}$ distinct bit-strings of length $\log|T|+o(\log|T|)$. Hence, only $2^{[\log|T|+o(\log|T|)]}$ distinct graphs (elements of T) can be compressed to this level. By a similar argument, it is easy to see that using the above compression machine the vast majority of elements in S will need at least $\log|S|$ bits to be encoded. Hence, the chance that a randomly selected element from S will achieve near-optimal compression is $\dfrac{1}{2^{[\log|S|-\log|T|-o(\log|T|)]}}$, which is negligibly small. Notice, that even if we bound $o(\log|T|)$ by some constant c, theoretically we can only say that the set T^* on which the compression machine achieves near-optimal compression is of size $|T^*| = 2^c|T|$. However, this is not a problem in practice, since any practical compression machine would achieve continuous compression rates on the elements of S. Hence, we can use it as an identifier of membership in T. It follows that if near-optimal compression is achieved on a graph then, with high probability, the graph will be in T.

Our purpose is to recognise SONIS. Since the distinctive feature of SONIS is their locally coherent structure, the compression machine must use the property of *local coherence* to achieve near-optimal compression on T.

In the next section we illustrate the principles laid-out above by a calculation on a class of graphs with a specific local coherence property. We do this using the recently published FIND-REFERENCE algorithm - a compression algorithm for web-graphs [1] as the compression machine.

4   The Find-Reference Compression Algorithm

A directed graph is completely described by a list of out-neighbours for each node —such a list is referred to as the *adjacency list* of the node. The FIND-REFERENCE algorithm as described in [1] uses similarity of the adjacency lists by using the list of one node to encode the list of another. The adjacency list of a node v can be encoded by reference as follows: (1) the reference node u is listed, (2) a bit string which indicating for each neighbour in the adjacency list of u, whether this node is also a node of v is generated and finally, (3) any neighbours of v that are not in u's list are listed. If there is large overlap between the lists of u and v, then encoding by reference will take far fewer bits of memory space than encoding all the neighbours explicitly. The experiments in [1] show that, for a sample web graph, the compression rate is considerable.

Since the compression obtained by FIND-REFERENCE is based on overlap between the neighbourhoods of nodes, this method will work well on graphs that have many nodes with similar neighbourhoods. Therefore, it is reasonable to assume that FIND-REFERENCE can be used to recognise a class of locally coherent graphs, where the local coherence property is based on only one node. We will call this property *node coherence*. The formal definition follows: Let $N(v)$ be the neighbourhood of a node v, and d_v^+ be the degree of node v.

DEFINITION. *A graph G is node-coherent with error q if, for every node v of G, there exists a another node u, so that*

$$|N(u) - N(v)| \leq qd^+(u).$$

Let $G_{n,d}$ be the class of all directed graphs with n nodes and average out-degree d. Note that each graph in $G_{n,d}$ has nd edges and average in-degree d. For the remainder of this section, n and d are considered to be fixed. n is large, while d is a constant very much smaller than n. These are consistent with the parameters of most networked information spaces. For example, in a recent crawl of the World Wide Web [5], $n \approx 2 \times 10^8$, while $d \approx 8$.

The size of $G_{n,d}$ equals:

$$|G_{n,d}| = \binom{n(n-1)}{dn} \geq 2^{dn \log(n) - o(n)}.$$

The inequality is derived from Stirling's formula (see e.g. [10,7]).

The size of $G_{n,d}$ implies that almost all graphs on n vertices with average degree d cannot be compressed to less than $nd \log(n)$ bits. Hence FIND-REFERENCE cannot possibly achieve better compression than this for most graphs in $G_{n,d}$. However, let T_q be the set of all graphs in $G_{n,p}$ that are locally coherent with error q. It can be shown by a straightforward counting argument, which is omitted here, that Find-Reference needs at most $(qd + 1)n \log(n) + nd + 2d \log^2(n)$ bits to compress any element of T_q. The size of T_q is commensurate with this compression rate. Namely, for small q:

$$|T_q| \geq 2^{(qd+1) \log(n) - o(n \log(n))}.$$

So, FIND-REFERENCE uses at most $t + o(t)$ bits to compress any element of T_q, where $t = \log |T_q|$, so the discussion of the previous section applies here. For any randomly chosen graph from $G_{n,d}$, the probability that any compression algorithm needs less than $t + o(t)$ bits is at most $2^{t-n+o(t)} \approx n^{(1-(1-q)d)n}$. If $(1-q)d > 1$ (a reasonable assumption for small q), then the probability that the algorithm compresses a random element that is in $G_{n,d}$, will become very small as n get large.

5 Further Work

We have described, in general terms, how compression may be used to recognise thematically unified clusters from the link structure of the cluster. The next step, of course, is the application of our proposed method to real-life data. In first instance, the algorithm FIND-REFERENCE can be used as the compression machine, because of its simplicity and speed. At a later stage fine-tuned compression machines could be developed.

The definition of local coherence can be refined and adapted to different kinds of networked information spaces. The concept of node- coherence may well be too restrictive in many cases. We can imagine, for example, that a web page copies most of its links from not just one other page, but from a small set of other pages. It has been shown in [1] that there is no efficient, generalised version of FIND-REFERENCE for this case. However, slightly sub-optimal compression methods may be sufficient for the purposes of pattern recognition.

Finally, the use of compression methods, to improve search engines or build focused crawlers for the WWW; develop a structural filter to detect patterns for calling graphs and financial transactions; or infer information about research communities from the citation structure in scientific databases, should be investigated.

References

1. Micah Adler and Michael Mitzenmacher. Towards compressing web graphs. In *Proceedings of the IEEE Data Compression Conference (DCC)*, 2001.
2. Yuan An, Jeannette Janssen, and Evangelos Milios. Characterizing and mining the citation graph of computer science literature. Technical Report CS-2001-02, Faculty of Computer Science, Dalhousie University, Halifax, Canada, 2001. http://www.cs.dal.ca/main/research/techreports/2001/CS-2001-02.html.
3. Per Bak. *How Nature Works: The science of self-organised criticality*. Copernicus, Springer Verlag, New York, 1996.
4. A. Barabasi and R. Albert. Emergence of scaling in random networks. *Science*, 246:508–512, 1999.
5. A. Broder, R. Kumar, F. Maghoul, P. Raghavan, S. Rajagopalan, R. Stata, A. Tomkins, and J. Wiener. Graph structure in the web. In *WWW9*, Amsterdam, 1999. http://www9.org/w9cdrom/160/160.html.
6. Harry Buhrman, Ming Li, John Tromp, and Paul Vitányi. Kolmogorov random graphs and the incompressibility method. *SIAM J. Comput.*, 29(2):590–599, 1999.

7. Thomas A. Cover and Joy. A. Thomas. *Elements of Information Theory*. Wiley, New York, 1991.
8. S. Dill, R. Kumar, K. McCurley, S. Rajagopalan, D. Sivakumar, and A. Tomkins. Self-similarity in the web. In *Proceedings of the 27th VLDB conference*, Roma, Italy, 2001.
9. S. Grumbach and Fariza Tahi. A new challenge for compressing algorithms: Genetic sequences. *Inf. Proc. and Management*, 30(06):875–886, 1994.
10. R.W. Hamming. *Coding and Information Theory*. Prentice-Hall, 1986. second edition.
11. Steve Lawrence, Kurt Bollacker, and C. Lee Giles. *ResearchIndex*. NEC Research Institute, http://citeseer.nj.nec.com.
12. S. Rajagopalan R. Kumar, P. Raghavan, and A. Tomkins. Extracting large-scale knowledge bases from the web. In *Proceedings of the 25th VLDB Conference*, Edinburgh, Scotland, 1999.
13. S. Rajagopalan R. Kumar, P. Raghavan, and A. Tomkins. Trawling cyber communities automatically. In *Proceedings of the 8th World-wide web conference*, Edinburgh, Scotland, 1999.
14. J. Ziv and A. Lempel. A universal algorithm for sequential data compression. *IEEE Trans. Inf. Theory*, IT-23:337–343, 1977.

On the Spectrum and Structure
of Internet Topology Graphs[*]

Danica Vukadinović, Polly Huang, and Thomas Erlebach

Computer Engineering and Networks Laboratory (TIK)
Swiss Federal Institute of Technology (ETH), Zurich, Switzerland
{vukadin,huang,erlebach}@tik.ee.ethz.ch.

Abstract. In this paper we study properties of the Internet topology on the autonomous system (AS) level. We find that the normalized Laplacian spectrum (*nls*) of a graph provides a concise fingerprint of the corresponding network topology. The *nls* of AS graphs remains stable over time in spite of the explosive growth of the Internet, but the *nls* of synthetic graphs obtained using the state-of-the-art topology generator Inet-2.1 is significantly different, in particular concerning the multiplicity of eigenvalue 1. We relate this multiplicity to the sizes of certain subgraphs and thus obtain a new structural classification of the nodes in the AS graphs, which is also plausible in networking terms. These findings as well as new power-law relationships discovered in the interconnection structure of the subgraphs may lead to a new generator that creates more realistic topologies by combining structural and power-law properties.

1 Introduction

Significant research efforts have recently been invested in the analysis of the Internet topology. The current Internet is the result of rapid, distributed growth without controlled planning by a central authority. Therefore, its topology reflects in great parts the choices and decisions made by individual organizations whose subnetworks form the Internet. As a consequence, the characteristics of the Internet topology can only be investigated by analyzing the available data about the current connectivity of routers or autonomous systems or snapshots of that connectivity taken at an earlier time.

Gaining additional knowledge about the properties of the Internet topology is important for several reasons. In particular, optimization problems related to resource allocation, call admission control, routing, and Distributed Denial of Service (DDoS) attack prevention (see [13]) that are provably difficult to solve for general topologies might allow efficient solutions for a class of networks containing the real Internet. Furthermore, a good understanding of the Internet topology can lead to improvements in network topology generators in order to generate "Internet-like" networks of various sizes for simulations. Network

---

[*] Partially supported by European Commission - Fet Open project COSIN IST-2001-33555, with funding provided by BBW Switzerland.

H. Unger, T. Böhme, and A. Mikler (Eds.): I²CS 2002, LNCS 2346, pp. 83–95, 2002.
© Springer-Verlag Berlin Heidelberg 2002

simulations with realistic topologies can again help to design, tune and evaluate new protocols, applications, and algorithms.

1.1 Related Work: Topology Models and Generators

Until 1999, one of the most popular network generators was GT-ITM [3], a generator that combines the hierarchical models called Transit-stub and Tiers with popular random graph models such as Waxman's model [18]. However, a major new insight into properties of the real Internet topology was gained by Faloutsos et al. [7]. They found four power-laws[1] that appear to hold for various relations between popular graph metrics in the Internet (both on the router level and on the AS level): node degree vs. node rank, degree frequency vs. degree, number of nodes within a certain number of hops vs. number of hops, and 20 largest eigenvalues of the the adjacency matrix vs. their ranks. Thus it became clear that realistic topology generators must produce graphs satisfying these power-laws.

Exploring the power-law degree distribution in WWW and Internet graphs, Barabási and Albert [1] proposed *incremental growth* – the fact that the nodes are added incrementally – and *preferential connectivity* – which means that the probability of connecting a new node to node i is proportional to the degree of i – as two main reasons for the appearance of power-laws. Based on this model, the BRITE topology generator was created [12].

Jin et al. [11] proposed a model called Inet. For a given number of nodes and percentage of nodes with degree 1, the power-law exponents from the real AS Internet graphs are used to determine the degree distribution of the resulting graph. A spanning tree using only nodes with degree at least two is created. The degree 1 nodes are then attached to the tree with proportional probability.

A generalization of the linear preference in the Barabási–Albert model and a comparison of different power-law topology generators can be found in [2].

Tangmunarunkit et al. in [15] compared structural generators based on hierarchical models (such as GT-ITM) to "purely" power-law degree-based generators (such as BRITE or Inet). Using different graph-theoretic metrics, they argued that the degree-based generator models are more realistic than structural ones and that, surprisingly, a certain hierarchical structure is present even in the degree-based generator models.

A simple model for the Internet topology consisting of five layers determined by node degrees is given in [16]. They noticed a power-law in the connection of degree-one nodes to their neighbors, which is related to our observation of other power-laws in the structure of the Internet topology (see Section 4).

A specific behavior of the spectral density of different "real-world" graphs has been noticed in [8]. They also propose spectral analysis as a promising tool for network topology classification. Correlations among nodes in the real AS Internet graphs have been studied in [14].

---

[1] A power-law holds between two properties y and x if y is roughly proportional to x^c for some constant exponent c. If (x, y) data pairs are plotted with both axes in logarithmic scale, the resulting points lie close to a straight line with slope c.

1.2 Topology Data: Real and Synthetic

The Internet topology is usually represented as a graph. On the router level, individual hosts and routers are the nodes and physical connections between them are the edges, but it is difficult to obtain accurate snapshots of the Internet on this level.

On a more abstract level, the AS level, each node of the graph represents an autonomous system (AS, see [10]), i.e., a subnetwork under separate administrative control. An edge between two nodes means that there is at least one direct connection between the two AS domains.

AS-level topology data of the Internet can be inferred from BGP routing tables and is available on the NLANR website (http://moat.nlanr.net/AS/). In this work, we used snapshots of the AS topology from November 8, 1997 (a graph with 3015 nodes and 5156 edges) to March 16, 2001 (10515 nodes and 21455 edges) taken roughly every 3 months. We downloaded the corresponding files (ASconnlist.*) from the NLANR website and treat the graphs as simple, undirected graphs (i.e., we remove parallel links).

We are aware that the data from the NLANR website is potentially incomplete and inaccurate. However, we believe that the results of our analysis would not change drastically for more complete AS graphs. An alternative approach that determines the AS-level topology using router-level path traces was recently proposed in [4], but the coverage of their graphs is only around 60%. Since we are interested in using real AS graphs with large coverage, we found it more appropriate to use the AS-level topologies obtained from BGP routing data as explained above.

In order to compare properties of the AS graphs with graphs produced by a state-of-the-art network topology generator, we selected Inet-2.1. For each of the AS graphs we generate an Inet graph with the same number of nodes. Inet-2.1 allows to specify the fraction of vertices with degree 1. We specified this fraction identical to the one measured for the corresponding AS graph. Nevertheless, the Inet-2.1 generator produces graphs with a small amount of parallel edges. We removed those parallel edges since we deal specifically with simple, undirected graphs. As an effect, the fraction of nodes with degree 1 in these normalized Inet graphs was slightly higher than specified.

1.3 Outline

The remainder of the paper is structured as follows: In Section 2 we give the definitions and basic properties of the normalized Laplacian spectrum of a graph. Then we derive a lower bound on the multiplicity of eigenvalue 1 that turns out to be close to the real value on the AS graphs and Inet graphs. In Section 3, the quantities used in the computation of this lower bound lead us to a new structural classification of AS graphs that can be explained also in networking terms. In Section 4, statistics and comparisons based on the structural model are presented, and first steps towards a hybrid graph generation model are proposed. Finally, in Section 5, we summarize our results and discuss future work.

2   The Normalized Laplacian Spectrum

Previous studies in the context of network models mostly have considered the largest eigenvalues of the adjacency matrix of a graph, but it was noted in [12] that these eigenvalues seem to satisfy a power-law relationship for many different topologies. We propose to look not only at the largest eigenvalues, but at the (multi-)set of all eigenvalues, called the *spectrum*. In addition, we do not use the standard adjacency matrix, but the normalized Laplacian of the graph [5]. Among other reasons, this has the advantage that all eigenvalues are contained in the interval $[0, 2]$ (see [5]) so that it becomes easy to compare the spectra of different graphs even if the graphs have very different sizes.

Let $G = (V, E)$ be an undirected, simple graph, where V is the set of vertices and E is the set of edges. Let $\|V\| = n$, $\|E\| = m$, and d_v be the degree of node v.

Definition 1. *The normalized Laplacian of the graph G is the matrix $\mathcal{L}(G)$ defined as follows:*

$$\mathcal{L}(G)(u, v) = \begin{cases} 1 & \text{if } u = v \text{ and } d_v \neq 0, \\ -\frac{1}{\sqrt{d_u d_v}} & \text{if } u \text{ and } v \text{ are adjacent}, \\ 0 & \text{otherwise}. \end{cases}$$

Note that if A is the adjacency matrix of the graph G (where $a_{ij} = 1$ if there is an edge between v_i and v_j, and $a_{ij} = 0$ otherwise) and D is a diagonal matrix having $d_{ii} = d_{v_i}$, then $\mathcal{L}(G) = D^{-\frac{1}{2}}(D - A)D^{-\frac{1}{2}}$. The normalized Laplacian spectrum (nls) is the set of eigenvalues of $\mathcal{L}(G)$, i.e., all values λ such that $\mathcal{L}(G)u = \lambda u$ for some $u \in \mathbb{R}^n$, $u \neq 0$. More about its characteristics can be found in [5].

A first natural question is: What is the normalized Laplacian spectrum for simple topologies such as stars, chains, grids and random trees on n nodes? The nls of a star S_n is 0, 1 (with multiplicity $n - 2$), 2, and the nls of a chain P_n is $1 - \cos(\frac{\pi k}{n-1})$, $k = 0, \ldots, n - 1$. For grids and trees, plots of the numerically computed spectrum are shown in Fig. 1 (a) and (b). To generate our nls plots, we compute all n eigenvalues with MATLAB, sort them in non-decreasing order, and plot them so that the i-th smallest eigenvalue λ_i, $1 \leq i \leq n$, is drawn at (x, y) with $x = (i - 1)/(n - 1)$ and $y = \lambda_i$. In this way, the plot is always within $[0, 1] \times [0, 2]$ and it becomes convenient to compare the nls of graphs with different numbers of nodes.

We found remarkably similar plots of the nls for all real Internet AS-level snapshots from November 1997 to March 2001 (see Fig. 1(c)). The same consistency was detected for Inet graphs with different numbers of nodes, but the nls of Inet graphs was clearly different from the nls of real AS graphs (also shown in Fig. 1(c)), in particular with respect to the multiplicity of eigenvalue 1. (There are other differences as well, but the investigation of these differences is work in progress.) Together with the known spectra of chains and stars and the plots of the nls of grids and random trees (Fig. 1 (a) and (b)), this indicates that the nls can be used as a kind of "fingerprint" for network topologies (or other arbitrary large graphs that are difficult to compare directly).

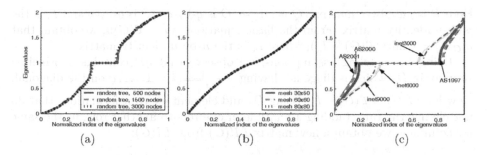

Fig. 1. (a) The *nls* of random trees that were generated by starting with one node and then repeatedly adding a new node and making it adjacent to an existing node chosen uniformly at random. (b) The *nls* of mesh graphs (grids). (c) The *nls* of AS and Inet-2.1 graphs.

2.1 A lower bound on the multiplicity of eigenvalue 1

AS graphs and Inet graphs both have a relatively large multiplicity of eigenvalue 1, but the multiplicity is considerably higher for AS graphs. This has motivated our interest in bounding the multiplicity of eigenvalue 1 in terms of structural properties of graphs.

We will use a technique of [9] (where the standard adjacency matrix is considered instead of $\mathcal{L}(G)$) to find a lower bound on the multiplicity of eigenvalue 1. Denote by $P(G) = \{v \in V \mid d_v = 1\}$ the set of leaves in G, called *pendants*, and by $Q(G) = \{v \in V \mid \exists w, (v, w) \in E, w \in P(G)\}$ the set of the neighbors of the leaves, called *quasi-pendants*. Let $R(G) = V \setminus (Q(G) \cup P(G))$ be the set of nodes that are not leaves and that are not neighbors of leaves, called *inners*. Let p, q, r respectively be the cardinalities of the sets $P(G)$, $Q(G)$, and $R(G)$. We call the subgraph of G induced by $R(G)$ *Inner(G)*. By *inn* we denote the number of isolated vertices in *Inner(G)*. Let $m_G(1)$ denote the multiplicity of the eigenvalue 1. Then we obtain the following lower bound.

Theorem 1. *The multiplicity of eigenvalue 1 of the normalized Laplacian is bounded from below by the sum of the number of pendants, the number of isolated inner nodes, and the negative of the number of quasi-pendants:*

$$m_G(1) \geq p - q + inn \tag{1}$$

Proof. We can assume the following labeling of the nodes, because the eigenvalues are independent of the labeling: $v_1, ..., v_n$ where $v_1, \cdots, v_r \in R(G)$, $v_{r+1}, \cdots,$ $v_{r+q} \in Q(G)$, and $v_{r+q+1}, \cdots, v_n \in P(G)$. Also, we can assume that (v_{r+i}, v_{r+q+i}) $\in E, i = 1, \ldots, q$. Then, the structure of the normalized Laplacian is

$$\mathcal{L}(G) = \begin{pmatrix} R & rQ & 0 \\ rQ^T & Q & qP \\ 0 & qP^T & I_p \end{pmatrix}$$

Here R is an r-by-r matrix, rQ is r-by-q, Q is q-by-q, qP is q-by-p and I_p is the p-by-p identity matrix. From the basic equations $\lambda u = \mathcal{L}(G)u$, we obtain that $m_G(1) = \text{nullity}(\mathcal{L}(G) - I_n)$, where I_n is the n-by-n identity matrix.

Using the labeling assumptions, we observe that qP contains a principal submatrix D_q which is diagonal, having $-\frac{1}{\sqrt{d_{v_{r+i}}}}, i = 1, \ldots, q$ on the diagonal. Now let $LI(G) = \mathcal{L}(G) - I_n$. Using D_q and elementary transformations that do not change the rank (adding a multiple of one row to another row, or the same for columns), we obtain a new matrix $LI'(G)$ from $LI(G)$:

$$
LI'(G) = \begin{pmatrix} R - I_r & 0 & 0 & 0 \\ 0 & 0 & D_q & 0 \\ 0 & D_q^T & 0 & 0 \\ 0 & 0 & 0 & 0 \end{pmatrix}
$$

Now it is enough to prove that $\text{nullity}(LI'(G)) = n - \text{rank}(LI'(G)) \geq p - q + inn$. We have that $\text{rank}(D_q) = q$, thus $n - \text{rank}(LI'(G)) \geq n - 2q - \text{rank}(R - I_r) = p - q + r - \text{rank}(R - I_r)$. Now, if inn is the number of isolated vertices in $Inner(G)$, each row that contains an isolated vertex will have 0 at the first r columns of $LI'(G)$, thus $\text{rank}(R - I_r) \leq r - inn$ and the statement follows. $\qquad\square$

3   A New Structural Classification of AS Nodes

The lower bound of Theorem 1 is given in terms of pendants, quasi-pendants, and isolated inner nodes. We found that this lower bound is close to the real multiplicity observed in the AS graphs and Inet graphs. Therefore, we classify the nodes of the graphs into sets P, Q, R and I as follows, and investigate their cardinalities. A node is in P if its degree is 1 (i.e., if it is a leaf) and in Q if it has at least one neighbor in P. Let $Inner(G)$ be the subgraph of G induced by nodes not being in P or Q. A node in $Inner(G)$ is in I if it is an isolated node in $Inner(G)$ and in R otherwise (i.e., if it is contained in a connected component of $Inner(G)$ with at least 2 nodes).

3.1   Physical Interpretation

The classes P, Q, R and I are defined in graph-theoretic terms motivated by Theorem 1. To relate these notions to ASs in the real Internet, we now propose plausible interpretations of the four node sets in networking terms. Further evidence supporting our interpretations can be derived from AS name tables and is given in the technical report [17].

Q Nodes, Best-Connected Nodes of the Internet. The class Q contains only a small number of nodes compared to the size of the whole graph and to the sizes of the other classes, but the best-connected nodes (largest degree) belong to Q. The subgraph induced by Q nodes has a similar structure for all observed graphs: it contains a big connected component with a characteristic nls (see [17]), and about 5% of isolated nodes.

We interpret the nodes in the big connected component of Q as core nodes. Note that Q nodes have leaf neighbors by definition. The isolated nodes, which have no Q neighbors, can be explained as exchange points serving to connect P, R, and I nodes.

R Nodes, Core, and Alliances. The subgraph induced by R consists of a larger number of connected components. Their size and frequency exhibit power-law relationships (see Section 4). The biggest connected component dominates by its size and node degrees. We interpret the connected components of R nodes, with the exception of the biggest one, as *AS alliances*. Alliances can be built on national, regional, commercial, or other grounds.

In order to gain further insights, we investigated the k-cores of the AS graphs. The k-core of a graph is defined to be the subgraph obtained by recursively deleting all nodes with degree less than k. Intuitively, the deeper cores of an AS graph (i.e., the k-cores for larger values of k, say $k \geq 5$) should correspond roughly to more well-connected "backbones" of the Internet at that time. We found that most of the nodes in the deeper cores are in Q and some are members of the biggest R component. This fact motivates an interpretation of the biggest component of R as being made up partly of AS domains belonging to the core and partly of multi-homed stubs or alliances. Note that core nodes in R do not have any leaf neighbors.

P and I Nodes, Stub Domains. P nodes are leaves (nodes with degree 1) by definition. Therefore, they must be stub nodes (nodes that do not forward traffic that neither originates in that node nor is destined for that node). I nodes, whose degree is small in most cases (i.e., they have just two or three neighbors in Q), are mostly multi-homed stub domains. The percentage of I nodes is increasing in the AS graphs over time, and the percentage of P nodes is decreasing. Currently, the I class is the biggest part of the Internet. It became bigger than the P class at the beginning of 2001. This positive trend in the number of I nodes and negative trend in the number of P nodes agrees with the fact that more and more leaf domains want to become multi-homed for better fault-tolerance [6].

The number of I nodes with higher degree (degree about 10) is rather small. These nodes are mainly big companies or universities with multiple connections to the backbone, but not providing forwarding services.

In summary, the classes P and I represent the outskirts of the Internet, and in a sense they correspond to the stub domains in the Transit-Stub model. Although the smaller alliances in R are arguably also the outskirts of the Internet, for the sake of simplicity and since some nodes in the biggest R component are found in the deeper cores of the AS graphs, from now on we refer to $Q \cup R$ as the *core* and to $P \cup I$ as the *edge* of the Internet.

4   Statistics and Comparisons

Having proposed a structural classification of AS nodes in the previous section, now we investigate how the Internet evolves in this structural sense and how it compares to graphs generated by Inet. Through our analysis, we find that both structural and power-law properties are important. We also observe new power-laws in the internal structure of R and the interconnection between P and Q. These findings represent first steps towards a hybrid generator model that encompasses both power-laws and structural properties.

4.1   Methodology

The set of graphs undergone analysis has been described earlier in Section 1.2. To observe how AS graphs evolve structurally and how they compare to Inet graphs, we look at the following three sets of metrics.

1. Ratio of nodes in P, I, Q, R
2. Ratio of links connecting PQ, IQ, QQ, RQ, RR
3. Average node degree (number of neighbors) in the whole graph, average node degree of the edge nodes ($P \cup I$), and average node degree within the core (subgraph induced by $Q \cup R$).

It is not to our surprise that the numbers of nodes in each component and the numbers of links inter-connecting the components are increasing. Thus we focus our analysis on how the components expand or shrink relatively to the whole graph and omit discussions on absolute numbers.

Results are depicted in Figs. 4, 5, and 6, respectively, which can be found at the end of this paper. Each plot shows changes of the AS graphs in the corresponding metric (Y axis) in time (X axis). In the next two subsections, we highlight important trends in the evolution of AS graphs and significant differences to Inet graphs.

4.2   Evolution of AS Graphs

Observation 1. We see from the top plots of Fig. 4 that the ratio of nodes in P is decreasing while that of I is increasing. That means, applying our interpretation of P and I, the area of single-homed leaf nodes is shrinking while that of multi-homed stub nodes is rapidly increasing.

Observation 2. The ratio of nodes in P and I combined has increased from approximately 67% to 74%. The ratio of nodes in R remains stable. The combined ratio of Q and R components, containing the core of the Internet, decreases from 33% to 26% (bottom plots of Fig. 4). In terms of ratio of nodes, the edge of the Internet is growing faster than the core.

Observation 3. Given that the ratio of nodes in P is decreasing, it is not surprising to see the ratio of links (edges) interconnecting QP decrease, and similarly to see the ratio of links QI increase as I increases (top plots of Fig. 5).

QP and QI combined increases from 54% to 60%. QQ, QR, and RR each remains relatively stable and the combined ratio decreases from 46% to 40%. This shows that in terms of the ratio of links, the edge of the Internet is again growing faster than the core.

Observation 4. More interestingly, the ratio of links in Q and R decreases by 6%, which is slightly lower than the 7% decrease in ratio of nodes. The ratio of links out-growing the ratio of nodes in the core indicates that the average node degree within the core (subgraph induced by $Q \cup R$) is increasing. This can be confirmed by the middle plot of Fig. 6.

4.3 Comparison to Inet Graphs

Difference 1. While we see the ratios of I and QI expand in AS graphs, they remain stable in Inet graphs (top-right plot of Fig. 4 and 5). This is also reflected in the left plot of Fig. 6, where we observe that the average number of neighbors of a node in the edge components (P and I) is increasing in AS graphs whereas it remains stable in Inet graphs.

Difference 2. The ratio of R remains stable in AS graphs while it expands significantly in Inet graphs (bottom-right plot of Fig. 4). Similar contrasts can be found in link statistics in Fig. 5: QR (bottom-middle) and RR (bottom-right).

Difference 3. Inet graphs, similar to AS graphs, have rather stable Q and QQ ratios, but the ratio level is higher than that in AS graphs (bottom-left plot of Fig. 4 and 5).

Difference 2 and 3, contrary to the evolution of AS graphs, indicate that the core of Inet graphs is not only larger but also expanding while the edge is losing its ground.

Difference 4. It appears that in the core of Inet graphs the ratio of links is growing just as fast as the ratio of nodes, thus resulting in a rather constant average degree within the core (middle plot of Fig. 6). This is in contrast with the average degree within the core of AS graphs, which is increasing significantly over time.

These differences show that although successful in modeling some of the power-law properties, Inet fails to capture structural changes in AS graphs. In particular, the core of the Internet is becoming relatively smaller and the edge larger, but the evolution of Inet graphs shows the exact opposite. More interestingly, the Internet is structured so that the average node degree is increasing within the core as well as for edge nodes. On the contrary, these average degrees remain constant for Inet graphs.

4.4 New Power-Laws and First Steps Towards a Hybrid Model

These structural differences are potentially critical when studying properties of routing protocols, for example quality of path, route convergence, and fault tolerance. To be more concrete, one can expect global effectiveness of an alternative route computation algorithm to be different when evaluated using graphs with a higher ratio of multi-homed stub nodes (I) and better connected core (Q and R). Below we outline a structural model that will allow us to verify this conjecture in the future.

Our premise is to model AS graphs encompassing both statistical and structural properties. By that, we mean to 1) generate a degree sequence that obeys power-law properties observed earlier, 2) form P, I, Q, and R clouds based on the size dynamics, and finally 3) inter-/intra-connect these clouds with analysis of their connectivity.

First results show that a power-law exists not only in the overall degree sequence but also within the structure. For instance, while investigating ways to form the R cloud, we find that the sizes of the connected components in R have a power-law distribution. Fig. 2 shows the sizes of the connected components in R ranked from the largest to the smallest (rank-size plot), and occurrences of different sizes (size-occurrence plot).

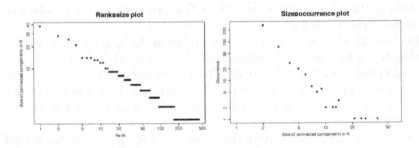

Fig. 2. Power-law in sizes of connected components in R

A power-law is also present in the way P and Q clouds are inter-connected. The left plot in Fig. 3 shows, for each node in Q, its rank on node degree (Y axis) and rank on number of degree-1 neighbors (X axis). Those Q nodes with one degree-one neighbor are ranked the 411th (lowest) in X axis; those with 2, 3, 4, and 5 degree 1 neighbors are ranked 275th, 191st, 147th, and 109th, gradually improving. Each column in the plot shows that a variety of Q nodes, with different node degrees, may have the same amount of P neighbors. The right plot of Fig. 3 illustrates the distribution of such Q nodes. The linear relationship in the log-log scale plot hints on a power-law distribution for Q nodes having one P neighbor.

This power-law property persists across different degree 1 neighbor ranks, until data points are too few to show a clear linear relationship in log-log plots. Further analysis verifies that the same power-law property between P and Q clouds exists in other snapshots of the Internet.

Another power-law in the interconnection of P and Q (relating the number of degree-1 neighbors of a Q node to the rank of that node in the sorted list of all Q nodes) has been discovered independently in [16]. These power-law properties within or between sub-structures of the AS graphs could be the missing links

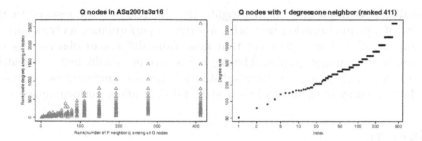

Fig. 3. Power-law in PQ inter-connection

between the state-of-the-art generators, i.e., Inet and GT-ITM. Each of them identifies one important aspect of the Internet topology — Inet for the statistical aspect and GT-ITM for the structural aspect — but unfortunately misses out on the other.

5   Conclusions and Future Work

We have investigated the normalized Laplacian spectrum of Internet topology graphs. It turned out that the nls can be used as a concise fingerprint of a graph. Real AS graphs from 1997 to 2001 produced nearly identical nls plots in spite of the significant difference in the number of nodes. Similarly, graphs generated with the Inet-2.1 generator had a characteristic nls, but different from the nls of real AS graphs, in particular with respect to the multiplicity of eigenvalue 1. We gave a lower bound on the multiplicity of eigenvalue 1 in terms of the cardinalities of different node sets P, Q, R, and I. For the real AS graphs, we found plausible interpretations for the nodes in P, Q, R, and I. In particular, the classification of nodes into these four types provides a structured view of the graph, featuring leaf domains, multi-homed stub domains, alliances, and core nodes.

Besides, while analyzing the subgraphs induced by P, Q, R and I and their interconnections we obtained new, previously unobserved power-law relationships with respect to the sizes of connected components in R and with respect to the degree rank of Q nodes with the same number of P neighbors.

Our results provide several immediate starting points for future work. First of all, we intend to use the insights we obtained from our analysis for improving the quality of the Inet-2.1 generator (with respect to the similarity to real AS graphs) and to explore the potential of a newly designed random topology generator based on our structural view in terms of P, Q, R and I nodes. We are aware that many aspects of the AS graphs are yet to be investigated thoroughly, for example the structure of the connections within Q and those between Q and R.

Furthermore, it will be interesting to identify additional characteristics of the nls (e.g. occurrence of other multiplicities, convex and concave regions) that can be interpreted in terms of graph theory or networking concepts.

Finally, it is important to investigate the differences with respect to the *behavior* of a communication network (in terms of performance metrics such as throughput, delay, fault-tolerance) that arise from differences observed in the corresponding topology graphs. Thorough case studies could help to identify which of the graph properties have substantial effects on network performance and which are only of theoretical interest and do not affect performance.

References

1. A. Barabási and R. Albert. Emergence of scaling in random networks. *Science*, 286:509–512, 1999.
2. T. Bu and D. Towsley. On distinguishing between Internet power law topology generators. In *INFOCOM 2002*, 2002. To appear.
3. K. Calvert, M. Doar, and E. W. Zegura. Modeling Internet topology. *IEEE Communications Magazine*, June 1997.
4. H. Chang, S. Jamin, and W. Willinger. Inferring AS-level Internet topology from router-level path traces. In *SPIE ITCom 2001*, Denver, CO, August 2001.
5. F.R.K. Chung. *Spectral Graph Theory*. Conference Board of the Mathematical Sciences, Providence, Rhode Island, 1997.
6. C. Diot. Sprint tier 1 IP backbone: Architecture, traffic characteristics, and some measurement results, 2001. http://talk.epfl.ch/talkdetail.php?talkId=42.
7. M. Faloutsos, P. Faloutsos, and C. Faloutsos. On power-law relationships of the Internet topology. In *SIGCOMM'99*, 1999.
8. I. Farkas, I. Dernyi, A. Barabási, and T. Vicsek. Spectra of "real-world" graphs: Beyond the semicircle law. *Physical Review E*, 64, August 2001.
9. R. Grone, R. Merris, and V. Sunder. The Laplacian spectrum of a graph. *SIAM Journal on Matrix Analysis and Applications*, 11(2):218–238, April 1990.
10. J. Hawkinson and T. Bates. RFC 1930: Guidelines for creation, selection, and registration of an autonomous system (AS). IETF, March 1996.
11. C. Jin, Q. Chen, and S. Jamin. Inet topology generator. Technical Report CSE-TR-433-00, EECS Department, University of Michigan, 2000.
12. A. Medina, I. Matta, and J. Byers. On the origin of power laws in Internet topologies. *ACM Computer Communication Review*, 30(2):18–28, 2000. April 2000.
13. K. Park and H. Lee. On the effectiveness of route-based packet filtering for distributed DoS attack prevention in power-law internets. In *SIGCOMM 2001*, August 2001.
14. R. Pastor-Satorras, A. Vázquez, and A. Vespignani. Dynamical and correlation properties of the Internet. *Physical Review Letters*, 87(25):258701–1, 2001.
15. H. Tangmunarunkit, R. Govindan, S. Jamin, S. Shenker, and W. Willinger. Network topologies, power laws, and hierarchy. Technical Report 01-746, Computer Science Department, University of Southern California, 2001.
16. L. Tauro, C. Palmer, G. Siganos, and M. Faloutsos. A simple conceptual model for the Internet topology. In *Global Internet*, San Antonio, Texas, November 2001.
17. D. Vukadinović, P. Huang, and T. Erlebach. Spectral analysis of Internet graphs. Technical Report 118, TIK Institute, ETH Zürich, 2001.
18. B.M. Waxman. Routing of multipoint connections. *IEEE Journal on Selected Areas in Communications*, 6(9):1617–1622, 1988.

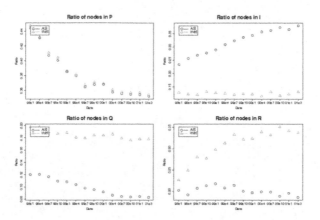

Fig. 4. Ratio of nodes in P, I (top), Q, R (bottom)

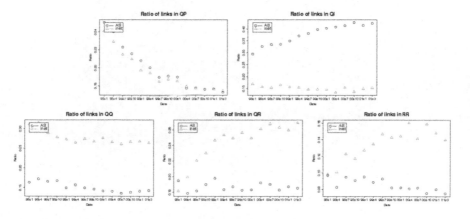

Fig. 5. Ratio of links in QP, QI (top), QQ, QR, RR (bottom)

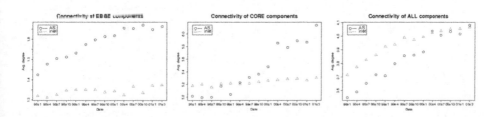

Fig. 6. Average node degree of edge nodes, within the core, and in the whole graph

Characterizing the Citation Graph as a Self-Organizing Networked Information Space

Yuan An[1], Jeannette C.M. Janssen[2], and Evangelos E. Milios[1]

[1] Faculty of Computer Science, Dalhousie University
Halifax, NS, Canada
{yuana,eem}@cs.dal.ca
[2] Dept. of Math. and Stats., Dalhousie University
Halifax, NS, B3H 3J5 Canada
janssen@mscs.dal.ca

Abstract. Bodies of information available through the Internet, such as digital libraries and distributed file-sharing systems, often form a self-organizing networked information space, i.e. a collection of interconnected information entities generated incrementally over time by a large number of agents. The collection of electronically available research papers in Computer Science, linked by their citations, form a good example of such a space. In this work we present a study of the structure of the citation graph of computer science literature. Using a web robot we build several citation graphs from parts of the digital library *ResearchIndex*. After verifying that the degree distributions follow a power law, we apply a series of graph theoretical algorithms to elicit an aggregate picture of the citation graph in terms of its connectivity. The results expand our insight into the structure of self-organizing networked information spaces, and may inform the design of focused crawlers searching such a space for topic-specific information.

1 Introduction

Thanks to the expansion and growing popularity of the Internet, a rapidly increasing amount of information is available electronically and in networked form. Thanks to the open and distributed nature of the World Wide Web, bodies of information are often created in a self-organizing way: the information entities are created by independent agents, and each agent links its information to the entities of a limited number of other agents. Hence we can refer to such bodies of information as *self-organizing networked information spaces*. The body of web pages and their hyperlinks forms a canonical example of such an information space, but the same principle applies, for example, to digital libraries and distributed file-sharing systems.

An interesting property of networked information spaces is that information is not only encoded in the entities themselves, but also in the link structure. Many properties of the entities can be inferred from the link structure. Graph-theoretic methods to study this link structure have therefore become popular. Since self-organizing networked information spaces are the product of a similar

H. Unger, T. Böhme, and A. Mikler (Eds.): I²CS 2002, LNCS 2346, pp. 97–107, 2002.

generative process, one would expect that their link structure will have certain common characteristics. Previous studies have focused mainly on the World Wide Web; we present here a study of an electronic library of scholarly papers in Computer Science.

A body of scientific literature can be seen as a networked information space. Here the information entities are the scientific papers, and they are linked together by citation relations. The link structure of this networked information space can be represented by a directed graph, which is commonly referred to as the *citation graph*. Each node of the citation graph represents a paper, and a directed link from one node to another implies that the paper associated with the first node cites the paper associated with the second node.

Citation graphs representing scientific papers contain valuable information about levels of scholarly activity and provide measures of academic productivity. A citation graph has the potential of revealing interesting information about a particular scholarly research topic: it may be possible to infer research areas and their evolution over time, measure relations between research areas and trace the influence of ideas that appear in the literature.

In this paper we report the results of examining various aspects of connectivity of the citation graph of computer science literature with graph theoretic algorithms. To build the citation graph, we implemented a web robot to query the online computer science library *ResearchIndex*.

Research in bibliometrics has long been concerned with the use of citations to produce quantitative estimates of the importance and impact of individual scientific publication and journals. The best-known measure in this field is Garfield's impact factor [7]. The impact factor is a ranking scheme based fundamentally on a pure counting of the in-degree of nodes in the citation graph. Redner [9] has focused on the statistical distribution of the number of citations of the scientific literature. Chen [4,5] developed a set of methods that extends and transforms traditional author co-citation analysis by heuristically extracting structural patterns from scientific literature for visualization as a 3D virtual map.

As to structural analysis of other networked information spaces, Broder et al. [2] studied various properties of Web graph including its diameter, degree distributions, connected components, and macroscopic structure, proposing a bow tie model of the Web. Earlier work, exploring the scaling properties of the Web graph, has been done by Barabasi [1]. More recent work, comparing properties of the Web at various levels, can be find in [6]. Exploiting the link topology of networked information space for information discovery has been recently proposed for the Web [3].

The following considerations motivated our study. Understanding the link topology of the citation graph using graph-theoretic tools may facilitate knowledge discovery relying on link information such as similarity calculation and finding communities, help in citation graph visualization, and help evaluate the evolution of specialties or research themes over time. Moreover, comparing the structure of a citation graph with that of other networked information spaces such as the Web will increase our understanding of the factors that influence the link structure of such spaces. This sort of understanding will lead to improved methods for Web navigation and data mining.

1.1   Main Results

We performed three sets of experiments on our collection of citation graphs obtained from different research areas. The main result of our analysis was that these citation graphs showed remarkably similar behavior in each of our experiments. Moreover, the results of the experiments performed on the union of the three graphs was again similar to that of each of its parts, indicating the self-similarity of the citation graph.

We first constructed a robot for querying *ResearchIndex* [8], and using the robot we built a collection of three local citation graphs by starting with papers from three different topics. We also merged the three graphs into the union graph: the combined citation graph of the three individual ones.

The first set of experiments computed the in-degree distributions and demonstrated that they follow a power law. Specifically, the fraction of articles with k citations is proportional to $1/k^e$, where the exponent e is close to 1.7 for each of the four graphs. We also investigated the average shortest path length between nodes, concluding that, if direction of the links is ignored, the citation graph classifies as a *small-world network*.

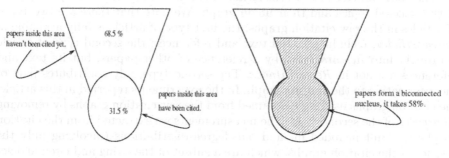

(a) 68.5% of the nodes have no incoming link

(b) 58% of the nodes in the giant Weakly Connected Component(WCC) account for a big Biconnected Component(BCC)

Fig. 1. The connectivity of the citation graph

The second set of experiments investigated the connectivity of the citation graph. It was found that approximately 90% of the nodes form a single Weakly Connected Component (WCC) if citations are treated as undirected edges. Within this giant WCC, almost 68.5% of the nodes have no incoming link, suggesting that 68.5% of the publications in the giant WCC have not been cited (yet). See Figure 1(a) for a representation of this result. Furthermore, within the giant WCC, around 58% of its publications form a large Biconnected Component(BCC), and almost all the remaining nodes of the giant WCC fall into trivial BCCs, each of which consists of a single distinct node. The aggregate picture that emerges is shown in Figure 1(b).

2   Measurements on the Citation Graph

2.1   Building the Citation Graph

The first step is to extract citation graphs from a citation database. *Research-Index*[8] is a Web-based digital library and citation database of computer science literature and provides us easy access to citation information for our study. We constructed a Web robot for querying *ResearchIndex* autonomously. We chose three areas within computer science as starting points: *Neural Networks, Automata and Software Engineering.*

Our procedure for creating the citation graphs started from a base set, obtained via keyword search, containing thousands of nodes that are not necessarily connected. We then expanded this base set by following incoming links and outgoing links of the nodes in the base set. The crawling process was terminated when space and time limitations were reached. About 100,000 papers were parsed for each topic.

The above process leads to the formation of three raw citation graphs for each of the selected topics and their union graph. We note that there are two types of articles in the raw citation graphs: the first type of article is fully available in *ResearchIndex*, including its full text and references; the second type of article is brought into *ResearchIndex* by a reference of other papers, but its text and references are not in *ResearchIndex*. The second type only contributes part of the information to the citation graph. In the experiments reported in this article, the citation graphs used were obtained from the raw citation graphs by removing all articles of the second type. The measurements we extracted from the citation graphs we built included in- and out-degree distributions (involving only the articles in the citation graphs, which are a subset of the citing and cited articles respectively) and diameters.

2.2   Degree Distributions

We begin by considering the in-degrees of nodes in the citation graph. We observed that the in-degree distributions follow a power law; i.e. the fraction of papers with in-degree i is proportional to $1/i^\gamma$ for some $\gamma > 1$. Our experiments on all citation graphs built from the different topics as well as the union citation graph confirmed this result at a variety of scales. In all these experiments, the value of the exponent γ in the power law for in-degrees is a remarkably consistent 1.7.

Figure 2(a) is a log-log plot of the binned in-degree distribution of the union citation graph for extracting the exponent γ. The value $\gamma = 1.71$ is derived from the slope of the line providing the best linear fit to the data in the figure.

The out-degree distribution in the union citation graph follows a more complex distribution, shown in 2(b). It peaks at 16, and after 18 it follows a power

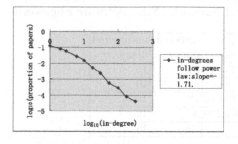

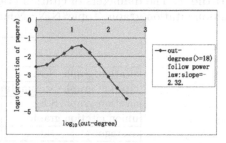

(a) The in-degree distribution subscribes to a power law with exponent=1.71

(b) The out-degree distribution

Fig. 2. In- and outdegree distribution in the union citation graph

law distribution with exponent 2.32. This outcome is not surprising, as there are very few papers, typically tutorial in nature, with a large number of references, while the majority of the papers have references in the range of 20 to 50. It should be noted that the out-degree of a paper in our citation graph is less than its number of references, since we only include in the citation graph the papers that are fully available in the *ResearchIndex* database. This affects older papers more, since their references are less likely to be available in electronic form.

2.3 Diameter

We turn next to the diameter measurement of citation graphs. In this study, the diameter is defined as the maximum over all ordered pairs(u, v) of the length of the shortest path from u to v in the citation graph. We measured two types of diameter for the citation graph: directed diameter and undirected diameter. Directed diameter is measured by the directed shortest path or dipath, while undirected diameter is obtained by treating edges as undirected.

Our connectivity tests revealed that the citation graph is not connected. This means that there are nodes which cannot be reached by a path from other nodes, implying that the diameter is infinite. However, the tests also revealed that ≈ 80% − 90% of the nodes are in one giant connected component, while the rest form a few very small components. Details are described in Section 3. We therefore considered the diameter of this giant connected component as the undirected diameter of the graph.

The diameters obtained by applying Dijkstra's shortest path algorithm on the giant connected components of the citation graphs built for the three topics and their union are shown in Table 1.

Ignoring the orientation of edges, we observe that the citation graph is a 'small world' with an undirected diameter of around 18. The result is consistent at a variety of scales and topics.

Table 1. The diameters of citation graphs built from different topics as well as union citation graph. Topic: N.N.: Neural Networks, S.E.: Software Engineering

	graph size	directed diameter	undirected diameter
citation graph–N.N.	23,371	24	18
citation graph–Automata	28,168	33	19
citation graph–S.E.	19,018	22	16
union citation graph	57,239	37	19
average		29	18

In contrast, we do not obtain such a 'small world' property in the *directed* citation graph. Our statistical study shows that the probability of having a directed path between any pair of nodes is only *2%*. The directed diameter was calculated by taking the maximum only over those pairs of nodes that are connected by a directed path. This diameter turned out to be around 30 (see Table 1). This is an outcome of the temporal nature of the citation graph. In almost all cases, references can only be made to papers that appeared previously, and therefore directed cycles are unlikely. (Some directed cycles arise in special circumstances, see Section 3.2)

3   Reachability and Connected Components

We now consider the connectivity of our citation graphs of computer science literature. This involves examining the various types of its connected components and reachability of nodes. Given a citation graph $G = (V, E)$, we will view G both as a directed graph as well as and undirected graph (the latter by ignoring the direction of all edges). We now ask how well connected the citation graph is. We apply a set of algorithms that compute reachability information and structural information of directed and undirected citation graphs: *Weakly Connected Components (WCC)*, *Strongly Connected Components (SCC)* and *Biconnected Components (BCC)*.

3.1   Weakly Connected Components

The first of our connectivity experiments showed that the citation graph is not, in general, connected. This can be explained in the context of our construction of the citation graphs: we started building each citation graph from a base set containing a number of documents which are not necessarily connected, and while the expansion of the base set serves to connect many of these documents, others remain in small isolated components. Moreover, our cleaning up process of removing those articles, whose text and references are not available, produced more isolated components.

Mathematically, a *Weakly Connected Component(WCC)* of an undirected graph $G = (V, E)$ is a maximal connected subgraph of G. A WCC of a citation graph is a maximal set of articles each of which is reachable from any other if links may be followed either forwards or backwards. In the context of a citation graph, links stand for the citations from one article to other articles cited in the former one. The WCC structure of a citation graph gives us an aggregate picture of groups of articles that are loosely related to each other.

The results drawn from the weakly connected component experiments on citation graphs are shown in Table 2. The results reveal that the citation graph is well connected–a significant constant fraction $\approx 80\% - 90\%$ of all nodes fall into one giant connected component. It is remarkable that the same general results on connectivity are observed in each of the three topic subgraphs. In turn, the same behavior is observed for the union graph, suggesting a certain degree of self-similarity. (The term *self-similarity* is used here, as in [6], to denote similar statistical behavior at several levels.)

Table 2. The results of Weakly Connected Component experiments on different citation graphs: the majority ($\approx 90\%$) of articles are connected to each other if links are treated as without directions.citation graph:N.N stands for Neural Networks; S.E. stands for Software Engineering

	graph size	size of largest WCC	percentage of largest WCC	size of second largest WCC
citation graph–N.N.	23,371	18,603	79.6%	21
citation graph–Automata	28,168	25,922	92%	20
citation graph–S.E.	19,018	16,723	87.9%	12
union citation graph	57,239	50,228	87.8%	21

3.2 Strongly Connected Components

We turn next to the extraction of *Strongly Connected Component(SCC)* of the connected components of the three topical citation graphs and their union graph. A *Strongly Connected Component(SCC)* of a directed graph is a maximal subgraph such that for all pairs of vertices (u, v) of the subgraph, there exists a directed path (dipath) from u to v. An article cannot cite articles that have not been written yet, so if article u directly or indirectly cites article v, then v must be older than u, so, under normal circumstances, v will not cite u. As a result, we might expect that there is no SCC in the citation graph. But contrary to our expectation, the results of SCC experiments on the collection of citation graphs reveal that there exist one to three sizable SCC's in each of the citation graphs, as well as a few very small SCC's. The results drawn from the experiments are shown in Table 3.

In order to know how the directed cycles were generated in those citation graphs, we extracted some SCCs from citation graphs and searched the corresponding articles of these SCCs directly in *ResearchIndex*'s database. Our study shows that several types of publications formed SCCs: (1) publications written by same authors tend to cite each other, they usually produce self-citations, (2) publications which are tightly relevant tend to cite each other, e.g., publications,

Table 3. The results of Strongly Connected Component experiments on different citation graphs: there exist many small SCCs, among them there are one -three bigger SCC(s), the rest are even smaller comparing those bigger ones. citation graph:N.N stands for Neural Networks; S.E. stands for Software Engineering

	graph size	size of largest SCC	size of second largest SCC	size of third largest SCC
citation graph–N.N.	18,603	144	14	10
citation graph–Automata	25,922	192	29	24
citation graph–S.E.	16,723	17	11	8
union citation graph	50,228	239	155	60

whose authors in same institute, dealing with same specialty and getting published concurrently are highly relevant and tend to cite each other, (3) publications which were published in several different forms, such as journals, conference proceedings or technical reports, at different times often formed directed cycles with other publications. The different forms of the publication were considered as one node during our creation process of the citation graph. (4) books or other publications which were published in several editions at different times, where the newer editions contained more recent references, often acted as jump points in the citation graph. The jump points formed by publications of type (4) caused large directed cycles in the citation graph; this is the reason of the existence of one to three bigger SCCs. Types (1)–(3) of articles usually gave rise only to small SCCs containing 2–5 articles.

A conceptual map arising from the analysis of the results of the SCC experiment on the union citation graph is depicted in Figure 3. A number of small SCCs are embedded in a well connected background net. This background net is a directed acyclic structure, i.e., there is no directed cycle in the background net.

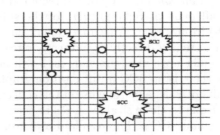

Fig. 3. The directed connectivity of a citation graph: a number of small SCCs embedded in a background net;the background net is a directed acyclic graph

3.3   Biconnected Components

We now turn to a stronger notion of connectivity in the undirected view of the citation graph, that of biconnectivity. A *Biconnected Component(BCC)* of an undirected graph is a maximal subgraph such that every pair of vertices is biconnected. Two vertices u and v are biconnected if there are at least two disjoint paths between u and v, or, equivalently, if u and v lie on a common cycle. Any biconnected component must therefore lie within a weakly connected component. Applying the biconnected component algorithm on the giant connected components of citation graphs, we find that each giant connected component of each citation graph contains a giant biconnected component. The giant BCC acts as a central biconnected nucleus, with small BCCs connected to this nucleus by cut vertices, and other single trivial nodes connected to the nucleus or a small BCC.

The numerical analysis of sizes of BCCs indicated that $\approx 58\%$ of all nodes account for the giant biconnected nucleus, the rest $\approx 40\%$ of the nodes are in trivial BCCs each of which consists of single distinct node, and the remaining $\approx 2\%$ of the nodes fall into a few small BCCs.

4   Does Connectivity Depend on Some Key Articles?

We have observed that the citation graph is well connected–90% of the nodes form a giant connected component which in turn contains a biconnected nucleus with 58% of all nodes. The result that the in- distributions follow a power law indicates that there are a few nodes of large in-degree. Moreover, our analysis of the out-degrees implies that there are also some nodes with large out-degree. We are interested in determining whether the widespread connectivity of the citation graph results from a few nodes of large in-degree acting as "authorities" or a few nodes of large out-degree acting as "hubs". We test this connectivity by removing those nodes with large in-degree or out-degree, and computing again the size of the largest WCC. The results are shown in Table 4 and Table 5.

Table 4. Sizes of the largest Weakly Connected Components(WCCs) when nodes with in-degree at least k are removed from the giant connected component of union citation graph

size of graph	50,228							
k	200	150	100	50	10	5	4	3
size of graph after removing	50,222	50,215	50,152	49,775	46,850	43,962	42,969	41,246
size of largest WCC	50,107	49,990	48,973	43,073	26,098	14,677	9,963	1,140

These results show that the widespread connectivity does not depend on either hubs or authority papers. Indeed, even if all links to nodes with in-degree 5 or higher are removed (certainly including links to every well-known article

Table 5. Sizes of the largest Weakly Connected Components(WCCs) when nodes with out-degree at least k are removed from the giant connected component of union citation graph

size of graph	50,228							
k	200	150	100	50	10	5	4	3
size of graph after removing	50,225	50,225	50,224	50,205	48,061	43,964	42,238	39,622
size of largest WCC	50,202	50,202	50,198	50,131	46,092	37,556	33,279	26,489

on computer science), the graph still contains a giant Weakly Connected Component(WCC). Similarly, if all links to nodes with out-degree 3 or higher are removed, the graph is still well connected. We conclude that the connectivity of citation graph is extremely resilient and is not due to the existence of hubs and authorities, which are embedded in a graph that is well connected without their contributions.

5   Discussion

We have reported the results of our examination of the self-organizing networked information space formed by electronically available scientific articles in Computer Science. The link structure of this space (referred to as the citation graph) can potentially be used in a variety of ways, for example to infer research areas and their evolution over time, measure relations between research areas, and trace the influence of ideas that appear in the literature.

For our analysis of the citation graph we applied graph-theoretic algorithms. We verified that the in-degree distribution follows a power law, a characteristic observed in various experimental studies to hold for other networked information spaces. We also studied the connectivity by extracting weakly and strongly connected components, as well as biconnected components. The aggregate picture emerging here differs from that of the Web, since citations, unlike hyperlinks, generally are restricted by the time in which a paper was written (older papers cannot reference newer papers). We measured the diameter of the graph, and verified that it is lower than would be expected of a random graph of comparable sparsity, classifying a citation graph as a "small world network". We also found evidence that the citation graph is quite robust in terms of connectivity; when nodes with low degree were removed, the graph still stayed mostly connected. In general, we found that the citation graph displays many of the characteristics of other networked information spaces, though it differs in some aspects due to the specific, time-dependent nature of citations. A suggestion for further research is the use of the observed characteristics of the citation graph to develop tools for better navigation, mining and retrieval in networked information spaces, such as the World Wide Web or corporate intranets.

In a follow-up of this study, we computed minimum cuts between authority papers in different areas, with the hope that this would enable us to separate the different research communities represented by the graph. These naive attempts were largely unsuccessful. The extraction of communities from the citation graph is an important area of further study. Our intuition and experience tells us that papers on a specific research topic must be more densely interconnected than random groups of papers. Hence research topics or "communities" should correspond to locally dense structures in the citation graph. However, our work shows that the connectivity of citation graphs as a whole is such that it is not possible to extract such communities with straightforward methods such as minimum cut. More sophisticated methods are needed if we wish to succeed in mining the community information encoded in the link structure of a citation graph or other networked information spaces.

Another important subject of further study is the evolution of the citation graph over time. Knowledge about the temporal evolution of the local link structure of citation graphs can be used to predict research trends or to study the life span of specialties and communities. Such knowledge can also be used for the development of dynamic models for the citation graph. Such models can, in turn, give insight into the self-organizing processes that created the citation graph, and serve as a tool for prediction and experimentation.

References

1. A-L.Barabasi and R.Albert. Emergence of scaling in random networks. *Science*, 286:509–512, October 1999.
2. A.Z. Broder, S.R. Kumar, F. Maghoul, P. Raghavan, S. Rajagopalan, R. Stata, A. Tomkins, and J. Wiener. Graph structure in the web: experiments and models. In *Proc. 9th WWW Conf.*, pages 309–320, 2000.
3. Soumen Chakrabarti, Byron E. Dom, David Gibson, Jon Kleinberg, Ravi Kumar, Prabhakar Raghavan, Sridhar Rajagopalan, and Andrew Tomkins. Mining the Link Structure of the World Wide Web. *IEEE Computer*, 32:60–67, 1999.
4. Chaomei Chen. Visualising semantic spaces and author co-citation networks in digital libraries. *Information Processing and Management*, 35:401–420, 1999.
5. Chaomei Chen. Visualising a knowledge domain's intellectual structure. *IEEE Computer*, 34:65–71, 2001.
6. S. Dill, R. Kumar, K. McCurley, S. Rajagopalan, D. Sivakumar, and A. Tomkins. Self-similarity in the web. In *Proceedings of the 27th VLDB conference*, Roma, Italy, 2001
7. E.Garfield. Citation analysis as a tool in journal evaluation. *Science*, 178:471–479, 1972.
8. Steve Lawrence, Kurt Bollacker, and C. Lee Giles. *ResearchIndex*. NEC Research Institute, http://citeseer.nj.nec.com (accessed on Sep.30, 2001), 2001.
9. S.Redner. How Popular is Your Paper? An Empirical Study of the Citation Distribution. *European Physical Journal B*, 4:131–134, 1998.

Characterization and Management of Dynamical Behavior in a System with Mobile Components

Christian Erfurth and Wilhelm Rossak

Computer Science Department
Friedrich Schiller University Jena, D-07740 Jena, Germany
Ch.Erfurth@computer.org

Abstract. A mobile agent system network is, in our definition, a dynamical system where so called agent servers are loosely coupled. In such an environment (mobile) agents may offer and consume services and act on behalf of a (human) user. This paper characterizes the dynamical behavior of such a network. Aspects of dynamical behavior are discussed, dynamical components are characterized, and a "cartography" method to handle dynamics is introduced. The resulting "maps" can be used to support the autonomy of agents by calculating itineraries and suggest migration strategies. The application of the map described in this paper is based on one of our current research projects in the context of the mobile agent system Tracy.

1 Motivation

Over the past years, research in the area of mobile agent technology as a new paradigm of distributed programming has focused on suitable programming languages [11, 5] and languages for agent communication [1]. Very much effort was put into security issues [18], control issues [16, 2], and in agent cooperation [13]. Several prototypes of real-world applications in the area of information retrieval, management of distributed systems, and mobile computing are in development [14, 15].

To our understanding, a mobile agent is any kind of software entity that is able to initiate a migration on its own within a network of heterogeneous computer systems. In addition, it works autonomously and communicates with other agents and host systems. At the university of Jena, we have developed the mobile agent system *Tracy* [4] to support our research. Thereby the autonomy of agents is one focus.

Dynamical behavior (mobility) of the agents or any dynamics in the surrounding environment, e.g. mobile platforms or dynamic services on-demand, increase the complexity of the system as an integrated entity. In spite of the system's dynamics an agent needs to be able to navigate within the network. This paper will describe and analyze the dynamical behavior of such systems with the goal to achieve the highest possible level of autonomy per agent in a volatile environment.

H. Unger, T. Böhme, and A. Mikler (Eds.): I²CS 2002, LNCS 2346, pp. 109–119, 2002.

In the following section 2 we analyze the dynamical behavior of a mobile agent system network and its components. The section contains fundamental thoughts as a general basis for a method to handle these dynamics, as discussed in section 3. The application of this method based on one of our current research projects is provided in section 4. In section 5 we provide a summary and outlook.

2   Dynamical Behavior

Within this section the phrase *dynamical behavior* is the focus. We try to categorize a system's possible dynamical behavior and identify the substantial dynamical components within our mobile agent system (MAS). A formal description of those dynamics is not the goal of our current research. We want to be able to react but not to simulate that behavior.

2.1   Aspects of Dynamical Behavior

In general, dynamical behavior means any kind of change in a well structured and otherwise stable environment. Dynamical behavior is typically triggered by some external or internal event and leads to a variation within the system's configuration with the goal to adapt to the changing needs that were signaled by those events.

The term *system* is a very general, abstract one, which is used in philosophy, science, technology etc., with different meanings. A system is always a set of "elements" which are connected with each other. After defining system limits a system may have certain input and output parameters (see [8], [17]).

The system mentioned here is a mobile agent system (MAS) network. Thus, the elements of our system are hardware and software components. In addition we have "humanware", denoting the set of human users. In this environment we now want to take a closer look at the involved components and the dynamics of their interaction.

As in most other systems in our framework of existence, there are two major types of dynamical behavior: *temporal dynamics* and *spatial dynamics*.

Temporal dynamics is "quite normal" in software or hardware systems. Amongst other things it is characterized by a component's "up time", availability, reachability, etc, thus characterizing the possibility of an active involvement in the systems interaction patterns. As we will discuss later, some components of our system will be high dynamical with regards to the temporal aspect, especially if we consider small and mobile platforms.

Spatial dynamics reference things like physical coordinates or logical net affiliation. This is again interesting especially in the case that mobile devices are involved or if the end user changes location within the network.

It would, of course, be valid to argue that these two forms of dynamical behavior are not separate types of dynamics but simply basic attributes/aspects that apply to any action involved in a dynamical process and that they should be discussed together. For example, a mobile device changes its location (spatial aspect) and thereby logs out of a specific context (is not any more available) to log in within a new context (is "suddenly" available in that context: temporal aspect). While the device is up and running all the time (in its own local perspective), its spatial dynamics trigger a temporally dynamical behavior (limited availability) for the the involved systems/networks (system perspective),

In the following subsection we pinpoint the elements of our system more precisely and also discuss them with regards to the very basic aspects of dynamical behavior we have identified.

2.2   The Dynamics of MAS Components

As mentioned above a system consists of several elements which may interact. We also mentioned that these elements are mainly software and hardware components. "Humanware" is a special "element" that will not be the focus in this paper.

Our system is a network of possibly multiple mobile agent systems (MAS). This means that there is computer hardware, multi-purpose platforms, and special MAS software components. As a point of reference and to ground our discussion we will refer to *Tracy* the MAS developed by our software group at the University of Jena (see [4] and [3] for details).

Such a network of MASes can be described as a mathematical graph with nodes and edges and we can identify the following components:

- computer hardware ("nodes" in the net/graph)
- connection between nodes (physical and logical)
- agent server running on nodes
- agents (stationary as well as mobile)
- domains (a logically connected set of agent servers within Tracy)

The nodes of the graph are computer systems/devices, i. e. physical platforms, which can host one or more mobile agent server(s). The edges in the graph are network connections between these nodes.

Computer Hardware. The temporal dynamics of computer hardware is basically defined as the availability of these components in the network. There are many different types of platforms available today with different goals and characteristics. Temporal dynamical behavior must, therefore, be adapted to the platform's planned utilization. A data base server, for instance, will have a high availability profile as opposed to a hand-held PDA. As a consequence, we can find any level of temporal dynamics in a MAS network, ranging from a very low level of dynamics (statical, high availability server) to pretty high dynamics (dynamical, temporal server/client with short online time-slots).

Spatial dynamics can be found in case of "mobile" hardware like handhelds, PDAs, laptops etc., but also in hardware that changes its net affiliation, e.g. computers which use a dial-up connection ("logical" change of location). Thus, there is a set of computer hardware platforms, like application servers, that is more static and there are platforms which change their net affiliation and (often simultaneously) their location.

As discussed before, a high level of spatial dynamics seems to trigger automatically a high level of temporal dynamics. An overview of platforms and corresponding dynamic aspects is summarized in Fig. 1 at the end of this section.

Physical and Logical Connections. A connection between nodes may be physical, e.g. a cable or an established wireless connection. However, there are also logical connections that are defined rather by a level of fast and reliable reachability via the ISO/OSI stack.

A physical connection is responsible for the direct, low-level accessibility/ availability of a node. In case of mobile nodes this physical connection may change (temporally disconnected or connected), possibly triggered by a spatial movement.

However, the physical connection is not the major point of interest. Usually data is transmitted via dynamic routing algorithms that mask the actual physical topology to a large extend. Thus, it is not so much necessary to consider physical connections; it will do to consider the platform itself as long as it has any logical connection to the desired network (sub-)domain. There is always a logical connection between two nodes as long as the nodes are available and are able to communicate with each other due to a compatible protocol.

Form this perspective, connections are at a lower level of interest – nodes are the primary points of interest with regards to system dynamics.

Agent Server. An agent server is a software component which enables a computer hardware to execute agents and in case of a MAS to send and receive agents. It is the agent's execution and communication environment. There may be more than one agent server running on the same platform.

The considerations here are the same as in case of computer components. Temporal dynamics depend on the up-time, the availability of an agent server, which in turn is linked to its platform's availability and spatial movement: An agent server can only move spatially and be available if its hardware is able to do so.

While spatial dynamics are, therefore, the same as the spatial dynamics of the underlying hardware, the level of temporal dynamics of an agent server is higher than that of the underlying computer hardware, simply because the agent server may go "offline" without switching off the hardware. Again see Fig. 1 for an integrated overview.

Agents. Agents are software components which may provide (intelligent) services. Basically, we distinguish two kinds of agents – stationary and mobile. Only mobile agents are able to migrate within the network from agent server to agent server (multiple "hops").

The temporal dynamics of an agent is characterized by the availability of the services provided by the agent. A service is available as long as the agent is running on a (fixed) server. Stationary agents can only be executed if the agent server *and* the computer hardware is running. The same holds for mobile agents (up-time or residence time at the considered mobile agent server) but the service (the mobile agent) can migrate to another running server.

A stationary agent can only move together with its agent server and, therefore, only with its hardware platform. Mobile agents are able to migrate and, as a consequence, exhibit their own spatial dynamics (that's why they are "mobile"). These agents may be highly dynamical from the point of view of a network's temporal dynamics, i. e. have very short timeframes of residence on an server, but may still potentially live longer than any agent server or local computer hardware (regarding up-time).

The level of temporal dynamics of the services provided by an agent at a considered platform is directly dependent but usually even higher than the dynamics of the underlying agent server and computer hardware. The spacial dynamics of stationary agents is as high as the dynamics of the agent server and computer hardware. Mobile agents are spatially more dynamical due to the ability of migration (see Fig. 1).

Mobile Agents and Domains. Domains are a logical concept within the Tracy MAS to join a set of agent servers together and to handle large MAS networks better by providing a means to construct smaller sub-networks. within a domain there is always a domain manager which holds certain information about the domain, e.g. regarding available services (of mobile agents) and their location within the domain, and which is the extern (and intern) contact point (more information about this in [3]).

Inside the domain there are the same dynamics as within an unrestricted network. However, the spatial dynamics of mobile agents can be controlled better: As long as the service provided by a mobile agent is executing somewhere within a domain, the service seams to be stationary within the domain – only the actual agent server has to be known to the domain manager to redirect a request of an interested party.

However an affiliation of an agent server or an agent to a domain can change, either by a domain split (see [3]) or in case of a moving mobile device (with executing agents on the platform, but without a migration of the mobile agent itself).

Selection of Interesting Components/Layers. So far we have pinpointed the components of a typical MAS network and have described the dynamical behavior of the components involved. Now we can reduce the overall component list to a smaller list that includes only components that are interesting with regards to their dynamical behavior. Interesting are only nodes which host at least one running agent server:

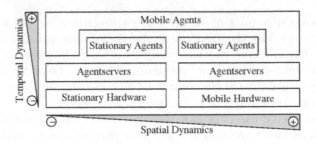

Fig. 1. Overview: A Framework of Component Dynamics

- agent servers running on stationary or mobile hardware/platforms
- stationary agents
- mobile agents

In addition, domains are interesting as they serve as a logical concept to handle dynamics better.

In Fig. 1 you can see the dynamical components of the MAS network in relation to the temporal and spatial dynamics. The figure also tries to summarize the dynamical behavior of the components. Thereby the y-axis marks the level of temporal dynamics and the x-axis shows the level of spatial dynamics. The left lower corner means less dynamics and the right upper corner means high temporal and spatial dynamics.

A basic distinction is made by the type of platform used (stationary or mobile), as this influences directly the dynamics of agent servers and stationary agents that reside on those platforms. Mobile agents are very independent, as they may migrate from platform to platform or simply move together with the platform they currently use.

The tasks and functionalities of the layers in MAS environment are:

- Hardware
  - Basic environment for running agent servers
  - connection to other nodes
- Agent server
  - provide basic functionalities for agents and infrastructure services
  - host agents
  - gateway to other applications
- Stationary Agents
  - extend agent server functionality
  - provide services
- Mobile Agents
  - have mobility capabilities
  - provide services
  - can fulfill a user given task (act on behalf of a user)

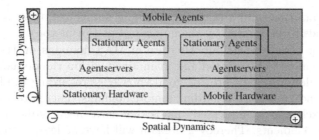

Fig. 2. Levels of Complexity in Mapping Dynamical Behavior

3   Discussion of Implications: Dynamic Domain Maps

Having characterized the dynamical behavior of the MAS network components, we now search for methods to handle these dynamics and the potential problems involved. Within the MAS network, services are the most important resource for the users (humans or agents which act on behave of a human). Services are provided by a more or less dynamical component in the network (agent server, agent). To use a service, you have to locate it. Thus, we need something like a map to be able to navigate and to find services. In contrast to the real world, where a map is a pretty static concept, a map in a system of MAS domains can change dynamically. Thus, we can not create a map once and then rely on delayed updates. What we need is a dynamic map, one that reflects the dynamics of the network. But what should/can we actually map?

Fig. 1 gave us some hints. On the map there have to be services and their location within the network. Perhaps only services which have a predictable and fairly stable dynamical behavior can be mapped. That would mean services with a long enough "up-time" and relatively low spatial dynamics can be registered. In Fig. 2, a refinement of our earlier figure, we indicate areas which can be mapped without problems (more statical) and areas which possibly can not (need not) be mapped (too dynamical). The darker the area is marked, the more difficult it is to map services provided by these components. If the location of a service is fixed, it is easier to map. If a service is highly available, it is again easier to map. Services with temporal and spatial dynamics can be mapped only if the level of dynamics is not too high. It should be mentioned that in this situation spatial dynamics are more difficult to handle than temporal ones. Lucky enough, most systems we are aware of exhibit attributes that provide a chance to map them at least to a large extend.

Useful dynamic maps can, thus, be created. However, due to the potential size of the MAS network it is not possible to have a single map of the complete network; problems with data acquisition are inherent in large networks. In addition, the highly redundant data has to be held up to date. Thus, the size of the map has to be reduced. Here, the Tracy domain concept helps us to create maps of a usable size – i. e. a dynamic map of the local domain with its limited number of platforms (and a potentially infinite number of agent servers, which in reality tends to be limited by the number of platforms too).

Due to the strictly distributed nature of MAS domains in Tracy, dynamic domain maps have to be created and maintained within the domain itself. As a consequence, domain maps provide good knowledge regarding the local domain but basically no knowledge regarding remote domains. Therefore, domains must be able to exchange "compressed" maps that have been reduced to the most essential data elements. Thereby a domain will have at least a rough, perhaps out-dated knowledge regarding remote domains (see also [6] or [7] regarding maps and reduced information).

Another advantage of the domain concept is to handle better the spatial dynamics within the domain. The services provided by mobile agents or services on top of a mobile device which migrate within the domain are easier to map than services which move between domains. In the local map the location of services can be kept up-to-date at a fairly low expense, as our experiments show. From the perspective of the complete network, each domain can then be regarded as a node on a higher level.

Dynamic domain maps have to be available to the agents (or to a human user) in the domain for searching services and planing itineraries. The next section will introduce the application of dynamic maps, based on one of our current research projects.

4   Application of Dynamic Domain Maps

Agents are designed to support humans. To approach this goal the autonomy of an agent is important. Thus, the agent needs support by the agent system to increase its autonomy e.g. by infrastructure services.

Dynamic domain maps should help the mobile agents to fulfill a task. The result's quality depends on the quality of the map. The data on the map should hold information about services (and their location). This can also include further information like service availabilities, node information, line quality (bandwidth, latency), etc, and the map may provide forecast modules to upgrade (enhance) the actually measured data.

In our project such a map is located at the domain manager or, in an upgraded version, even at every node within the domain to shorten response times. With it the agents can search locally for services provided within the domain and search for further information on the local domain. Additional modules support the agent to plan the itinerary and the migration. Fig. 3 illustrates the corresponding scenario. This is also an overview of our project's structure – while some of the modules are operational as prototypes, other, higher level modules are still under development. The map module constructs the domain map. As already indicated, the collected node information is enhanced by additional characteristics of the network (latency, bandwidth, availability, migration) and different forecast modules can be added. Due to the inherently dynamical be-

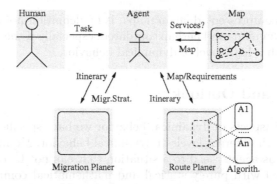

Fig. 3. Overview – Collaboration of Modules

havior of the domain, data is refreshed in suitable time intervals (intervals can be set to fit different situations and levels of dynamics in the domain).

The routing module is able to calculate a possible migration path for the agent by matching the map data and the values given by the forecasts to the agents job specification. Basically this is the traveling sales man problem and hard to solve with an increasing number of nodes. However, there exists a set of quite good algorithms which calculate nearly optimal tours quickly: [9], for example, covers selected tour construction heuristics, classical local optimization algorithms (2-Opt, 3-Opt, Lin-Kernighan), simulated annealing, tabu search, genetic algorithms, and neural net algorithms. To be able to test different algorithms, the routing module has an interchangeable calculation component. Our current results indicate that local optimization algorithms seem to be the best fit for our application ([10] compares various algorithms). Thereby, in order to improve a feasible tour it is modified by deleting some edges, thus breaking the tour into paths, and then reconnection those paths in an other possible way [12]. Neural nets are too slow, and genetic algorithms are too complex and, therefore, also not fast enough.

The migration optimization module calculates a suitable migration strategy i.e. how migration is done in Tracy (pull code, push code, etc.; see [4]). For this task mainly the line data on the map is used. Tracy supports migration strategies which are able to limit transmissions during migration to the code that is actually needed on the target node(s).

Any mobile agent in the domain may use all the modules listed above as an externally available resource. The modules are independent and can also be used separately. Results are considered to be suggestions for the invoking agent, but the agent's autonomy to make the final decision itself is strictly observed. The agent can recalculate its itinerary at every agent server it visits, should that be its decision, e.g. in case of high network dynamics in the current domain. In case the mobile agent leaves the local domain by migration, it should update its information at the first remote node, because the knowledge on remote domains (summarized in "compressed" domain maps) is by definition not as complete as that in local domain maps and perhaps outdated, especially if the agent migrates into a domain with a high level of dynamical behavior.

5 Summary and Outlook

After introducing aspects of dynamical behavior we have specified areas within a MAS network with different levels of dynamical behavior. Mobile components, platforms as well as agents, lead to a situation that can not be controlled completely or analyzed with purely statical and mathematical complete concepts. A certain level of uncertainty and incompleteness must be accepted to remain operational. Thus, we have established dynamic domain maps ("snap shots" of the domain) to manage behavioral and system dynamics better, to support the autonomy of agents, and to achieve higher quality results from agents. Nevertheless, there are highly dynamical components (temporal/spatial) which can still not be mapped, e.g. mobile agents with an extremely short execution time that migrate to and leave an server very fast. Despite very encouraging first results, we need to determine what actually is "too fast" for our dynamic maps in more depth by further experimentation. We also need to pinpoint more precisely how much network traffic and calculation time is caused as an overhead to guarantee an up-to-date map (and what "up-to-date" actually means in that context). On a higher level of reasoning, where we talk about end-user satisfaction, we also need to establish a metric that provides for a rough estimate how expensive it is to calculate an agent's itinerary automatically and "complete enough". Different approaches, ranging from neural networks to graph based mathematics, may be useful and will be tested in more detail.

References

1. J. Baumann, F. Hohl, N. Radouniklis, K. Rothermel, and M. Straßer. Communication concepts for mobile agent systems. In Rothermel [15], pages 123–135.
2. J. Baumann and K. Rothermel. The shadow approach: An orphan detection protocol for mobile agents. Technical Report 1998/08, Universit¨at Stuttgart, Fakultät für Informatik, 1998.
3. P. Braun, J. Eismann, and W. Rossak. A Multi-Agent Approach To Manage a Network of Mobile Agent Servers. Technical Report 12/01, Friedrich-Schiller-Universität Jena, Institut für Informatik, 2001.
4. P. Braun, C. Erfurth, and W. Rossak. An Introduction to the Tracy Mobile Agent System. Technical Report Math/Inf/00/24, Friedrich-Schiller-Universität Jena, Institut für Informatik, Sept. 2000.
5. G. Cugola, C. Ghezzi, G. P. Picco, and G. Vigna. Analyzing mobile code languages. In J. Vitek and C. Tschudin, editors, *Mobile Object Systems: Towards the Programmable Internet (MOS'96), Linz, July 1996*, volum 1222 of *Lecture Notes in Computer Science*, pages 93–110, Berlin, 1997. Springer Verlag.

6. C. Erfurth, P. Braun, and W. Rossak. Migration Intelligence for Mobile Agents. In *Artificial Intelligence and the Simulation of Behaviour (AISB) Symposium on Software mobility and adaptive behaviour. University of York (United Kingdom), March 2001*, 2001.

7. C. Erfurth, P. Braun, and W. Rossak. Some Thoughts on Migration Intelligence for Mobile Agents. Technical Report 09/01, Friedrich-Schiller-Universität Jena, Institut für Informatik, 2001.

8. N. Fliege. *Systemtheorie.* Teuber, Stuttgart, 1 9 9 1.

9. D. Jonhson and L. McGeoch. *Local Search in Combinatorial Optimization*, chapter The Traveling Salesman Problem A Case Study in Local Optimization, pages 215–310. John Wiley and Sons, Ltd., 1997.

10. D. Jonhson and L. McGeoch. *The Traveling Salesman Problem and its Variations*, chapter Experimental Analysis of Heuristics for the STSP. Kluwer Academic Publishers, 2002. To appear in: The Traveling Salesman Problem and its Variations.

11. F. C. Knabe. *Language Support for Mobile Agents.* PhD thesis, Carnegie Mellon University, Paittsburgh, Pa., Dec. 1995.

12. S. Lin. Computer Solutions of the Traveling Salesman Problem. *Bell System Technical Journal*, 44:2245–2269, 1965.

13. A. Oricini, F. Zambonelli, M. Klusch, and R. Tolksdorf, editors. *Coordination of Internet Agents: Models, Technologies, and Applications.* Springer-Verlag, 2001.

14. E. D. Pietro, O. Tomarchio, G. Iannizzotto, and M. Villari. Experiences in the use of Mobile Agents for developing distributed applications. In *Workshop su Sistemi Distribuiti: Algoritmi, Architetture e Linguaggi (WSDAAL'99), L'Aquila (Italy), September 1999*, 1999.

15. K. Rothermel, editor. *Proceedings of the First International Workshop on Mobile Agents (MA'97), Berlin (Germany), April 1997*, volume 1219 of *Lecture Notes in Computer Science*, Berlin, 1997. Springer Verlag.

16. K. Rothermel and M. Straßer. A protocol for preserving the exactly-once property of mobile agents. Technical Report 1997/18, Universit"at Stuttgart, Fakultät für Informatik, 1997.

17. R. Unbehauen. *Systemtheorie.* Oldenbourg-Verlag, 1997.

18. G. Vigna. *Mobile Agents and Securtiy*, volume 1419 of *Lecture Notes in Computer Science*. Springer Verlag, New York, 1998.

Ergotracer: An Internet User Behaviour Tracer

Carlos Gregorio Rodríguez[*1] and Pedro Palao Gostanza[2]

[1] Department of Sistemas Informáticos y Programación
Universidad Complutense de Madrid
`cgr@sip.ucm.es`
[2] Department of Computer Security, Bankinter
`papalao@bankinter.es`

Abstract. Many research areas related to Internet (resource discovery, intelligent browsing and navigation, data search and retrieval...) are developing agents and adaptive systems whose main target is to help the user to manage the large quantity of information available through Internet. A detailed knowledge of users behaviour when navigating or using services provided by Internet is a vital component for many of these agents and systems. There are other areas (data mining, data caching, web design...) where getting a thorough knowledge of Internet dynamics and ergonomics is advisable. They could also profit by a precise description of the user behaviour. Nowadays Internet user behaviour traces are mainly collected at the servers or proxies. Detecting the behaviour at the server-side provides just a partial vision of the user, where only the behaviour inside the server is controlled. Furthermore, many behaviour features which appear at the client-side are impossible to detect by the server. In this paper we introduce **Ergotracer**, a distributed, cross-platform, lightweight tool that gathers in detail the behaviour of a user navigating the web.

1 Introduction

Internet is becoming the largest information and knowledge repository ever created. The short and medium-term expectations state that the information volume continues growing [BB98, ISC01, NUA01]. According to *Internet Software Consortium*, the number of Internet servers has grown from 1,313,000 in January, 1993, to 125,888,197 in July, 2001. The *Nua Internet Survey* estimated in August, 2001, that the world's Internet users were over 500 million people. Additionally, new technologies such as next generation cell-phones and Internet terminals offered by phone companies will allow Internet access to an even wider range of users and increase the demand of Internet services. This increase makes it essential for Internet technology to become more sophisticated in order to cope with information overflow.

In many areas such as resource discovery, data search and retrieval, intelligent browsing and navigation, data caching, etc. many efforts are being made in order

---

[*] Research partially supported by the CICYT project TIC 2000-0771-C02-01.

H. Unger, T. Böhme, and A. Mikler (Eds.): I²CS 2002, LNCS 2346, pp. 121–132, 2002.

to design adaptive systems and agents to help Internet users to survive in a sea of information [Lie95, JFM97, Nwa95, Bru96]. These new tools should identify the features and needs belonging to each user in order to make decisions: they should *know* their users in order to *customize* their services.

This need has been highlighted in the literature [CP95, TNP97, Mul97]. For instance, [BDMS94] compiles the results from projects carried out by members of the Internet Research Task Force Research Group on Resource Discovery and Directory Service. It identifies the main problems and proposes research focus. One of the paper proposals is "Third, the range of user expertise and needs require that user interfaces and search strategies be highly customisable" and below "the first type of customisation involves tracking a person's search history."

Information about Internet user behaviour is mostly collected on the server-side. There are dozens of products intended to provide log files from web servers and proxies. This information is valuable and already in use. But regarding the end-user behaviour and experience there are restrictions: only the user behaviour concerning a particular server is logged and information about the user history, in a broad sense, is not available. Besides, it is impossible for servers to obtain an adequate insight into the user behaviour. Therefore, many details are missing.

This paper describes a tool called Ergotracer[3] that accurately gathers and informs of the user behaviour and performance when navigating or using services on Internet. Ergotracer is based on technology present in current Internet browsers and can therefore be distributed easily and widely.

In section 2, some related work is presented and the design principles that have drawn our tool are outlined. In section 3, Ergotracer capabilities are described and an overview of the execution of the tool is shown. Some technical details concerning design and implementation are also covered. In section 4, privacy and security issues are taken into consideration. In section 5, some possible applications of Ergotracer are enumerated in order to show the versatility and generality of the tool. Finally, we offer our conclusions in section 6.

2   Related Work and Design Decisions

There are many products that produce server or proxy logs, analyse the obtained data and prepare reports and statistics. An Internet server can collect package and route-related information. This knowledge is very important and helpful for routing, cloning, and so on. Some user-server interaction can also be collected. Data about the number of users connected, the amount of time a user is connected, pages visited per session, time per page, etc., are usually logged.

Almost all tools whose goal is to help the user or customise a website are based on the click stream analysis [SF99, Sane, Quest]. These tools study the user characteristics detectable by the server: time spent on a page, linking graph within the server, etc. But many details of the user behaviour are out of the

---

[3] Ergo- from the Greek *ergon*, work and -trace from the Latin *trahere*, to draw.

server's reach: number and size of open navigation windows, movements of the cursor on the pages, etc. In order to design intelligent agents, accurate user behaviour is necessary. Papers, such as [Dav99, CP95], describe the shortcomings of conventional proxy log formats.

An alternative to collect server-side behaviour is to enhance a browser, for instance in [CP95]. This solution can be applied only for experimental purposes: browsers source code is not always available and, even more important, it is difficult to deploy an instrumented browser among a large and representative number of Internet users. As far as we know, no simple and cross-platform tool to collect user behaviour has been developed.

A tool with an adequate insight into the Internet user's behaviour and experience should have a number of properties. One of the main ones should be its client-side aspect, in order to be closer to the user and get to know his or her behaviour in detail. This includes not only their visited links but more sophisticated data such as: the number of browser windows and information contained in each of them, the way in which the mouse is moved toward a link, whether the scroll is used or not, etc. Furthermore, collecting the information at client-side means an increase of generality, since that information can be used at different levels: by tools or agents located at the client-side; it can be sent back in real time to the page or service server, so that it has a better knowledge of its user; or it can be sent any place to be stored or analysed. Therefore, this data can be used by a large amount of tools. Other important properties are: cross-platform and easy installation, in order to be potentially usable for a large number of Internet users; lightweight, so it does not affect the user performance.

Ergotracer was constructed with these principles in mind. In order to develop a client-side tool, we have focused on the natural workplace of the user: the browser. Ergotracer works on the browser and uses Javascript, present in almost every navigator due to its compatibility with HTML. In spite of being a script language, when used at its maximum force and combined with sophisticated programming techniques, it allows us to collect highly detailed user behaviour. Since Javascript main concern is dynamic web pages manipulation, it lacks some fundamental capabilities like network access. Therefore, when sending data though Internet Ergotracer relies on Java language because it is also cross-platform.

In short, Ergotracer solves the problem of detecting and storing the information related to navigation through Internet on the clients who carry out the navigation. And it only uses technology implemented by almost all browsers, that is, technology at client level: HTML, Javascript and Java, [AGH00, Netscape].

3   Ergotracer at Work

In this section we describe Ergotracer. First, we present an overview of the tool capabilities: the kind of events that can be detected, the way the context for each event is determined and the log generation. Execution features are also described. Finally, some technical issues and details are discussed.

3.1   An Overview

Ergotracer is very easy to install in the client: the browser only has to load a specific page with the code of Ergotracer. From then on, and until desired, this window is *infected* and starts detecting and gathering the events produced in that window while navigating. Ergotracer source code can be stored in the client and used by the client when desired or an Internet server can send it to the client.

The events that are detected can vary from the exact position of the mouse pointer to the change of a form field in a web page or the movement or resize of any of the browser windows. The whole context in which an event were produced can be gather at any given moment. This provides a precise vision of the behaviour.

Events	Description
abort	The loading of an image is aborted
blur	A form element, window or frame loses focus
change	A select, text, or textarea field loses focus and its value has changed
click	An object on a form is clicked
closewindow	A browser window is closed
dblclick	A form element or a link is doubled clicked
dragdrop	An object is dropped onto the browser window
error	The loading of a document or image causes an error
eventchange	The set of detected events has changed
focus	A window, frame, or form element receives focus
keydown	A key is depressed
keypress	A key is pressed or held down
keyup	A key is released
load	A window or all of the frames within a window finish loading
mousedown	A mouse button is depressed
mousemove	The cursor is moved
mouseout	The cursor leaves an area or link from inside
mouseover	The cursor moves over an object or area from outside
mouseup	A mouse button is released
newwindow	A new browser window arises
reset	A reset button is clicked
resize	A window or frame is resized
scroll	A window is scrolled
select	Some of the text within a text or textarea field is selected
submit	A submit button is clicked
unload	A document is unloaded
urlchange	A window or frame has changed the document it is showing
windowmove	A window is moved through the screen

Fig. 1. Events controlled by Ergotracer

A client's navigation control mainly uses Javascript in order to detect and control certain events produced in the navigation windows of visited pages. But Javascript is not enough for Ergotracer's needs and, therefore, the tool defines and manages its own events. Figure 1 shows a list of the events that are controlled. In boldface those defined by our tool.

Among the events detected by Ergotracer that go beyond the capabilities of Javascript, are those dealing with the detection of the closing and opening of new navigation windows. Every new window emerging from an infected window will also be infected and it will start to detect and analyse the events produced in it. Because there are multiple possibilities of opening new windows in a browser, this detection requires the use of various techniques.

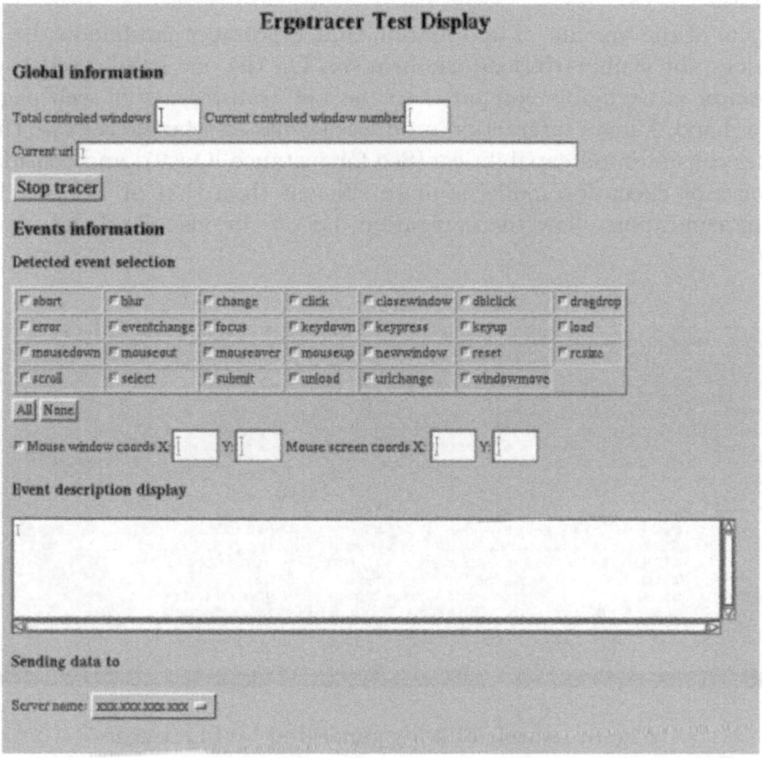

Ergotracer Test Display

Global information

Total controled windows [ ]   Current controled window number [ ]

Current url [ ]

[Stop tracer]

Events information

Detected event selection

☐ abort	☐ blur	☐ change	☐ click	☐ closewindow	☐ dblclick	☐ dragdrop
☐ error	☐ eventchange	☐ focus	☐ keydown	☐ keypress	☐ keyup	☐ load
☐ mousedown	☐ mouseout	☐ mouseover	☐ mouseup	☐ newwindow	☐ reset	☐ resize
☐ scroll	☐ select	☐ submit	☐ unload	☐ urlchange	☐ windowmove	

[All] [None]

☐ Mouse window coords X: [ ] Y: [ ]   Mouse screen coords X: [ ] Y: [ ]

Event description display

[   ]

Sending data to

Server name: [XXX.XXX.XXX.XXX ▾]

Fig. 2. Execution test display for Ergotracer

To identify the origin and the context of the events that are produced is not an easy task. On one hand, several windows can be controlled; on the other hand, pages that contain frames involve the navigation through different pages within the same window. Ergotracer detects and identifies the event in a unique way that pin-points the exact place of origin and therefore the context is perfectly defined.

This way, the data storage is thorough and could even replay the navigation carried out, step by step.

The amount of information that Ergotracer can potentially provide is so detailed that on many occasions it will suffice —or might be desired— to select a certain number of events to control. Ergotracer allows for this detection to take place quite selectively since it can be independent for each user, as well as for each navigation window controlled; it can also be changed dynamically. Figure 2 shows a simple interface to test or to inspect Ergotracer's behaviour while collecting information from the browser. The checkboxes indicate the event selection and can be dynamically switched on/off. The server to which data are sent can also be changed dynamically. The display at the bottom shows information about the collected events. This information is similar to that saved into the log files (see Fig.3).

In spite of the amount of information that Ergotracer can handle, its performance does not visibly overload the browser. On the one hand, execution time of Ergotracer is negligible compared to the net transference of web pages. On the other hand, human interaction produces events at a far slower rate than the computer consumption capabilities. (See for instance [Ous91] and consider that the Javascript execution model is more efficient than that of Tcl.) Such good operating conditions allow the navigation data to be visualised/used instantaneously.

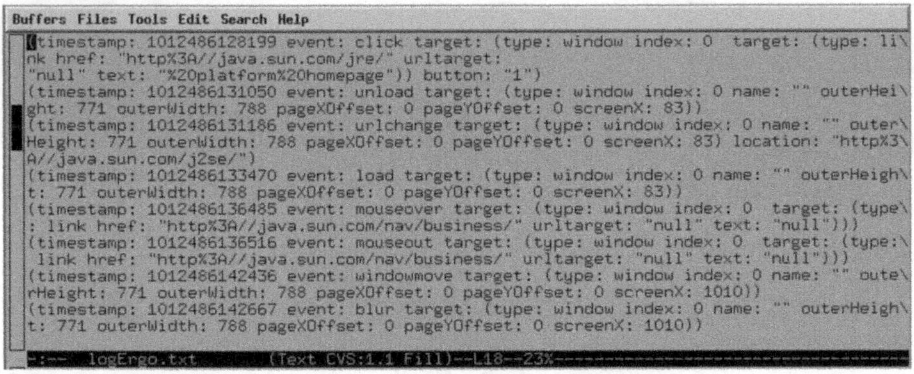

```
Buffers Files Tools Edit Search Help
(timestamp: 1012486128199 event: click target: (type: window index: 0  target: (type: li\
nk href: "http%3A//java.sun.com/jre/" urltarget:
"null" text: "%20platform%20homepage")) button: "1")
(timestamp: 1012486131050 event: unload target: (type: window index: 0 name: "" outerHei\
ght: 771 outerWidth: 788 pageXOffset: 0 pageYOffset: 0 screenX: 83))
(timestamp: 1012486131186 event: urlchange target: (type: window index: 0 name: "" outer\
Height: 771 outerWidth: 788 pageXOffset: 0 pageYOffset: 0 screenX: 83) location: "http%3\
A//java.sun.com/j2se/")
(timestamp: 1012486133470 event: load target: (type: window index: 0 name: "" outerHeigh\
t: 771 outerWidth: 788 pageXOffset: 0 pageYOffset: 0 screenX: 83))
(timestamp: 1012486136485 event: mouseover target: (type: window index: 0  target: (type\
: link href: "http%3A//java.sun.com/nav/business/" urltarget: "null" text: "null")))
(timestamp: 1012486136516 event: mouseout target: (type: window index: 0  target: (type:\
 link href: "http%3A//java.sun.com/nav/business/" urltarget: "null" text: "null")))
(timestamp: 1012486142436 event: windowmove target: (type: window index: 0 name: "" oute\
rHeight: 771 outerWidth: 788 pageXOffset: 0 pageYOffset: 0 screenX: 1010))
(timestamp: 1012486142667 event: blur target: (type: window index: 0 name: "" outerHeigh\
t: 771 outerWidth: 788 pageXOffset: 0 pageYOffset: 0 screenX: 1010))
-:--  logErgo.txt       (Text CVS:1.1 Fill)--L18--23%-----------------------------------
```

Fig. 3. Sample of a log generated by Ergotracer

Once the events are detected and controlled a log to keep track of them is generated. To store data in the client memory or to send it through the web the Java language capabilities are used.

The basic pattern to define the log for each detected event is `(timestamp: event: target: )`. Timestamp and event tags contain the information on the event name and the time at which it was produced. The target tag provides a detailed and hierarchical description of the context in which the event occurred:

the object to which the detected event was originally sent and all other objects in which this first object is contained. Figure 3 shows a sample of a log file (browsed with emacs) when navigating java.sun.com. The first event in the sample is a click over a link. This event is followed by an unload event, a urlchange event, and a load event. Next events (mouseover and mouseout) show that the mouse was over a link (but did not press it). Last events show that the browser window was moved (windowmove), and finally the mouse left the browser window raising a blur event.

Finally, the execution or running of Ergotracer can be stopped at any moment without interfering with the navigator behaviour. Figure 4 shows Ergotracer at work. In this case two navigation windows are under control. The display is active and shows the information collected at every moment. The information

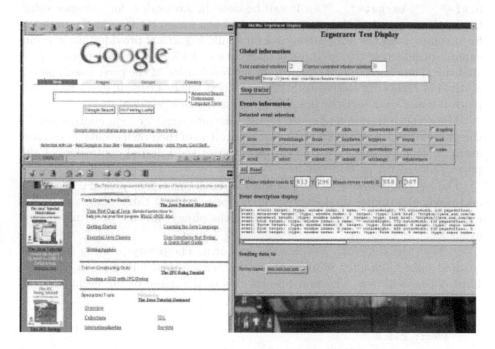

Fig. 4. Ergotracer at work

shown on the event description display is the same that is gather in the log files but has not timestamp information.

3.2   Some Technical Details

Among the functions used by Ergotracer we can differentiate three fundamental tasks: window infection; event control and log generation.

The window infecting functions have several purposes. They are in charge of running the event controllers which will deal with the subsequent task. They also open the connections with the possible receivers of generated data. Sockets are used to communicate with those receivers. Finally, the window-infecting functions have to create the data structures necessary for the rest of Ergotracer's execution. The main data structure is a list where the information about every controlled window is maintained and updated.

Plenty of small functions make up the event control task. Each is in charge of detecting an determined event. As previously mentioned, apart from the events that Javascript can control, new events are added: windowmove, urlchange, scroll, newwindow, eventchange and closewindow. Ergotracer's detection of the newwindow event gives rise to multiple challenges since the generation of a new browser window can take place in very different ways. It can be done in HTML, for instance using the feature target in the hypertext tag (<a href="..." target="...">). It can be done in Javascript, for instance using the method open() of the window class. And can it also be done in the browser, for instance using the left button click on a link. Ergotracer provides mechanisms capable of detecting the intention of opening a new window for each of these possibilities. These mechanisms range from the redefinition of the predefined open() method in Javascript to the study of the context where a certain event has taken place in order to detect the possible creation of a new window.

The event detection and control must take into consideration another detail: the pages visited can be designed to use controllers of their own events. Ergotracer event controllers allow the correct operation of the internal controllers of the pages visited with no interference.

The log generation involves a number of functions whose primary mission is accurately identifying the location where a certain event takes place and giving a detailed description of the context where the object that has determined that event is.

In Fig.5 the trace of a click event is shown. The pretty-printing is just for reading sake. Character sequences use the hexadecimal encoding in the ISO-Latin-1 character set. The first line informs of the name of the event and the

```
(timestamp: 1012210977837
    event: click
   target: (type: window index: 0
            target: (type: link href: "http%3A//java.sun.com/"
                     urltarget: "null"
                     text: "Java%20support"))
   button: "1")
```

Fig. 5. Trace for a click event

time at which it was produced. Then the attributes of the event are shown. The most significant attribute for many of the events is the target that informs of the context. In this case the click event has also a button attribute that informs that the click was done using the button 1 of the mouse. The target has a top-bottom structure that gathers the context. In Fig.5 the target informs that the click event was produced in a window whose index in the data structure was 0 and inside that window on a link that has a number of attributes: the url that would follow, the target tag, if any, in the HTML page and the hypertext read in the page.

Trace in Fig. 5 does not specifies window attributes. This is not an Ergotracer lack, but just a decision (easy to change if necessary) of the shown information for a determined event. Although quite significant, an event trace is not intended to be read in isolation. Information not present in an event trace is present in a previous event trace and has not changed ever since.

4   Privacy and Security Issues

The issues related to privacy and security of the generated data should be thoroughly discussed.

As for privacy issues, Ergotracer is not a tool designed to *spy* on the users' behaviour (in the negative sense of the word). The tool we have developed has the mission of obtaining detailed information of people's behaviour when using Internet in an easy and general, but also powerful, manner. The primary goal is to create agents and adaptive systems that might help these people to get by in an ever-changing and ever-growing information structure.

Ergotracer may be employed by the user, him or herself, for example, to inform an adaptive interface. In such a case there is no privacy problem: the user always controls the operation of Ergotracer; and could decide whether to send data to external servers or not.

It is a different case when a user is navigating and enters a server that wants to know his/her navigation data and, therefore, wants Ergotracer to start working with the client. For a use of the whole Ergotracer capabilities, due to the sort of operations Ergotracer needs to carry out, Java and Javascript's security system warns the user of the contingency. Some light uses of Ergotracer that do not affect the security are transparent for the users. For instance a web page server can use Ergotracer just to collect the events occurred into the served pages without explicit user permission.

Javascript's security system is based on the digital signature of the scripts. This model allows the user to confirm the validity of the certificate used to sign the script. It also allows the user to ensure that the script has not been tampered with since it was signed. The user then can decide whether to grant privileges based on the validated identity of the certificate owner and validated integrity of the script. The technique, although more complex, is quite similar to those of cookies. A user may accept or deny cookies, or may also be selective with the cookies he/she accepts.

We believe that if researchers are able to create authentically useful agents and adaptive systems whose goal is to help users and not only to engross the marketing databases, then people will not hesitate to give details of their behaviour to these kinds of tools. Much like we all give personal details to the doctor who is responsible for healing us.

As for security, one aspect to consider is the secure transfer of data through the net. Fortunately, Java provides standard methods for protecting web communications (Secure Sockets Layer). Therefore, data encryption, server authentication, and message integrity can be achieved.

5   Possible Uses

There are many areas where good comprehension of user knowledge would be advantageous to the existing tools. It is not our intention to exhaustively enumerate all the possible applications which could be improved thanks to the information compiled by Ergotracer. On the other hand, we want to provide some examples of its uses, which would help to better understand the versatility and generality of the tool introduced in this article.

The Ergotracer-generated data can be used in many different ways; individually, by a single user, or collectively; they can be dynamically managed at the moment of their collecting or statically analyzed later; they can be used on-line or off-line. . .

Some fields where they can be used are: sociological research, intelligent browsing and navigation, resource discovery, data search and retrieval, data caching, data-mining, security, and web sites and services design and evaluation.

A dynamic use would be appropriate for providing agents and adaptive systems with necessary material. Based on this material, certain decisions to help the user can be made: concerning the kind of search, the way data are shown, interesting related links. . .

A static use concerning the user's transactions would be also appropriate for the aforementioned areas, but in particular for data-mining and caching in the identification of strategies, users communities and habits and so on.

Detailed logs generation could be used in security and in the confirmation of the services rendered as an electronic verification. Finally, it would be an extremely helpful tool when it comes to determine web metrics to evaluate the design quality of web servers or service providers.

In the following paragraphs, we are going to give a few extended examples where the detailed information collected by Ergotracer would make a great difference with respect to traditional data gathering methods.

A team of psychologists and sociologists at our university was preparing a set of studies on Internet usability and ergonomics and they asked us how much user behaviour could be collected. Ergotracerwas the answer. Unfortunately, the collaborative project did not find adequate financial support and several interesting work paths are still untread. For instance, we know that an eye-tracker and Ergotracer can record the user behaviour experience when navigating and reproduce the experiment from the collected data, including the precise position of the eyes and the mouse pointer on the screen.

In order to develop intelligent agents, a profile of the user's preferences is required. In a closed context, for example a bookstore, it is not difficult to find the correlation between preferences and activities: users buy what they like. In a wider context, finding the right correlations becomes a much more difficult task and every activity has to be collected and considered. Usually this information is gathered in a plug-in that is platform dependent (browser+OS). Ergotracer collects accurate information, is cross-platform and does not need explicit installation.

Ergotracer is proof of concept. So we will explain a stand-alone application in another area that we are currently developing and can benefit from Ergotracer ideas: ANote (an annotated documental database). ANote is oriented towards a small and closed working group. Its goal is to avoid printed documents without losing its main quality: you can write on its margin all your notes. ANote is a winner for ecological reasons and because it allows notes sharing. So it is possible to use ANote as a distributed editor to develop documents. A lot of Ergotracer ideas can be reused in ANote because the natural document source is the Internet. An user could insert a document in ANote while browsing the Internet and immediately start to insert notes and sharing them within a user group. Even more, ANote should allow the user to add notes to remote documents without downloading them into the local database. ANote needs inspect user activity while browsing in order to respond with a sensible and immediate action. For instance, a right click should open a popup menu with possible actions in the current context. One action could be to add the current document to the database; another one could be to activate automatic database loading, so that every page that we reach from the current one will be added to the database.

6 Conclusions

This paper describes Ergotracer a tool that accurately gathers and informs of the user behaviour and performance when navigating or using services on Internet.

Unlike most of the existing tools, Ergotracer collects the user interaction at the client-side. This feature allows a thorough knowledge of the user behaviour and make it possible the use of collected data by tools both inside and outside the client.

Ergotracer is based on technology present in current Internet browsers, it is cross-platform and lightweight and can therefore be widely used and deployed.

Agents and adaptive systems in many research areas related to Internet (resource discovery, data search and retrieval, intelligent browsing and navigation. . .) could take advantage of the on-line information collected by Ergotracer. Many other areas (security, data mining, data caching, web design. . .) could find in the Ergotracer-generated log files appropriate material for study.

Acknowledgments

The authors would like to thank Bernabé Hornillos Ramos and Javier Varela for their undeniably earth shattering contributions to this paper.

References

[AGH00]   Ken Arnold, James Gosling, and David Holmes. *The Java Programming Language.* Addison-Wesley, June 2000.

[BB98]   Krishna Bharat and Andrei Broder. A technique for measuring the relative size and overlap of public web search engines. In *Proceedings 7th World-Wide Web Conference (WWW7).* Special issue of Computer Networks and ISDN Systems, Volume 30, 1998.

[BDMS94]   C. Mic Bowman, Peter B. Danzing, Udi Manber, and Michael F. Schwartz. Scalable internet resource discovery: Research problems and approaches. *Communications of the ACM*, 37(8):98–107, 1994.

[Bru96]   Peter Brusilovsky. Methods and techniques of adaptive hypermedia. *User Modeling and User Adapted Interaction*, 6(2–3):87–129, 1996.

[CP95]   Lara D. Catledge and James E. Pitkow. Characterizing browsing strategies in the World-Wide Web. *Computer Networks and ISDN Systems*, 27(6):1065–1073, 1995.

[Dav99]   Brian D. Davison. Web traffic logs: An imperfect resource for evaluation. In *Proccedings of the Ninth Annual Conference of the Internet Society (INET'99)*, 1999.

[ISC01]   Internet domain survey. http://www.isc.org/ds/, 2001.

[JFM97]   Thorsten Joachims, Dayne Freitag, and Tom Mitchell. Webwatcher: A tour guide for the world wide web. In *Proceedings of IJCAI97*, 1997.

[Lie95]   Henry Lieberman. Letizia: An agent that assists web browsing. In Chris S. Mellish, editor, *Proceedings of the Fourteenth International Joint Conference on Artificial Intelligence*, pages 924–929. Morgan Kaufmann publishers Inc.: San Mateo, CA, USA, 20–25 1995.

[Mul97]   Jorg P. Muller. *The Design of Intelligent Agents: A Layered Approach*, volume 1177 of *Lecture Notes in Computer Science*. Springer Verlag, 1997.

[Netscape]   Netscape. Client-side JavaScript guide. http://developer.netscape.com/docs/manuals/js/client/jsguide/.

[NUA01]   Nua internet survey. http://www.nua.ie/surveys/, 2001.

[Nwa95]   Hyacinth S. Nwana. Software agents: An overview. *Knowledge Engineering Review*, 11(2):205–244, 1995.

[Ous91]   John K. Ousterhout. An x11 toolkit based on the tcl language. In *Proceedings of the 1991 Winter USENIX Conference*, 1991.

[Quest]   Quest Software. Funnel web analyzer. http://www.quest.com/funnel_web/analyzer/

[Sane]   Sane Solutions. Nettracker. http://www.sane.com/products/NetTracker/.

[SF99]   Myra Spiliopoulou and Lukas C. Faulstich. WUM: A tool for Web utilization analysis. *Lecture Notes in Computer Science*, 1590, 1999.

[TNP97]   Michael Twidale, David M. Nichols, and Chris D. Paice. Browsing is a collaborative process. *Information Processing and Management*, 33(6):761–783, 1997.

A Friendly Peer-to-Peer File Sharing System with Profit but without Copy Protection

Rüdiger Grimm[1] and Jürgen Nützel[2]

[1] Technische Univerität Ilmenau, Institut für Medien- und Kommunikationswissenschaft
D-98693 Ilmenau, Germany
Ruediger.Grimm@TU-Ilmenau.de
[2] Technische Univerität Ilmenau, Institut für Theoretische und Technische Informatik
D-98693 Ilmenau, Germany
Juergen.Nuetzel@TU-Ilmenau.de

Abstract. Content providers try to restrict the usage of their products by their customers in order to prevent unlicensed distribution. On the other hand, customers ignore these restrictions and share files for free (Gnutella). Content providers and content users treat one another as enemies with conflicting interests. In this paper we bring customers and providers of content back together to a common economic interest. Content providers support their customers to re-distribute their products in that they pay for any re-distributed multimedia product a small percentage on commission. Customers have a choice to pay for a received copy or to use it freely. If they use it for free, they will get no commission on re-distribution. If they pay, they will become licensed re-distributors automatically. This paper describes a friendly peer-to-peer file-sharing model of customers, which brings profit to both, content providers and their customers. We will also specify a protocol for payment and re-distribution. We will describe open interfaces and file formats, which are needed for implementation.

1 Motivation and Introduction

Production and distribution of multimedia products is expensive. Content providers like BMG, Sony and Vivendi, as well as software producers like Microsoft or Oracle, take all the economic risk and depend on revenues. Distribution of illegal copies and unlicensed copies would undermine the model as we observe with the services of Napster (meanwhile domesticated by BMG), and Gnutella [4] or Freenet, and with unlicensed Microsoft software. There are even future scenarios where no high-level music products will exist any more; if there will be nobody to pay authors, composers and singers, because their products have no market price. People would get it for free in equal quality, so why pay for it?

For the time being, only one model for countermeasures is seriously discussed in the multimedia industry and standardization bodies. That is: prevention of copy and re-distribution. This brings the industry into a nasty dilemma. On the one hand, their products shall be sold and thus transferred into the end-user devices. There, they are no more under control of the publishers, but of the customers. On the other hand, however, although being in the end-user environment, the products shall not be under free control of the customers. The mechanisms to restrict usage, especially copy and

H.Unger, T.Böhme, and A.Mikler (Eds.): PCS 2002, LNCS 2346, pp. 133-142, 2002.
© Springer-Verlag Berlin Heidelberg 2002

re-distribution, are not in the hand of the publishers, but within the end-user devices. As we observe in reality, however, customers ignore the restrictions and re-distribute through file-sharing services or just directly from friend to friend.

This is regarded as misuse, and would be charged legally. It reflects the interest of users directly: they have the products in their hands, copy and re-distribution is cheap (almost no cost) and easy, so why pay money for products they get for free in equal quality? By contrast, the content providers experience a serious loss by free re-distribution of their products. Any copy given to another user is a loss of payment, the publishers believe.

2   The Standard Model of IPMP

The MPEG community develops the so-called IPMP model. IPMP stands for "Intellectual Property Rights Management and Protection" [1, 2] and is one method for the management of digital rights (DRM). It is based on end-user restriction. Users shall buy IPMP-standardized devices, which contain IPMP-tools that control the usage of the content in a way pre-specified by the publisher of the content. IPMP is flexible. Content streams contain an IPMP portion. The IPMP portion would specify, which IPMP-tools are the appropriate ones, how they should treat the content. A content stream may even contain the tools themselves within the IPMP portion, if they are not available locally in the end-user device.

However, this model has a drawback. Any multimedia product contains the elements of its decoding (and even of its encryption, if needed) in itself. End-user devices may be programmable. PCs are definitely programmable. Products and tools within an end-user device can thus be re-programmed in a way that they ignore the restrictions originally designed for a product. The multimedia industry knows this, of course. We observe it as an every-day behavior of users worldwide. However, the industry argues that once there is an accepted standard with powerful software and devices out in the world, a significant high number of customers will follow the rules and use the standardized functions. The others will not become too many, because (a) it costs efforts, and (b) they will be legally pursued. They can be ignored, economically.

We are implementing a first step towards the IPMP model in a Diploma thesis in our University in order to demonstrate that it works, from a functional point of view [3]. A simple tool in the end-user device is able to encrypt and decrypt content symmetrically. The symmetric key is transported within a "recoverable signature" on the basis of asymmetric cryptography. The sender of content would create a symmetric key, and encrypt the content with this key. The encrypted content, the recoverable signature of the encrypted key, and the certificate of the related public verification key comprise a "content transfer envelope" and can be transferred to other users.

The user tools are designed such that on reception of a content transfer envelope, the recoverable signature and the respective public key certificate are cut out of the content stream and stored in a local table of signatures and keys.

The next recipient would not be able to decrypt and consume the re-distributed content unless the sender has applied a signature with his own private key. This would not make it impossible to re-distribute content without payment, but at least re-distribution would be easily traceable by law enforcement mechanisms. Hopefully, users will avoid free re-distribution because they do not want to be part of illegal traces.

Of course, the mechanism of this tool can be broken easily. It can be re-programmed in several ways. For example, a re-programmed tool may store the content in clear on the device. It may re-distribute the content in clear. It may store the original signature together with the encrypted content. Or it may re-distribute an encrypted content and put the signature of the original sender into the content transfer envelope and hide the intermediate user from a trace. This is all possible. However, the rationale of the model says, if users want to attack the mechanism, they may do so. But it will cost some effort, and it is illegal. Most users will follow the standardized rules, they will use the original tool, and thus an economically significant number of users will not copy and re-distribute content without payment, at least not without signature.

We believe that this model is too weak, and that users will indeed break the rules, because it is easy, cheap, and in the interest of users to re-distribute content freely. Therefore, we need another model. We will criticize this model and then we will develop an alternative model in the next two sections.

3   Arguments against the IPMP Model

According to the IPMP model the security policy of the content provider is enforced by local tools within the end-user devices. The policy does not satisfy needs of the end-user, but of the content provider. In contrary, the end-user is restricted in his free usage of the content. This violates a fundamental principle of security models in open systems:

In an open environment of communication partners who underlie no central control, every party must have all the mechanisms at his disposal, which are required to enforce his interest. This is realized when partners exchange receipts or contracts. A contract serves as a proof, which helps to enforce one's right against the other party. Note that the proof is in the hand of the interested party, not in the hand of the pursued party, while the pursued party cannot repudiate the proof.

The construction of IPMP is the other way round. Those who have an interest in the DRM policy (the content provider) gives the mechanisms to enforce the policy out of his hands into the hands of those who have no interest in the policy (the consumer). Therefore, it can be expected as a tendency, that end-users will evade those mechanisms. Practice will necessarily turn into legal control. Content providers will pursue their customers, even with detective methods. Users will try to avoid those rules, as we already observed when Napster was sued and finally shut down and when Gnutella came up [4]. Gnutella is based on the individual interest of all users to receive data, and this works only when users provide data, this is the model of file sharing which serves the interests of the participating users.

As a summary, the IPMP model is not only "un-cool". It violates basic security rules and it is built against the file-sharing architecture of the Internet.

4   An Alternative Security Model

What can we do in order to put a DRM model back on sound feet? The best possibility we see is to link the self-restriction of end-users with their personal interest. One can think about discounts, money-back services or quality guarantees in exchange for well behaviour of customers. Stronger than this is an adequate reposition of interests. Re-distribution is obviously in the interest of end-users. It should be no longer against the interest of content providers, but in contrary, it must be placed in the interest of content providers as well. Content providers should be put in a position that they do not hinder their customers to re-distribute their products, but they should support them to re-distribute their products as widely as possible.

This is not out of place. Content providers want to sell their products. And selling means distribution. Therefore, content providers do have high interest in the distribution of their products. However, the products should be paid for. We suggest users to become re-distribution partners. A customer, who pays for a product, gets the right to re-distribute it. He will get a percentage (commission) of the payment, which the next recipients pay for. As a proof of this right a signed receipt is added. If the recipient does not pay the content provider, the re-distributor will get no commission from the content provider.

Why should a recipient pay for a product? The recipient wants to become a re-distributor himself. If the recipient does not pay, he will not be able to earn a commission on re-distribution. The important step in this procedure is that payment and registration for re-distribution are automatically linked. Commission is paid to the one who has paid the content. The signature of the receipt proves that the signer (the owner of the purchase rights, i.e. the creator or his authorized agent) has received payment for the product from the buyer who is named by the receipt. If the recipient does not pay for a product but re-distribute it anyway (he is free to do so), then the original sender from whom he has received the product, will earn the commission.

This model gives free choice to all users. A user may receive, consume and re-distribute multimedia content without care of DRM. In this case, he doesn't pay, and he won't earn (he may help others to earn, though). On the other hand, a user may choose to pay for a product. In this case he gets a receipt which establishes his official role of a licensed re-distributor of the product. Payment creates the opportunity to earn a percentage of the payment by any paying recipient of his re-distribution.

5   The Friendly Peer-to-Peer File-Sharing System

In this section we describe the complete system, which was developed at the Ilmenau Technical University in close cooperation with the 4FriendsOnly.com Internet Technologies AG (4fo AG) [5]. We will provide (client parts) and run (server part) a first reference implementation of the described system. The whole system specification will be open. This allows every publisher or even the developers themselves to distribute their content friendly.

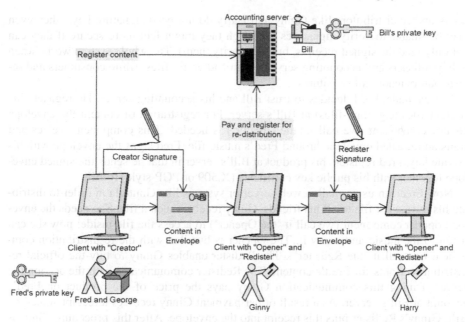

Fig. 1. A snapshot of the peer-to-peer friendly file-sharing system. Involved components and persons are shown

The system description is divided into three subsections. In the first subsection we enumerate all involved components and persons. The next subsection defines the file format which is used for file-sharing. The third subsection defines the underlying protocols.

5.1 Involved Components and Persons

In this paper we describe a first version in which a trusted person named Bill is involved. Bill acts as a trusted third party between content publishers (designers, composers or programmers) and their customers. Bill runs a central service. This service manages the registration and re-distribution for publishers. Let a designer Fred and a programmer George be two such publishers who sell their products with the help of Bill's service. Bill's server adds a signed receipt to the content as a proof of payment. Besides registration Bill manages also the payment for publishers like Fred and George, and for consumers and re-distributors like Ginny and Harry. We call Bill's server "accounting server", because it manages an account for every publisher and re-distributor.

Note that Bill is not needed, if Fred or George decides to run his own accounting service. Decentralized accounting in the hand of a publisher is practical if Fred and George are well known by most potential customers. If the customers do not trust unknown publishers a trusted third-party accounting service like Bill's is more useful. In this paper we will include Bill's central accounting server.

In this version, publishers like Fred and George, as well as the accounting service like Bill's, own signature keys. They are able to sign files and to verify signatures.

Users and re-distributors like Ginny and Harry do not need signature keys, they even may be unable to verify signatures (although they might feel more secure if they can not only read the signed receipts, but also verify them). The whole system works when only publishers and accounting services sign and verify files, while consumers and re-distributors ignore all signatures.

For example, Fred decides to trust Bill and his accounting server. He registers his content files (e.g. mp3-files) at Bill's server. For registration of content the envelope creator component (we call it 'the Creator') is needed. This component creates and signs an unsealed envelope around Fred's music-file. Fred signs the envelope with his private key. Fred registers his product at Bill's server in that he sends the signed envelope together with his public key certificate (X.509 or PGP-style) to Bill.

Now Fred can use e-mail, a web-server or systems like Gnutella in order to distribute his enveloped file to all his friends. Ginny receives such a file. She needs the envelope opener component (we call it 'the Opener') to access the file inside: now she can listen to the music and enjoy it. The Opener is bundled with the re-distribution component (we call it 'the Redister'). The Redister enables Ginny to buy the official re-distribution rights for Fred's content. The Redister communicates with the accounting server. During this communication Ginny pays the price of the product on Fred's account at Bill's server. As a result of her payment Ginny receives a receipt signed by Bill. Ginny's Redister puts this receipt into the envelope. After this procedure Ginny is official re-distributor. Now she receives commission for Fred's content as soon as Harry decides to pay for it. The receipt which Ginny added to the envelope serves two purposes: it informs Harry and it proves to Bill that she, Ginny, deserves the commission payment.

5.2   The Unsealed Envelope – File Format for Friendly File Sharing

We do not encrypt distributed content. We simply put the content into an unsealed envelope in clear. The format for this envelope is similar to the Java archive (JAR) format. The JAR file type is based on the standard cross-platform ZIP archive format. JAR provides structures for signatures made by different persons. Our archive format is as close as possible to JAR. We call it the "friendly archive (FAR)".

The FAR is transferred with the content stream from customer to customer. Bill is not interested in the content. Therefore, Bill will not store the full FAR, but the envelope elements of the FAR which identify the creator and the re-distributors of content.

The first file in a JAR is an ASCII file named MANIFEST.MF in the META-INF directory. For executable content in a FAR archive the manifest must contain a section for the executable file with the Install-Script keyword. In JAR this keyword indicates the executable installer.

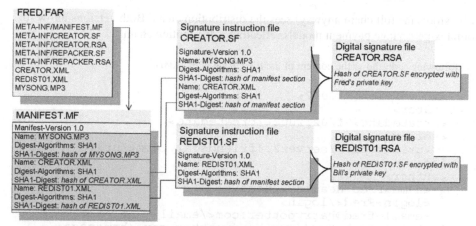

Fig. 2. Files involved in the FAR archive named FRED.FAR

A manifest file contains only a list of the files in the archive that are to be signed. The associated signatures are not contained in the manifest file, but they are stored outside in extra files. Among others, this is the function of the signature instruction files (*.SF) and of the digital signature files (*.RSA). A FAR archive (FRED.FAR in our example) has at least one pair of a signature instruction file and a digital signature file, namely the CREATOR file-pair. In our example this pair (CREATOR.SF and CREATOR.RSA) was made by Fred for his content file (MYSONG.MP3) and for his content description file (CREATOR.XML) in the archive. The other pairs (REDIST01,, REDIST02, etc.) are only created after a customer has re-distributed this file. In our example, a second pair (REDIST01.SF and REDIST01.RSA) is made and signed by the accounting server of Bill after Ginny has paid for it. The second pair and the corresponding receipt file (REDIST01.XML) are not included until Ginny has paid for it. If Harry also pays for it another set of files (REDIST02.SF, REDIST02.RSA and REDIST02.XML) is added, and so forth with any new recipient to come.

The CREATOR files are documents for the creatorship of content. They prove the registration as well as Fred's responsibility and rights for his product The REDIST01, REDIST02, etc. files are documents for the re-distribution rights of customers who have paid for the product.

What happens with the receipts if a product is re-distributed several times? We have two possibilities for the implementation of the Redister component. In a (simpler) first version, Redister stores and transfers only the latest receipt file in the envelope. For example, if Harry pays for the music file of Fred, Ginny would receive her commission payment due to Ginny's receipt read by Harry. But then, Ginny's receipt would be removed from the FAR stored in Harry's Redister. For further redistribution by Harry, Harry's recipients would only see Harry's receipt, not Ginny's receipt. However, in Ginny's FAR, Ginny's receipt would remain. Whenever Ginny redistributes the product, her receipt would be transferred. In a (more complex) second version the receipts of the complete distribution chain are left in the envelope. In the second version, a recipient would see the distribution chain, in the first version, only Bill (who stores the full chain anyway) sees the distribution chain. Both versions allow for complex percentage payment models reflecting a distribution chain.

The following code shows the content of the file CREATOR.XML.

```xml
<?xml version="1.0"?>
<creator>
  <createdate>01/02/2002</createdate>
  <server>
    <url>https://server3.4friendsonly.com</url>
  </server>
  <author>
    <name>Fred Weasley</name>
    <login>Fred</login>
    <email>fred@harrypotter.com</email>
    <homepage>http://www.harrypotter.com</homepage>
    <pubkey>
      <type>RSA</type>
      <length>2048</length>
      <keyid>0FF2168D</keyid>
      <fingerprint>E0017F15583564D0572DB4BBC989200A
      </fingerprint>
    </pubkey>
  </author>
  <price>
    <amount>2.5</amount>
    <currency>EUR</currency>
    <commission>20%</commission>
  </price>
  <filelist>
    <file>
      <name>MYSONG.MP3</name>
      <description>This is my first song</description>
    </file>
  </filelist>
</creator>
```

This code snipped shows the content of REDIST01.XML.

```xml
<?xml version="1.0"?>
<redister>
  <paydate>03/04/2002</paydate>
  <generation>1</generation>
  <server>
    <url>https://server3.4friendsonly.com</url>
    <pubkey>
      <type>RSA</type>
      <length>2048</length>
      <keyid>02FAA6B1</keyid>
      <fingerprint>5FFDB4BBC989564D0200AE0017F15123
      </fingerprint>
    </pubkey>
  </server>
  <actualredister>
```

```
    <login>Ginny</login>
    <email>ginny@harrypotter.com</email>
  </actualredister>
<redister>
```

5.3 Protocols and Interfaces

Opener and Redister are combined in one executable file (Opener.exe). On Windows systems this executable is registered for the FAR file extension. The Creator (Creator.exe) is a separated executable. The Creator and Redister (part of Opener.exe) communicate with the accounting server. These two protocols are fundamental for the whole system. Firstly we describe what happens, when Fred uses the Creator..

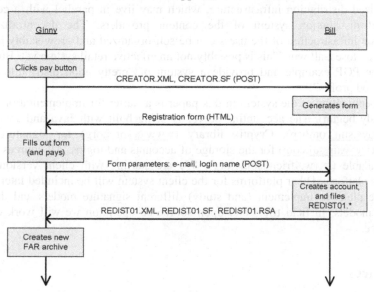

Fig. 3. Sequence diagram for the communication between Ginny's Redister component and Bill's accounting server

In contrast to the communication between Ginny and Bill, the communication between Fred and Bill is quite simple. After Fred has produced the music file, he starts the Creator. He enters the information for the file CREATOR.XML. After that the Creator builds the files MANIFEST.ML, CREATOR.XML, CREATOR.SF and CREATOR.RSA. The Creator uses Fred's private key to create the signature (CREATOR.RSA). Finally the FAR archive is build. At the end of the process the communication starts. The Creator sends the files CREATOR.XML and CREATOR.SF to Bill. Bill uses these files to create an account for Fred. Bill answers with an e-mail. The e-mail includes a password for Fred to access the account easily

When Ginny opens the FAR from Bill, the information of CREATOR.XML is shown. The file MYSONG.MP3 is stored temporarily on Ginny's hard-disk. Ginny is asked by the Opener to pay or play. If she decides to play, the MP3-player of the system is started with the temporary file. If Ginny decides to pay, the Redister component is invoked. See Fig. 3 for the detailed description of the communication between Ginny and Bill. The result of the communication leads to a new FAR, which includes additional information about Ginny`s re-distribution rights. When Harry opens this FAR from Ginny, the information of `CREATOR.XML` and `REDIST01.XML` is shown.

6   Conclusion

In the friendly file sharing model, the consumption of multimedia products is linked to an incentive for payment. Both, the content provider and the consumer would gain an economic profit from the payment. Re-distribution of content without payment is still possible: it is neither forbidden, nor technically blocked. However, it is not attractive.

Those who pay and re-distribute are the users themselves. They would build up a decentralized distribution infrastructure, which may live in parallel with a centrally controlled distribution system of the content providers. The decentralized re-distribution infrastructure of the users can be self-organized and grow stably bottom-up. Nobody loses, all win. This is possibly not an effective retail system yet. But it can follow the PGP example and provide a system of "pretty good distribution" with "pretty good profits".

The specification of the system in this paper is a starter for implementation (which has already begun). The accounting server is being built with Java and JavaServer Pages (java.sun.com/jsp), Cryptix library (www.cryptix.org) for signatures, and MySQL (www.mysql.com) for the storage of accounts and logins. All sources will be open available (www.4friendsonly.org). We are starting with client versions on a Windows platform. Other platforms for the client system will be included later. There are future plans to implement (and study) different signature models and different payment models. In field trials and open source co-operation we will work on user acceptance.

References

1. IPMP Ad-hoc Group, ISO/IEC JTC 1/SC 29/WG11: Coding of Moving Pictures and Audio. Study of Text of PDAM ISO/IEC 14496-1:2001, Dec 2001.
2. 3GPP S1-01 1197 V0.0.0 (2001-11-23). Proposed Stage 1, Release 6, Nov 2001.
3. S. Puchta: Untersuchung und Entwicklung von Sicherheitsmechanismen am Beispiel des Zugriffsschutzes MPEG-4 kodierter Audioströme. Diploma Thesis (in German), Technische Universität Ilmenau, Jan 2002.
4. Angelo Sotira: Step 1 – What is Gnutella? In: http://www.gnutella.com , 3 Dec. 2001.
5. Homepage of 4FriendsOnly.com Internet Technologies AG, http://www.4FriendsOnly.com

A Decentral Library for Scientific Articles

Markus Wulff

Dept. of Computer Science, University of Rostock
18059 Rostock, Germany
mwulff@informatik.uni-rostock.de

Abstract. Today, the management of information resources in the Internet is mostly realized by centralized services. Clients can contact the server and access these resources. Nevertheless, the classic client-server architecture suffers from some limitations caused by holding every data in one central place.

Internet communities are groups of individuals sharing a common interest or work scope. The connection between the members of a community creates a logical structure overlying the physical network structure. The community structure can be adapted and modified. This allows the appliance of some efficient and innovative algorithms and techniques. This is realized in the AWeb information management system.

In the contribution, a decentralized library for scientific articles based on the AWeb middelware is presented and the main concepts of the AWeb will be summarized in brief.

1 Introduction

The Internet is built by millions of connected computers all over the world. The substructure for the communication over the Internet is the TCP/IP protocol stack. It ensures that some arbitrary data can be transmitted form one computer to another one. Therefore, only the address of the target machine must be known, the routing through the network and the reliable transmission of the data is ensured by the basic protocols. This physical structure of the network cannot be changed by an Internet user and must be seen as a given condition for the development of almost all Internet applications.

In the early nineties, the World Wide Web (WWW) was introduced to support the users exchanging documents using the Internet. Documents could now be placed on any machine in the Internet and remotely accessed from any other computer in the Internet using a Web browser. For this, only the URL, consisting of the IP address of the source machine and the local path to the document on it, is required. A special communication server, the HTTP server, must be running on the source machine to answer the request for a document from the users Web browser. The real important new feature of the WWW was the possibility to link and access other documents, local or remote, inside a HTML document. Thus, the reader may follow these links to get related information located somewhere in the Internet. Today, millions of documents are placed in the Web and are mostly

H. Unger, T. Böhme, and A. Mikler (Eds.): I²CS 2002, LNCS 2346, pp. 143–152, 2002.

linking other documents or information resources. These linked documents are building a graph like structure on top of the underlying physical computer network [1], which helps the user to navigate through documents spread all over the Internet.

The disadvantage of the WWW structure is that it is relatively fixed and cannot be readjusted for individual needs of the user. Furthermore, it is not easy to find all information which are available on the Web. The content of the search engines are often outdated and does include parts of all available resources [2] only.

To overcome this problems, a new structure must be created which first of all can be adapted to the individual needs of every user and do also allow an efficient information management. There are always users on the Web sharing common interests or a common work scope and so on. These users are probably interested in the same or similar information. Such groups of users are often called *communities* [3,4,5]. Obviously, one can find interesting information on machines of other users inside such a community. So the users should be able to "link" other users and adapt the structure of this graph to their own needs. The result is again a network structure which overlies the physical computer network. But instead of the fixed structure of links between documents in the WWW this will create a network of users which can be modified by each user itself.

To realize this idea, every user needs his own personal communication daemon running on his machine, which supports the communication tasks. The user can now provide own information by making it accessible through the communication daemon. On the other side, every "member" running the same kind of communication program can access the information at the other users machines. These links consist of the IP address of the other machine and some path information. The address is necessary for the communication with the remote daemon and can be stored locally in a community address warehouse or neighborhood warehouse. After a while, every user knows some addresses of other users inside the community. This neighborhood relations build the *community graph* with the communication daemons as nodes and the edges are the links stored in the neighborhood warehouses on every machine.

The structure of the community network can be used to apply some efficient mechanisms for the information management. Newly emerging information can be propagated inside a community very fast and a query sent by a user can be answered quickly, always using the community network structure created through the links stored in the neighborhood warehouse of each node.

2   Related Projects and the Concept of the AWeb

2.1   Related Projects

The above described idea leads to a decentralized network structure, where every node acts as a server as well as a client. The concept is not new, but became well known to the public in recent years due to the emergence of file sharing facilities like Gnutella [6]. The main idea behind is that pairwise interacting users may exchange any kind of information over the network. Every participating user can be an information consumer and an information provider at the same time. All the data the network keeps are spread over the users machines. Not even a catalog of available resources is stored somewhere at a central server like it is done in client-server systems like Napster [7]. Moreover, peers may join and leave without any complicated registration mechanism and yet the system retains the ability to query the currently available peers for information. The network structure is flexible, reconfigurable and keeps the privacy and anonymity of the users.

Today, many projects using the described idea of a completely decentralized distributed systems to develop new protocols and application for a communication in the fast growing Internet. Freenet [8] for instance is a location-independent distributed file system across many individual computers. It allows files to be inserted, stored, and requested anonymously. As well as the quite similar Free Haven storage system [9], Freenet aims to provide security and anonymity for the user in the first place.

Gnutella [6] is a peer-to-peer file sharing protocol to enable users to provide and download any kind of data. The queries are protected and keep the anonymity of the user. The download of a file from one machine to the other is done with a direct connection for performance reasons, which will reveals the address of the peer and corrupt anonymity. A problem of Gnutella is the communication scheme. It uses inefficient "broadcasts" and produces a very high network load when the number of users increases.

There are also several other projects for the development of peer-to-peer file sharing software to be found on the Web, which will not be mentioned here. In the following, the main concepts of the AWeb are described.

2.2   The New Concepts of the AWeb

The goal of the AWeb is to provide a middelware for an efficient information management inside communities. It introduces some new ideas and algorithms using the logical community network structure.

Communities are inhomogeneous and mutable. The structure of the whole system changes over the time. Nobody knows these structure or the information kept on the nodes. Each node of a community holds information about an arbitrary part of the whole structure. Nevertheless, every member should be able to find information all other users provide and vice versa. The solution to this problem are *message chains* [10]. In fact, a message chain is a special communication mechanism to pass information from one node to another. Such a message can cause any kind of action at the destination node and will be forwarded to a neighbor of the current node. Thus, every node of the network is able to find information at previously unknown nodes and can learn about any other node in the community. Message chains are a very powerful communication method in a decentral environment. By using this uniform mechanism, every kind of inter-node communication task can be performed.

As mentioned above, communities are build by sharing common interests and information. That means that the information each node keeps form the community. For the case of the existence of two conflictive information, there must be an mechanism the community deals with that problem. Conflictive information can be for instance the decision whether a new resource is accepted to be relevant to the community or not. Communities can be splitted into subcommunities and on the other side, subcommunities can be combined to be one single community. This can be done using voting algorithms [11].

Furthermore, an efficient mechanism to collect and distribute new emerging information inside a community is required. Every member of a community is normally interested in new resources concerning his own interests or work content. The use of conventional search engines is here not the most efficient way because they cannot make use of the advantages the community structure offers. Based on the community structure, algorithms for decentralized search engine can be developed: "Ants" are constantly searching the community network and collecting new information of the nodes. These information are distributed inside the community and every member can be up to date without searching for new information by himself.

A user can be a member of more than one community depending on his interests. The different fields of interest (communities the user is member of) are called *horizontal communities*. They can be represented as nodes of a graph. The edges of this graph are connections between the different nodes representing the relationship between the different topics. This way, the user arranges his keywords and gets one or more connected graphs. These graph(s) can also be seen as communities and should be called *vertical community*. Vertical communities are connections between the "real" horizontal communities.

This structuring of the different communities can be used to accelerate the search for information inside the community and to improve respond and access times. On one hand, the request for a certain topic can be sent to a node inside the same community and on the other hand, the community network can be structured for a better routing through the community like described in Unger et. al. [12].

2.3 The AWeb Middelware

The AWeb is a middelware providing the above described concepts for the communication and the information management inside a community environment. It can be used to build decentralized applications.

As an example, a distributed de-central library for scientific publications should be introduced in the following. The difficulties of a central client-server system. In addition, a community based environment can adapt itself to the interests and needs of the actual user which can optimize the performance and resource consumption of the whole system. Therefore, the architecture shown in Fig. 1 is used to realize the AWeb idea.

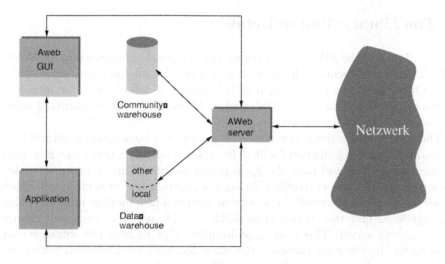

Fig. 1. Architecture of a AWeb node

An AWeb node consists of two main components — the *AWeb server* and the *graphical user interface* (GUI). The community server answers every incoming request by other community members and acts as communication client for the local user. The server uses the message chains described in Wulff et. al. [10] for all communication tasks. The particular services are provided by the modules which can be added to the server.

The community data is stored in the *community warehouse* and all locally stored documents residing in the *document warehouse* which is divided into one part for the documents provided by the local user and one part for the documents the user has downloaded from other community members. The latter part can also be called document cache. The warehouses are managed by the AWeb server Using the GUI the vertical and horizontal communities can be managed by the user. Furthermore, the search service interface is provided by the editor as well as the interface for adding own documents to the distributed library and viewing the locally stored and/or linked documents.

To become a member of the AWeb community, the knowledge of at least one address of a AWeb node is mandatory For this purpose, the address of several nodes should be announced. Then, through search activities of the user other nodes will be found and stored in the community warehouse. Hereby, the users community is created.

The AWeb software is implemented in the Java programming language to achieve a high portability and to due to the object oriented philosophy of this language it supports the modular, extendible structure of the software. The described software, the community editor and the community server, has to be installed on every machine which should become an AWeb node.

3   The Library Tool in Detail

An installation of the AWeb-server transforms a normal computer into an AWeb-node. This communication daemon is responsible for all communication of the node. Once the server is started, it is listening at a default port for incoming requests or replies from other AWeb nodes. All messages are constructed using the same message chain format.

The server itself is multi-threaded, i. e. each time a connection is established, a separate thread is launched for it. The new connection thread can now read the message header and load the appropriate module. This mechanism makes the server flexible and extendible. In such a manner, no connection can block the server. In order to install a new service, simply a new module must be added and registered and the service is available on this node without any change to the existing server. This plug-in philosophy helps to keep the software easy to maintain. In the next sections, the main modules are described which are necessary to make the AWeb distributed library work.

3.1   The Ping Module

The first service, the server should provide is similar to the well known *ping* service of the Internet Protocol. The only task this module has to fulfill is to answer incoming requests that the AWeb community server is running on the machine.

This function might not be interesting for the user but is necessary for the server to do its work.

3.2   The Search Module

Much more complex than the ping module is the module for the search on the community. In a community environment, every node keeps only a part of the "knowledge" of the whole community, in this particular case, a small number of documents of the library. A search is initiated every time the user is looking for new documents concerning a certain topic. Therefore, only a keyword must be supplied by the user. The search functionality is provided by the AWeb middelware.

If a search request comes in, the community server loads the search module which will then process the request. First, the local community warehouse is searched for the keyword given in the request and if it is found, the list of documents saved in the warehouse for the given keyword is sent to the requesting node. As said above, the reply might be affected by one or more flags given in the request.

If a reply comes in, it is evaluated and the results are presented to the user. On the replying node, the request is passed on to another randomly chosen node if the hop-counter of the request is greater than zero. This will restrict the time, a search message lives in the community.

3.3 The Community Graph Editor

The graph editor is the user interface for the management of the community warehouse. Figure 2 shows the main window of the graph editor. It represents the content of the users community warehouse, the vertical community, as a graph. Each keyword is pictured as a vertex and the relations between the keywords are the edges of this graph.

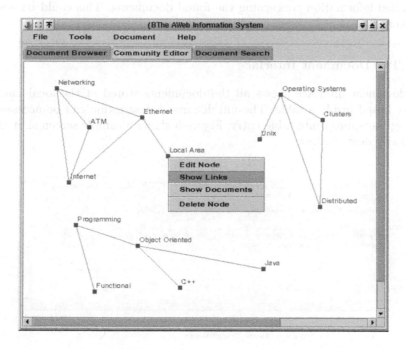

Fig. 2. The Community Graph Editor

The relationship between two keywords is not necessarily both-way. The outgoing edge of a node which "knows" the other one is marked with a different color. The edges can be weighted in order to express the strength of the pertinence of the relation. Within a search request it might be demanded to return the related keywords too. This can be restricted by assigning access right to the edges.

3.4 The Search Interface

In order to find new documents in the community library, the search function of the AWeb can be used. The search form of the library tool offers a keyword search for documents. The user must provide the keyword and the entry node of the community graph. That means that the address of the target node is taken from the list of addresses of the community to which the entry node belongs. If the user is not member of a related community, the address of an other AWeb node can be provided.

Furthermore, related topics can be required with the search message. This way, the user can make the search more detailed or generalized.

The results are presented in the result window. Now, the user can decide to store the links to interesting documents in the local community warehouse, to download documents and store them in the local document cache, and to get a detailed information concerning the found documents. This could be a short abstract, document keywords and so on.

3.5   The Document Interface

The document interface shows all the documents stored at the local machine or just linked inside a table. The full document description can be accessed by clicking the appropriate table entry. Figure 3 shows a sample screen shot of the document view window.

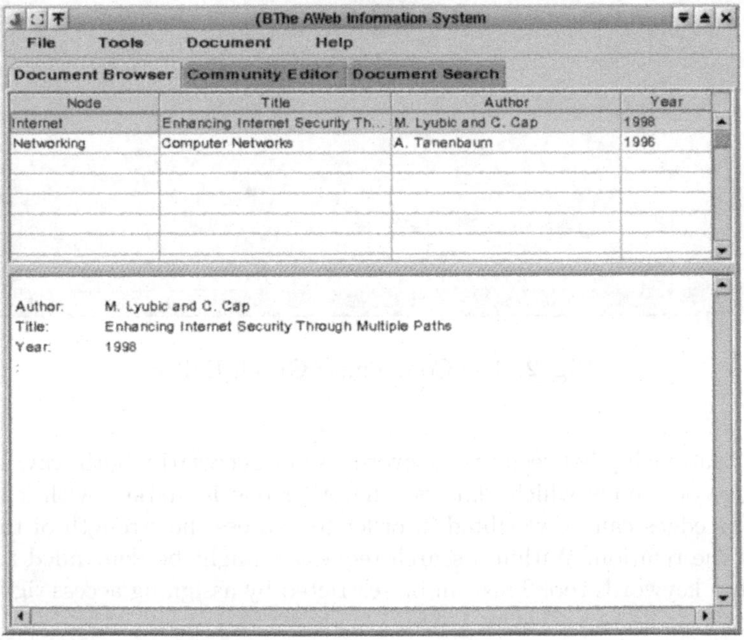

Fig. 3. The document view window

If the user wants to add a new document to the local document warehouse, the document interface should be used. This module makes sure, that the required information for a document are provided and will generate a proper entry for the local document warehouse.

3.6   The URL Verifying Module

The structure of an Internet community is subject to frequently changes at any time. New nodes are added, other nodes are removed from the community or the content of a node's warehouse changes. In every case, the information which the community holds is modified. So it might happen that the links stored in the local warehouse are not up to date and that a link points to a resource which was removed or has changed its location. The URL verifying module checks the links in the local warehouse for actuality.

Every time the module is launched it tries to reach the URLs stored in the local community warehouse. If an error occurs, it will retry to contact the URL for certain times and if the error persists, it is announced to the user. Then the user can decide whether to keep the warehouse entry anyway, to remove it or to search for the document again, in order to update the URL entry.

4   Conclusion

The AWeb system provides an decentralized and distributed environment for efficiently exchanging information. The system is able to provide the user with new information related to the given topics automatically but allows also the search for available information throughout the AWeb.

Nevertheless, the system lacks security and anonymity related features. The anonymity of the user can not be granted and the transfers are not encrypted. The AWeb is thought in the first place to publish scientific articles. In most cases, the author does not need to remain anonymous and the provided articles are not thought to be kept secret. A problem is, that the AWeb provides no accountability. This allows any user to publish any kind of data inside any community. The AWeb implementation is a first prototype which realizes the described information management in a community environment.

References

1. Kleinberg, J.M., Kumar, R., Raghavan, P., Rajagopalan, S., Tomkins, A.S.: The Web as a graph: Measurements, models, and methods. In Asano, T., Imai, H., Lee, D.T., Nakano, S., Tokuyama, T., eds.; Proc. 5th Annual Int. Conf. Computing and Combinatorics, COCOON, Springer-Verlag (1999)
2. Lawrence, S., Giles, C.L.: Accessibility of information on the web. Nature **400** (1999) 107–109
3. Flake, G., Lawrence, S., Giles, C.L.: Efficient identification of web communities. In: Sixth ACM SIGKDD International Conference on Knowledge Discovery and Data Mining, Boston, MA (2000) 150–160
4. Gibson, D., Kleinberg, J.M., Raghavan, P.: Inferring web communities from link topology. In: UK Conference on Hypertext. (1998) 225–234
5. Kumar, S.R., Raghavan, P., Rajagopalan, S., Tomkins, A.: Trawling the web for emerging cyber-communities. WWW8 / Computer Networks **31** (1999) 1481–1493
6. Gnutella. http://www.gnutellanews.com (2001)

7. Napster. http://www.napster.com (2000)
8. Clarke, I., Sandberg, O., Wiley, B., Hong, T.: Freenet: A Distributed Anonymous Information Storage and Retrieval System. In: ICSI Workshop on Design Issues in Anonymity and Unobservability, Berkeley, CA (2000)
9. Dingledine, R., Freedman, M.J., Molnar, D.: The Free Haven Project: Distributed Anonymous Storage Service. In: Workshop on Design Issues in Anonymity and Unobservability. (2000)
10. Wulff, M., Kropf, P., Unger, H.: Message Chains and Disjunct Paths for Increasing Communication Performance in Large Networks. In et al., K., ed.: Distributed Communities on the Web (DCW), Springer Verlag Berlin, Germany (2000)
11. Unger, H., Böhme, T.: Distribution of information in decentralized computer communitites. In Tentner, A., ed.: ASTC High Performance Computing, Seattle, Washington (2002)
12. Unger, H., Unger, H., Titova, N.: Structuring of decentralized computer communities. In Tentner, A., ed.: ASTC High Performance Computing, San Diego, CA (2002)

Optimisation of Distributed Communities Using Cooperative Strategies

Saiho Yuen[1], Peter Kropf[1], and Gilbert Babin[2]

[1] Informatique et recherche opérationnelle
Université de Montréal, Montréal, Québec, Canada
{yuensaih,kropf}@iro.umontreal.ca
[2] Technologies de l'information
HEC – Montréal, Montréal, Québec, Canada
Gilbert.Babin@hec.ca

Abstract. The complex structure of the Web requires decentralised, adaptive mechanisms efficiently providing access to local and global capacities. To facilitate the development of such mechanisms, it seems reasonable to build clusters of machines with similar structures and interests. In such a manner, communities of machines can be built. In a community, every machine contributes to the overall success through a division of management work and a respective collaboration. This article presents and analyses experimental results for algorithms optimising service response times in a community. It extends previously published results on the *Wanderer* optimisation algorithm; we describe variations of the *Wanderer* and present simulation results of these variations.

1 Introduction

The Internet represents a large pool of resources. However, these resources are difficult to access. Furthermore, the sheer size of the Internet makes it difficult, if not outright impossible to keep track of all these resources. One promising solution approach is to manage the information about resources using self-organising and adaptive information bases [5].

There are currently many projects underway which use this approach [1,2,4,3]. One such project is the Web Operating System (WOS) [3,6] which is built to support communities of client and server machines. These machines do not only share a common communication context, but also sets of similar parameters and interests. The WOS is an open middleware solution allowing for software services to be distributed over the Internet. The WOS infrastructure provides the tools to search for and prepare all the necessary resources that fulfil the desired characteristics for a service request (e.g., performance, storage, etc.).

In the WOS context, a community, or WOSnet, is a set of WOS nodes requesting or providing a specific service. This implies that there exists a dichotomy: within a community, nodes are either servers or clients. By client, we mean nodes requesting the service offered in a community. By server, we mean nodes

H. Unger, T. Böhme, and A. Mikler (Eds.): I²CS 2002, LNCS 2346, pp. 153–168, 2002.

providing the service offered in a community. Needless to say, WOS nodes may participate in many community and may therefore be both server and client.

A WOSnet is dynamically formed; nodes may dynamically join and leave a community. The WOSnet evolves through the location and execution activities performed by the different WOS nodes. The knowledge about the WOSnet, accumulated through these activities, is stored by the nodes in *warehouses*. These warehouses are the node's knowledge center. For example, a service location request will leave its result in the warehouses of the nodes visited. In general, service location requests are processed using message chains, transmitted in parallel [7].

In [8] we presented and analysed experimental results for two algorithms optimising service response times in a community, namely the *Whip* and *Wanderer* algorithms. This paper extend this previous work; it presents and analyses variations of the *Wanderer* algorithm. The simulation environment is briefly described in Section 2. We also define the notion of network community optimisation and we describe the *Wanderer* algorithm, on which the results presented herein are based. We also explain in that section why variations are necessary. In Section 3, we introduce the different variations developed and analyse them, based on simulation results. Finally, Section 4 concludes the paper with a discussion of the approach.

2   Simulating Communities

We developed a tool to simulate the behaviour of a community [8]. The service provided by the community is a simple data transfer service. Basically, client nodes request a data transfer and server nodes provide the requested data. The simulation tool represents a WOSnet as a randomly generated graph of nodes placed in a 2D grid. Each node has a warehouse containing the list of server nodes it knows, along with a measure of the quality of that node. The quality of the service is measured by the response time for a service request of client c to server s, denoted $t(c, s)$. For simplicity, we assume $t(c, s) = 1/b(c, s)$, where $b(c, s)$ is the bandwidth between client c and server s. We estimate $b(c, s)$ by using the euclidian distance between client c and server s in the simulation plane.

A simulation is divided in cycles. Within each cycle, the number of requests made by a client increases linearly. As the number of requests increases, servers have more difficulty in fulfilling all the requests received, and may therefore reject requests.

At any point during the simulation, a client may become unsatisfied with the response time of its current server or may even see his request rejected. When this occurs, the client will seek a better server to fulfil his requests. This is what we call a *community optimisation*. The goal of the optimisation is to minimise the response time for each client. To achieve this goal, the optimisation process reorganises the community by selecting a more suitable server for that client. It does so by recursively searching for server nodes the client does not know yet and by inspecting the warehouse entries at each server visited. During this process the warehouses searched are updated, thus dynamically restructuring the virtual network or community.

Many different parameters can be controlled by the simulation tool:

- the proportion of nodes acting as servers,
- the maximum number of entries in the warehouse (i.e., the length of the list of servers),
- the number of cycles in a simulation,
- the duration of a cycle, calculated in *units of time* (ut).

2.1 Evaluation of Optimisation Algorithms

Different algorithms may be defined to perform the optimisation process. In order to compare these algorithms, we use different measures.

- The effectiveness of the algorithm (E) is the ratio

$$E = r_{\text{avail}}/r_{\text{min}} * 100,$$

where r_{avail} is the average response time of requests, if all the clients of the network launch exactly one request simultaneously and the clients are using the server with the largest bandwidth in the network, and r_{min} is the average response time of requests, if all the clients of the network launch exactly one request simultaneously and the clients are using the server with the largest bandwidth that the algorithm was able to find. The effectiveness measures the distance between the configuration obtained with the algorithm and the optimal attainable configuration.
- The convergence time of the algorithm (t_c) is the time required for reaching r_{min}. It is measured in ut.

2.2 The Wanderer Algorithm

The *Wanderer* algorithm [6] is based on the transmission of a message, named a wanderer, from node to node. A wanderer w is a tuple (c, k, l, h), where c is the list of clients for which the optimisation is performed, k is the list of servers visited (k for knowledge), l is the identifier of the node on which the wanderer currently is located (l for location), and h is the hopcount of that message[3]. Given that S is the set of server node, C is the set of client nodes, and $\perp$ is an undefined identifier, we can formally define the set of all possible wanderers W as

$$W \subseteq \mathcal{P}(C) \times \mathcal{P}(S) \times (S \cup \perp) \times \mathbb{N}.$$

Therefore, $c \in \mathcal{P}(C)$, $k \in \mathcal{P}(S)$, $l \in S \cup \perp$, and $h \in \mathbb{N}$.

The *Wanderer* algorithm is launched by a client every time it wishes to find a better server. It proceeds in three distinct stages: initialisation, search,

---

[3] The hopcount h is defined for completeness but is not used herein.

and update stages. At the *initialisation stage*, the wanderer is initialised by the client: c contains the client launching the wanderer, k contains the list of servers known by the client, l contains the identifier of the first server to visit, and h is set to 0. At the *search stage*, the wanderer is sent to the node identified by l. Once there, k is updated with new information about servers, found on the current node. The value of l is set to the identifier of the next node to visit, if any. The value of h is incremented. It then proceeds with the search stage, until all nodes in k are visited. At the *update stage*, the client selects the node in k with the shortest response time. Formally, we have:

Let c_0: client launching the wanderer.
Let c_w: the client list c of wanderer w.
Let k_w: the knowledge list k of wanderer w.
Let l_w: the location l of wanderer w.
Let h_w: the hopcount h of wanderer w.
Let $k.append(k')$: appends knowledge k' to knowledge k.
Let $n.next(k)$: based on the information available in the warehouse of node $n \in S \cup C$ and on k, returns the next node to visit, if any; returns $\perp$ otherwise.
Let $c.update(k)$: update the warehouse of client c using knowledge k.

A-Initialisation stage

Let $c_w \leftarrow \{c_0\}$
Let $k_w \leftarrow \emptyset$
Let $l_w \leftarrow c_0.next(k_w)$
Let $h_w \leftarrow 0$

B-Search stage

While $l_w \neq \perp$
    "Send" wanderer w to node l_w
    $k_w \leftarrow k_w.append(\text{content of the local warehouse})$
    $l_w \leftarrow l_w.next(k_w)$
    $h_w \leftarrow h_w + 1$
End-While

C-Update stage

For each $c \in c_w$
    $c.update(k_w)$
End-For

A wanderer has been defined as a tuple or data structure upon which the above algorithm is executed. Since the algorithm includes communication, i.e. sending the tuple to another node where the same algorithm is executed, one might also define the tuple together with the algorithm as an entity that migrates from node to node. At each node, the tuple is updated using that nodes local information. Therefore, the wanderer tuple could, together with the code of the algorithm, be implemented as mobile agent. In the following sections, we use sometimes rather the notion of agent for reasons of simplicity of explanation.

3   Variations of the Wanderer Algorithm

From previous simulations [8], we observed that the *Wanderer* algorithm is very effective, even when varying all the simulation parameters. It turns out, however, that its convergence time changes greatly depending on these same parameters. The algorithm is also very demanding in terms of computational resources; since a wanderer is sent from node to node, it requires resources on every node it visits. The quantity of resources required is proportional to the number of wanderers currently in the network. In a larger network, that number can be extremely high. As a consequence, the *Wanderer* algorithm may create network congestion.

The main difference between the *Wanderer* algorithm and its variations is cooperation. The main goal of the cooperation is to eliminate the problems created by the original *Wanderer* algorithm described in the previous section, such as the computational resources required, network congestion, etc. We introduced two main strategies to alleviate these effects: sharing and merging.

Sharing. We define *sharing* as an exchange of knowledge in k. The process of sharing happens during the search stage (at the end of the loop) when there is more than one wanderer on the same node. Whenever two wanderers meet at a node, they will exchange information. Each wanderer will exchange at most once on each node visited. Formally, we can define the process of sharing as follows:

Let $w.sharing$(k,k'): the sharing function of wanderer w.

If $(l_w = l_{w'})$
$\quad k_w \leftarrow w.sharing(k_w, k_{w'})$
$\quad k_{w'} \leftarrow w'.sharing(k_w, k_{w'})$
End-If

As shown in Figure 1, wanderers W1 and W8, coming from different nodes, meet on node S4. Before choosing the next node to visit, they share their information. Before sharing, $k_{W1}=\{S3, S4\}$ and $k_{W8}=\{S2, S4\}$. After sharing, both wanderers have exactly the same contents, that is $k_{W1}=k_{W8}=\{S2, S3, S4\}$, and both wanderers continue their search process with that knowledge.

Merging. We define *merging* as an operation where one wanderer takes all the knowledge of another wanderer before destroying that wanderer. As is the case with sharing, merging also happens at the end of the search stage loop, when there is more than one wanderer on the same node. Furthermore, merging is not automatic. Different criteria may be used to determine whether merging should occur or not. Each wanderer will merge at most once on each visited node. Formally, we can define the process of merging as follows:

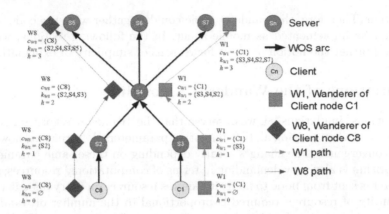

Fig. 1. Wanderers Sharing Information

Let $w.merging()$: the merging function of wanderer w.
Let $n.criterion(w, w')$: a boolean function indicating if wanderers w and w'
can merge on node n.

If $[(l_w = l_{w'}) \wedge l_w.criterion(w, w')]$
$\quad k_w \leftarrow w.merging(k_w, k_{w'})$
$\quad h_w \leftarrow \max(h_w, h_{w'})$
$\quad W \leftarrow W \setminus w'$
End-If

As shown in Figure 2, wanderers W1 and W8, coming from different nodes, meet on node S4. Before choosing the next node to visit, they verify if it is possible to merge. Wanderer W1 initiates the negotiation and both wanderers agree to merge. This corresponds to the evaluation of the merge condition described above. Thus W8 is merged with W1. Before merging, k_{W1}={S3, S4} and c_{W1}={C1}, while k_{W8}={S2, S4} and c_{W8} = {C8}. After merging, wanderer W1 remains, with k_{W1} = {S2, S3, S4} and c_{W1} = {C1, C8}, and wanderer W8 is destroyed.

Based on those two strategies, different variations of the *Wanderer* algorithm are defined. These variations can be broken into three categories:

1. the share category, where wanderers share their knowledge,
2. the merge category, where wanderers merge with the other wanderers,
3. the mixed category, where wanderers either share their knowledge or merge with other wanderers depending on different parameters.

We tested each variation under the same conditions and network configuration as the original *Wanderer* algorithm: the network comprises 2,000 nodes, of which 2% are servers. We ran from 5 to 20 simulations for each experimental parameter. The results from the different variations are compared to the results obtained from the original *Wanderer* algorithm, allowing us to assess the effect of sharing and merging.

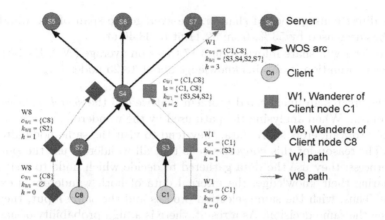

Fig. 2. Wanderers Merging

3.1 Share Category

There is only one variation in this category: the *Wanderer-Share*. In this algorithm, the wanderer uses the sharing strategy, as described in Sect. 3, i.e., at the end of the search stage loop, it tries to share its knowledge with other wanderers present on the current node. The results from the simulation are presented in Table 1 and can be summarised as follows:

Table 1. Comparison of the Wanderer and the Wanderer-Share Algorithms (2000 nodes; 2 % of server nodes)

	E (%)	t_c (ut)	t_l (ut)	K_g (%)	K_e (%)	N_s	K_s
Wanderer	99.81	440	82.11	100	0	–	–
W-share	99.61	380	38.46	27.67	72.33	3.17	18.25

- The efficiency (E) of the *Wanderer-Share* is almost identical to that of the *Wanderer* algorithm. This may be explained by the fact that both algorithms do a complete search through the network. Furthermore, the *Wanderer-Share* does not try to reduce the number of wanderers in the network.
- The convergence time (t_c) of the *Wanderer-Share* algorithm (380 ut) is 14 % lower than that of the *Wanderer* algorithm (440 ut). Recall that the client node performs its warehouse update only once the wanderer has finished its network walk-through. By sharing information, the search takes less time since the wanderers do not need to visit the whole network.
- Most of the information about the servers is exchanged, rather than being gathered. An average of 72 % of the wanderer's knowledge is exchanged (K_e), while only 28 % is gathered (K_g).

- As a direct consequence of sharing, the average life span of the wanderers (t_l) has decreased by 53 %, from 82.11 ut to 38.46 ut.
- A wanderer will share information 3.17 times on average (N_s). Each time it shares information it obtains knowledge about 18.25 nodes (K_s).

Sharing creates an unexpected problem that we call the *search path convergence* problem. When analysing the path used by the wanderers, we realize that each time two wanderers share data, they tend to visit the same node after the sharing. The reason for this convergence is that all wanderers use the same selection process: they use the data gathered to decide which node to visit next. After sharing their knowledge, the internal data of both wanderers is exactly the same. Thus, with the same selection process and the same input, they end up making the same decision. As a result, there is a high probability of network congestion. Network congestion occurs earlier with a large network, because the number of wanderers increases proportionally with the number of client nodes, which in turn increases the number of shares.

3.2   Merge Category

We have developed three variations in the Merge category, the *Wanderer-Merge-Random*, *Wanderer-Merge- Select*, and *Wanderer-Merge-Node* algorithms. In these algorithms, the wanderer uses the merging strategy, as described in Sect. 3, These variations differ in the way wanderers decide to merge with other wanderers, i.e., the $n.criterion(w, w')$ function. In the *Wanderer-Merge-Random* algorithm, the wanderer agent decides to merge randomly, using a binomial probability. In the *Wanderer-Merge-Select* algorithm, the wanderer's decision to merge is made according to the similarity with other wanderers. The similarity refers to number of nodes that two wanderers have in common; if two wanderers have visited the same nodes, their similarity would be 100 %. In the *Wanderer-Merge-Node* algorithm, the wanderer agent decides to merge based on the number of wanderer agents on the current node. In this case, merging occurs only if there is more than a certain number of wanderer agents on a node.

Wanderer-Merge-Random Algorithm. For this variation, we looked at how the algorithm's behaviour changes when changing the probability to merge. We tested with probabilities varying from 25 % to 100 %. Table 2 presents the results, which can be summarised as follows:

- The efficiency (E) of the *Wanderer-Merge-Random* algorithm does not differ from *Wanderer* algorithm. This result follows from the complete search of the network.
- The convergence time (t_c) of the *Wanderer-Merge-Random* algorithm is about 20 to 40 ut faster than the *Wanderer*. The increase seems to depend on the probability to merge.

Table 2. Comparison of the Wanderer and the Wanderer-Merge-Random Algorithms (2000 nodes; 2 % of server nodes)

	E (%)	t_c (ut)	t_l (ut)	N_w	K_g (%)	K_e (%)	N_m	K_m
Wanderer	99.81	440	82.11	27.90	100	0	–	–
W-Merge-R (25 %)	99.84	440	57.86	17.62	74.88	25.12	4.80	20.09
W-Merge-R (50 %)	99.92	420	54.67	10.97	75.22	24.78	17.91	19.82
W-Merge-R (75 %)	99.96	400	56.27	5.81	73.07	26.93	29.05	21.54
W-Merge-R (100 %)	99.91	400	59.03	5.44	70.78	29.22	36.99	23.38

- The number of wanderers in the network (N_w) for the *Wanderer-Merge-Random* is much smaller than for the *Wanderer*. Furthermore, it decreases significantly as the probability to merge increases. This is a logical outcome of merging.
- When varying the probability to merge, we observe that the average life of wanderers (t_l) decreases until the probability reaches 50 % and then increases again.

This last observation may be explained by the fact that when the probability is less than 50 %, there is a higher probability that the knowledge obtained through merging is not yet known, while that probability decreases when the probability to merge increases. This is confirmed by the knowledge exchanged when merging (K_e). Furthermore, as more merges occur, more time is spent updating client nodes in c_w.

Finally, if two wanderers have already visited the same nodes, merging does not accelerate the search process. This effect is shown in Table 2 where we can see that the number of merges (N_m) increases significantly with the probability to merge, but the information exchanged at each merge (K_m) remains relatively stable.

Wanderer-Merge-Select Algorithm. For this variation, we looked at how the algorithm's behaviour changes when changing the degree of similarity required to merge. We tested with similarity degrees varying from 25 % to 100 %. We obtained the following results (Table 3):

Table 3. Comparison of the Wanderer and the Wanderer-Merge-Select Algorithms (2000 nodes; 2 % of server nodes)

	E (%)	t_c (ut)	t_l (ut)	N_w	K_g (%)	K_e (%)	N_m	K_m
Wanderer	99.81	440	82.11	27.90	100	0	–	–
W-Merge-S (25 %)	99.01	440	60.81	4.95	78.05	21.95	41.14	17.56
W-Merge-S (50 %)	98.80	420	57.75	6.87	84.44	15.56	23.50	12.45
W-Merge-S (75 %)	99.65	420	57.85	16.67	84.26	15.74	7.41	12.59
W-Merge-S (100 %)	99.66	420	80.28	27.03	91.66	8.34	0.57	3.80

- The efficiency (E) of the *Wanderer-Merge-Select* algorithm is similar to the *Wanderer* algorithm.
- The convergence time (t_c) is constant but slightly faster (20 ut) than the *Wanderer*.
- As we increase the degree of similarity required to merge, the number of wanderers in the network (N_w) increases significantly, while the number of merges (N_m) decreases.
- We also observe that the amount of data exchanged (K_e) decreases as the degree of similarity increases. Indeed, when two wanderers merge and the degree of similarity required is 50 % or more, the knowledge gained by merging is necessarily lower than 50 %.
- The higher the required degree of similarity, the more difficult it is to merge.
- The life span of the wanderers (t_l) in this algorithm follows a pattern similar to that of the *Wanderer-Merge-Random* algorithm.

When the required degree of similarity is high, merging occurs in two situations:

1. Merging occurs at a very early stage of the search, when wanderers still have very little data. It is then easier to find other wanderers with similar content.
2. Merging occurs much later during the search stage. Wanderers need to visit more nodes before merging, otherwise they do not reach the required similarity degree.

However, neither situation helps in accelerating the search, because the knowledge exchanged by merging is not significant enough to have an impact on the convergence time. In the extreme case where the similarity is very high (around 100 %), the wanderers cannot even cooperate. Therefore, in order to have reasonable results with the algorithm, we need for the required similarity degree to be low. In addition, the time to evaluate similarity increases when the required similarity increases.

Wanderer-Merge-Node Algorithm. For this variation, we looked at how the algorithm's behaviour changes when changing the number of wanderers required before merging can occur. We tested with the number of wanderers needed varying from 5 to 80, which is from 10 % to 160 % of the "maximum" number of wanderers in the network. Since the distribution of wanderers follows a normal distribution, there is no maximum value. In most cases however (99 % of the time; see Fig. 3), this number is less than 50. For simplicity, we fix that maximum to 50 wanderers.

Results are illustrated in Table 4 and can be summarised as follows:

- The efficiency (E) of the algorithm is again very high.
- As the two other variations of this category, this algorithm has a significant effect on the population of wanderers in the network (N_w).

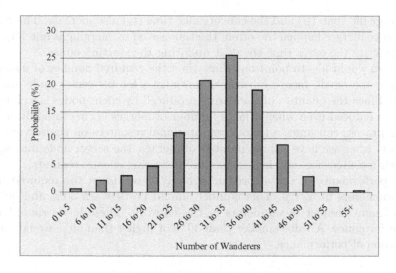

Fig. 3. Probability Distribution of the Number of Wanderers in the Network (2000 nodes)

When the number of wanderers required to merge reaches 100 %, there is almost no chance that merging will occur. Thus, without merging, the algorithm behaves exactly like the original *Wanderer* algorithm. Therefore, the required number of wanderers to merge should always be less than 100 % of the maximum number of wanderers in the network.

The most significant effect of using the number of wanderers on the node as a parameter of merging is that the number of wanderers (N_w) is efficiently controlled when the required number of nodes for merging is small. However, the reduction is not efficient when that number is too small. For instance, when the required number of wanderers is 5, the reduction is about the same as when that required number is 10. Furthermore, when that required number is too small,

Table 4. Comparison of the Wanderer and the Wanderer-Merge-Node Algorithms (2000 nodes; 2 % of server nodes)

	E (%)	t_c (ut)	t_l (ut)	N_w	K_g (%)	K_e (%)	N_m	K_m
Wanderer	99.81	440	82.11	27.90	100	0	–	–
W-Merge-N (5)	99.67	460	53.63	5.65	68.73	31.27	25.42	25.02
W-Merge-N (10)	99.23	400	49.58	7.06	67.94	32.06	12.88	25.65
W-Merge-N (20)	97.34	380	52.59	11.99	65.52	34.48	4.32	27.59
W-Merge-N (30)	99.60	440	59.39	17.39	62.99	37.01	1.97	29.61
W-Merge-N (40)	99.76	420	70.24	23.02	70.37	29.63	0.75	23.70
W-Merge-N (50)	99.87	400	79.50	26.71	91.66	8.34	0.19	6.67
W-Merge-N (60)	99.89	420	80.54	27.34	99.25	0.75	0.02	0.60
W-Merge-N (80)	99.87	400	81.43	27.62	100	0	0	0

the average life span (t_l) and the convergence time (t_c) also increase. The reason is that since merges happen too often, the time saved by merging is not sufficient to compensate the extra time spent at updating the starting nodes.

We also would like to point out that when the required number of nodes for merging is too small, merging becomes unrealistic for the server node and the network. Since the quantity of wanderers produced by client nodes is so large, it cannot be reduced even when a large number of merges occur. In addition, the merging process consumes a lot of computational resources on the server node. Therefore, when we have a large number of merges, the server node may spend too much resources for merging, instead of answering clients' requests.

The performance of the algorithm strongly depends on the required number of wanderers to merge. This number should be between 30 % and 50 % of the maximum number of wanderers in the network. These levels should yield good performance. A value smaller than 30 % or higher than 50 % would yield a degradation of performance.

3.3   Mixed Category

The goal of the mixed algorithms is to combine the advantages of sharing and merging. Whenever there is more than one wanderer on a node, either merging or sharing will occur, based on a selection criterion. Formally, algorithms of the mixed category work as follows:

> **If** $[(l_w = l_{w'}) \wedge l_w.criterion(w, w')]$
> $\quad k_w \leftarrow w.merging(k_w, k_{w'})$
> $\quad h_w \leftarrow \max(h_w, h_{w'})$
> $\quad W \leftarrow W \setminus w'$
> **Else-If** $(l_w = l_{w'})$
> $\quad k_w \leftarrow w.sharing(k_w, k_{w'})$
> $\quad k_{w'} \leftarrow w'.sharing(k_w, k_{w'})$
> **End-If**

We have developed three different algorithms in this category, which are the cross-product of the sharing and merging variations: the *Wanderer-Mixed-Random* algorithm, the *Wanderer-Mixed-Select* algorithm, and the *Wanderer-Mixed-Node* algorithm. As is the case with algorithms of the merge category, these algorithms are differentiated by the way they decide which strategy (sharing or merging) to apply (i.e., evaluating function $n.criterion(w, w')$).

The *Wanderer-Mixed-Random* algorithm selects sharing or merging using a binomial random variable. The *Wanderer-Mixed-Select* algorithm will choose to share or merge based on the similarity of wanderers. Finally, The *Wanderer-Merge-Node* algorithm makes that decision based on the number of wanderers currently on the node.

Wanderer-Mixed-Random Algorithm. For this combination, we looked how the algorithm's behaviour changes when changing the ratio of the strategy chosen. The algorithm applies merging with probability p and sharing with probability $1 - p$. The tests used probabilities p ranging from 20 % to 80 %. The results obtained are presented in Table 5 and can be summarised as follows:

- The efficiency (E) of the *Wanderer-Mixed-Random Algorithm* is similar to the previous variations of the *Wanderer* algorithm.
- The convergence time (t_c) is comparable to the one obtained by the *Wanderer-Share* algorithm. It thus appears that the sharing effect, where wanderers do not need to visit all the nodes, dominates with regard to the convergence time.
- Increasing the merge probability leaves the amount of data obtained through merging (K_m) fairly constant. On the other hand, the information gained by sharing (K_s) increases with increasing merge probability p. This is due to the increased elimination of redundant information by merging.
- The number of wanderers in the network (N_w) is governed by the merging component of the strategy and therefore than for the *Wanderer* and *Wanderer-share* algorithms.

Table 5. Comparison of the Wanderer and the Wanderer-Mixed-Random Algorithms (2000 nodes; 2 % of server nodes)

	E (%)	t_c (ut)	t_l (ut)	N_w	K_g (%)	K_e (%)	N_m	K_m	N_s	K_s
Wanderer	99.81	440	82.11	27.90	100	0	–	–	–	–
W-Share	99.61	380	38.46	22.67	27.68	72.31		–	3.17	18.25
W-Merge-R (50 %)	99.92	420	54.67	10.97	75.22	24.78	17.91	19.82	–	–
W-Mixed-R (20 %)	99.78	400	49.56	7.76	85.60	14.40	7.41	12.50	0.43	3.55
W-Mixed-R (40 %)	99.25	400	45.38	10.70	79.13	20.87	3.81	13.32	0.89	6.79
W-Mixed-R (50 %)	99.10	380	44.56	12.52	73.93	26.07	2.82	13.96	1.15	8.43
W-Mixed-R (60 %)	99.21	400	42.56	14.70	66.91	33.09	1.89	14.68	1.47	10.02
W-Mixed-R (80 %)	99.38	400	40.14	18.95	46.19	53.81	0.67	11.08	2.17	13.74

With this algorithm, we observe that the combination of the two strategies yields good results since both strategies are focused on distinct area. Sharing focuses on the exchange of knowledge and will maximise knowledge exchanged (K_e). Merging focuses on the control of the population (N_w); it will minimise the risk of network congestion and reduce computation resources needed by the algorithm.

The Wanderer-Mixed-Select Algorithm. For this combination, we looked at how the algorithm's behaviour changes when changing the ratio of merging and sharing. The degree of similarity to decide upon merging varies from 25 % to 100 %. If there is no merging, the sharing strategy applies. The results presented in Table 6 are summarised as follows:

- The efficiency (E) is of the same order as for the other strategies.
- The time to live of wanderers (t_l) is closer to the results obtained with the *Wanderer-Share* algorithm and thus better than in the case of the *Wanderer-Merge-Select* algorithm.
- Sharing increases the knowledge exchanged (K_e) and the life time of the wanderers (t_l) decreases accordingly.

Table 6. Comparison of the Wanderer and the Wanderer-Mixed-Select Algorithms (2000 nodes; 2 % of server nodes)

	E (%)	t_c (ut)	t_l (ut)	N_w	K_g (%)	K_e (%)	N_m	K_m	N_s	K_s
Wanderer	99.81	440	82.11	27.90	100	0	–	–	–	–
W-Share	99.61	380	38.46	22.67	27.68	72.31	–	–	3.17	18.25
W-Mixed-S (25 %)	99.60	400	46.37	9.21	77.05	22.95	4.90	11.29	0.84	8.41
W-Mixed-S (50 %)	98.03	420	42.66	15.35	50.32	49.68	1.89	9.93	1.82	16.38
W-Mixed-S (75 %)	99.66	400	40.83	19.58	42.05	57.95	0.94	7.90	2.24	17.18
W-Mixed-S (100 %)	99.84	380	39.13	22.88	38.33	61.67	0.17	0.77	2.80	17.35

This algorithm deals with the "late merge problem" of the *Wanderer-Merge-Select* algorithm, where it becomes more difficult to merge as the similarity degree increases. When two wanderers meet on the same node and do not have sufficient similarity, they share their data in the case of the mixed strategy. After exchanging information, they have the same knowledge and will thus tend to choose the same next node. In such a case, however, these two wanderers meet again on the next node, but this time their knowledge is identical. Therefore a merge occurs. This means that wanderers always end up merging. After the first sharing, the wanderer's knowledge is nearly the same, so a merge occurs sooner or later. Therefore, the threshold must be high in order to achieve good results. However, it should not be too high, otherwise the algorithm will be reduced to the *Wanderer-Share* algorithm. In some way, this algorithm also corrects the search path convergence problem: since only the wanderers who have a high degree of similarity will merge, the algorithm controls the wanderer population (N_w) by eliminating the "useless doubles."

The Wanderer-Mixed-Node Algorithm. For this case of combining merging and sharing, we varied the number of wanderers required for merging. Again, this number was varied from 5 to 80 wanderers, or from 10 % to 160 % of the "maximum" number of wanderers on the network. If the number of the wanderers on a node is higher than the number required, then wanderers will merge, otherwise they will share knowledge. Table 7 summaries the results obtained in this simulation.

- The efficiency (E) is similar to all the other algorithm variations.

Table 7. Comparison of the Wanderer and the Wanderer-Mixed-Node Algorithms (2000 nodes; 2 % of server nodes)

	E (%)	t_c (ut)	t_l (ut)	N_w	K_g (%)	K_e (%)	N_m	K_m	N_s	K_s
Wanderer	99.81	440	82.11	27.90	100	0	–	–	–	–
W-Share	99.61	380	38.46	22.67	27.68	72.31	–	–	3.17	18.25
W-Mixed-N (10)	99.21	380	44.70	9.38	72.43	27.57	3.52	14.98	1.03	6.87
W-Mixed-N (20)	99.57	360	39.48	15.27	46.00	54.00	1.04	17.86	2.00	12.67
W-Mixed-N (30)	99.49	400	37.70	19.43	38.70	61.30	0.32	6.31	2.70	15.28
W-Mixed-N (40)	99.73	400	38.41	22.02	29.53	70.47	0.06	1.20	3.05	18.09
W-Mixed-N (50)	99.77	400	38.30	22.91	27.48	72.52	0.01	0.12	3.16	18.32
W-Mixed-N (60)	99.69	400	38.30	22.91	27.45	72.55	<0.01	<0.01	3.18	18.25
W-Mixed-N (70)	99.83	400	38.29	23.20	26.80	73.20	0	0	3.15	18.59

- The number of wanderers (N_w) is slightly lower than for the *Wanderer-Share* algorithm.
- The same observations with regard to the choice of the number of wanderers required for merging (compared to the "maximum number" of nodes) yield as for the *Wanderer-Merge-Node* algorithm. If that number is too high, no merge occurs and the algorithm behaves like the *Wanderer-Share*.

The application of the *Wanderer-Merge-Node* and *Wanderer-Mixed-Node* algorithm requires the "maximum number" of nodes in the network to be known in order to determine the correct number of nodes for taking the merging decision. However, in a completely decentralised system as the WOS, this information, the "maximum number" of nodes, is not available. This suggests to introduce a mechanism for guessing or approximating that number locally at each node, based on the local information gathered over time.

4   Discussion

This work is related to the optimisation of communities. In previous experiments on the *Wanderer* algorithm [8], we showed that although this algorithm could easily adapt to changes in the network and showed high and constant efficiency, it required large amounts of computational and communication resources. Furthermore, the life span of wanderer agents is very large. In this paper, we presented variations of the *Wanderer* algorithm and analysed whether these variations resolved the problems observed with the original *Wanderer*. In order to address these limitations, we opted for cooperation among wanderer agents. We have focused on two strategies of cooperation: sharing and merging. Both strategies have their advantages and disadvantages. Sharing increases the gain of knowledge, but may create network congestion because of the path convergence problem. Merging decreases the population of wanderers of the network, but only shows small increases of performances; in some cases, performances may even decrease. From our observations, we conclude that the most appropriate solution is a combination of both strategies with a careful selection of thresholds between sharing and merging. The results obtained with the mixed *Wanderer* algorithms indicate that the resource, the performance and congestion problems can be satisfactorily resolved.

Acknowledgements

We are grateful to Dr. Habil. Herwig Unger, from University of Rostock (Germany), for is involvement in this project.

References

1. L.N. Foner. YENTA - A Multi-Agent Referral System for Matchmaking. In *First International Conference on Autonomous Agents (Agents'97)*, Marina del Rey, CA, 1997.
2. K. Kramer, N. Minar, and P. Maes. Mobile software agents for dynamic routing. *Mobile Computing and Communications Review*, 3(2), 1999.
3. P. Kropf, H. Unger, and G. Babin. WOS: An Internet Computing Environment. In *Workshop on Ubiquitous Computing*, PACT 2000 (IEEE International Conference on Parallel Architectures and Compilation Techniques), pages 14–22, Philadelphia, PA, 2000.
4. V. Menkov, D.J. Neu, and Q. Shi. Ant world: A collaborative web search tool. In P. Kropf et al., editor, *Distributed Communities on the Web (DCW 2000)*, LNCS 1830, pages 13–22, Quebec, Canada, 2000. Springer.
5. D. Milojicic. Operating systems - now and in the future. *IEEE Concurrency*, 7(1):12–21, 1999.
6. H. Unger. Distributed Resource Location Management in the Web Operating System. In SCS A. Tentner, editor, *High Performance Computing 2000 (ASTC)*, pages 213–218, Washington, DC, 2000.
7. Herwig Unger, Peter Kropf, Gilbert Babin, and Thomas Böhme. Simulation of search and distribution methods for jobs in a Web operating system (WOS^{TM}). In A. Tentner, editor, *High Performance Computing Symposium '98*, Boston, MA, USA, April 1998. SCS International.
8. Herwig Unger, Saiho Yuen, Peter Kropf, and Gilbert Babin. Simulation of communication of nodes in a wide area distributed system. In *Eurosim 2001 Congress*, Delft, The Netherlands, June 2001. Published on CD-ROM.

Proven IP Network Services:
From End-User to Router and vice versa[*]

Gerald Eichler[1], Anne Thomas[2], and Ralf Widera[1]

[1] T-Systems Nova, Technologiezentrum, D-64307 Darmstadt
{Gerald.Eichler,Ralf.Widera}@t-systems.com
[2] Technische Universität Dresden, Fakultät Informatik, Institut SMT, D-01062 Dresden
Anne.Thomas@inf.tu-dresden.de

Abstract. This paper analyses, using Unified Modelling Language, end-users'
and applications' common basic requirements towards a QoS enabled network.
It provides the basis for a QoS description language, the so called Application
Profile (AP) supporting mapping mechanisms between application, end-user
and network. Based on this analysis the paper introduces five practically
implemented Network Services (NS), designed for large networks with the aim
to manage the resources. The underlying mechanisms at network level and QoS
capabilities of routers, allowing appropriate handling of underlying Traffic
Classes (TC) by adaptation of scheduling and queuing parameters, are
presented. Considering the proof of the requirements active and passive
measurements with high precision are introduced. Data is collected in a central
database, verifying the specifications and allowing adjustments for admission
control as well as technical parameters at network level.

1 Introduction – The Expectations of End-Users

Business end-users are looking for reliable and provable network applications, while
private end-users focus on cheap and easy accessible infotainment offers. From the
network operators or Internet Service Providers (ISP) point of view, Quality of
Service (QoS) is definitely a business opportunity. An important prerequisite for QoS
offers towards the customer is a technique for precise specification of *Network
Services (NS)* and their support at network level. Using a generic template for Service
Level Specifications (SLS), the proposed specification and measurement methods can
in principle be transferred also to other service classifications than the one suggested
within this paper. An example are the Globally Well Known Services, which will be
defined in an upcoming IETF draft of the NSIS working group by the AQUILA [1]
consortium.

Chapter 2 compares end-user expectations with application requirements, which
lead to a grouping of applications. Chapter 3 introduces a proposed set of NSs, while
chapter 4 points out the network level support within routing entities supporting
Traffic Class (TC) handling. Sophisticated measurements to prove network QoS are
described in chapter 5. A summary and outlook with the next steps within the
AQUILA project concludes this paper.

---

[*] This work is partially funded by the European Union under contract number IST-1999-10077
'AQUILA'.

H.Unger, T.Böhme, and A.Mikler (Eds.): I²CS 2002, LNCS 2346, pp. 169-180, 2002.
© Springer-Verlag Berlin Heidelberg 2002

2   Applications – The Centre of the QoS Offer

2.1   Application Requirements

Although the default best-effort service, the standard offer in the Internet, is adequate for many accepted applications [10], it is inadequate to support real-time applications [6]. In the case of a congested network the end-user may not be able to use an application at all. For example, if packet delay and jitter increase too much, a phone call can degrade till the delivered message is incomprehensible. In the case of an online "real-time" action game playing can become impossible, when the players do not get the information in "real-time" and synchronised. This leads to a relatively low acceptance and usage [7] of such a priori economically interesting applications by end-users. To overcome this loss of profit possible solutions are the offer of access to over-provisioned networks or to QoS enabled networks, which this paper focuses on. One of the main challenges is to design a network in such a way that finally the applications work as expected and that the consumer is hopefully satisfied. The description of applications and their requirements at application level is the purpose of this section.

Applications are entities at the edge between the network and the end-user. The availability of network resources (bandwidth, buffers, etc.) at network level can affect and influence their behaviour. At application level these network resources correspond to the QoS parameters throughput, delay, jitter, error and loss, defined in Table 1. To work properly the different *service components* of an *application type* (Fig. 1) have various *QoS requirements* (Fig.1) in value (e.g. voice telephone call: delay <50 ms, jitter <20 ms) as well as in dependency. Some *application types* with their requirements are depicted in a non exhaustive application list in Table 2. These parameters build one part of a network independent QoS request/offer, ruled by a QoS description language at application and end-user level the so called *Application Profile (AP)*.

Table 1. Definition of QoS parameters that are affecting application appearance

Parameter	Definition
Throughput	amount of user information performed and transmitted in a certain period of time
Delay	overall time between a query and its response
Jitter	unwanted variations of the speed of an information flow
Error	unwanted modification of information
Loss	unwanted loss of information

Beside these general *QoS requirements* independent from a network implementation each concrete *application* produces *traffic* (Fig. 1). As will be later shown in chapter 4 the network QoS implementation mainly relies on traffic handling: the handling is determined by the incoming traffic. Therefore, in a request scenario, for mapping activities at network level explained in chapter 3, traffic information is required for each concrete application. This traffic prediction is mainly possible for non adaptive applications. Table 3 depicts network independent traffic parameters, the so called *traffic specification* from Figure 1, with opposite alternatives as example values.

Table 2. QoS parameter requirements of some popular, commonly used applications. Strong dependencies (*and weaker dependencies (*are indicated

Application Type - Concrete Application	Throughput	Delay	Jitter	Error	Loss
Real-time audio – VoIP		*	*	*	
Real-time video - Video conference	*	*	*	*	*
Audio on demand - MP3	*		*		*
Video on demand - Internet TV	*		*		*
Online banking		*		*	*
Online games		*	*		*
Online trading		*	*		*
Chat and TELET		*			*
Web browsing		*			
E-mail					

Table 3. Parameters characterising the applications traffic and possible alternatives

Parameter	Alternative 1	Alternative 2
Traffic type	Stream: time integrity preservation	Elastic: loose time requirements
Burstiness	Bursty	Constant
Connection rate	High rate	Low rate
Life time	Long	Short
Bit rate	Constant bit rate	Variable bit rate
Packet size	Large	small

This section emphasises that applications have strong requirements towards the network that can be expressed in a network independent manner.

2.2   End-Users Expectations

Within the scope of a Service Level Agreement (SLA) negotiation with the customer, which is a prerequisite for QoS selling, it is important for a network operator or ISP to argument using adequate terms. As example a private customer using multimedia applications is taken. This basic scenario can be extrapolated to more professional environments. The end-user, who is likely not a network specialist, can only express verbally the QoS he perceives at application level. As depicted in Fig. 1, an end-user talking about concrete *applications* (like Microsofts NetMeeting) probably refers to general *application types* like "video conferencing", "MP3", etc. A video conferencing *application type*, for example, again is described by the *service component types*: "video", "voice"and "data." As the perception of QoS is highly subjective [2] and relies on the human senses (mostly sight and hearing) and on the perception of time-related behaviour (e.g. lip-sound synchronisation, or long waiting time) the quality levels of an application are expressed again in non technical terms with metaphors (e.g. "picture size", "standard TV quality", etc.), which is depicted in Fig. 1 with *session characteristic (type)*. A user-friendly QoS description is related to its universal apprehension and in a residential context ideally refers to well-known similar services from everyday life like: tv, vcr, hi-fi, phone, etc. At end-user level an ISP needs a description language for presenting applications and their different quality levels.

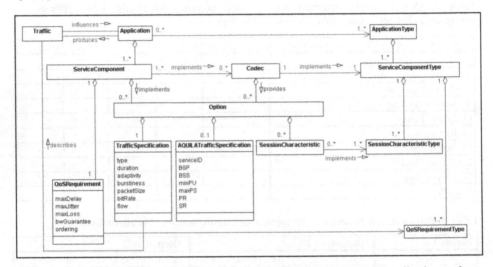

Fig. 1. UML class diagram depicting the relations between a concrete application and an application type. Generic, predictable, and unpredictable factors are part of the description

An AP is a network independent QoS specification. It can be interpreted as a QoS description language that enables the characterization via metaphors of applications and QoS at end-user level in the scope of a QoS offer/request and their *QoS requirements* as well as their *traffic specification*. The description of concrete applications using the AP takes the form of files listing the possible quality options (incl. *traffic specification* and *QoS requirements*) supported by an application and the corresponding end-user metaphors (*session characteristic*).

Firstly, the QoS offer/request is related to the quality perceived by the end-user, secondly determined by the application QoS requirements and thirdly described by its traffic. At network level the offer/request solution takes the network implementation into account, and the request coming from the end-user/application, specified with the AP has to be mapped by a converter into parameters corresponding to the engineering of the network via so called *Network Services* and *Traffic Classes* explained in the following chapter.

3   Network Services – The Network Operator's Offer

This chapter introduces proposed parameter sets and service specific settings to verify service qualities at the edge between application and network level.

3.1   Network Services

The AQUILA consortium [1], that operates a Differentiated Services (DiffServ) aware testbed, defined four manageable premium transport options beside best effort for IP user traffic, as listed in Table 4, the so called *Network Services (NS)*.

Table 4. Premium Network Services as defined within the AQUILA project

Services	Goals
PCBR Premium Constant Bit Rate	designed to serve a constant bit rate traffic. Examples of applications: voice trunking and Virtual Leased Lines. This service should support circuit emulation and meets hard QoS requirements with respect to packet loss ratio (not greater than 10^{-8}) and packet delay (not greater than 150 ms, low jitter).
PVBR Premium Variable Bit Rate	designed to provide effective transfer of streaming flows of variable bit rate type. The traffic description of a flow has two parameters to declare, the Sustainable Rate (SR) and Peak Rate (PR). Policing assumes double token bucket. For the purpose of admission control algorithm, the notion of effective bandwidth (evaluated on the basis of SR, PR and dedicated for this service link capacity) is used.
PMM Premium Multi-Media	designed to support greedy and adaptive applications that require some minimum bandwidth to be delivered with a high probability. Although the PMM service is not primarily targeted for applications using TCP, but there is optimisation regarding the TCP transport protocol.
PMC Premium Mission Critical	designed to support non-greedy applications. The sending behaviour may be very bursty. This requires a very low loss and low delay service to be delivered with a high probability. Throughput is of no primary concern for PMC applications. There is an optimisation regarding the TCP transport protocol.

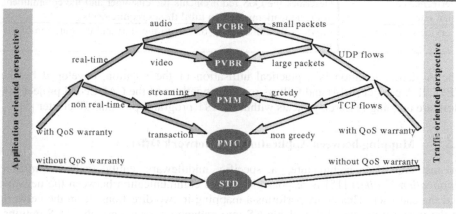

Fig. 2. Correspondence between the application point of view of the NSs and the traffic oriented one

Figure 2 describes the choice of NSs following decisions about typical alternatives from application and traffic oriented perspectives. If there is no QoS requirement best effort, the standard NS (STD) is applied.

The NS and their detailed characteristics are defined by the network operator. The idea of these NS is to provide a few specific offerings from the network operator to the customer, which are relatively easy to understand, suitable for a specific group of applications, and maintainable in large scale networks.

3.2   The Service Level Specification (SLS)

At network level an operator needs a formalism in order to express technically what can be offered to its customers. The AQUILA project has submitted an Internet Draft, which proposes to use a generic *Service Level Specification (SLS)* [11], capturing all possible service offerings that can be provided by the DiffServ network. Such a powerful generic description template helps to simplify the mapping process inside the network and the negotiation between the customer and the network.

An instance of the generic SLS, e.g. each AQUILA NSs, contains concrete values for the parameters, represents a selected service offer by the network operator and can be defined as predefined SLS types." The semantic content of the generic SLS template is composed of attributes at the top level, listed in Table 5. For details refer to [12].

Table 5. Attributes of the AQUILA SLS content

Attribute	Description
Scope	Indicates the typology of the ongoing reservation with reference to the end-points of the traffic flows
Flow identification	Focuses on the association between packets and SLSs
Traffic description, conformance testing	Describes the traffic relevant to the reservation
Performance guarantees	Describes the QoS requirements the customer and the commitment of the network operator to fulfil theses requirements
Service schedule	Provides the information related to the start and the duration of the service

The AQUILA notation is a practical utilisation of the notation, developed by the TEQUILA project [8,14] and follows recommendations of the CADENUS project [3]. Both are ongoing research projects within the IST programs premium IP cluster [5].

3.3   Mapping between Application and Network Offer

In the AQUILA architecture, a specific middleware entity (called *End-user Application Toolkit*) [15] is responsible for the communication between the network and the end-user. This entity performs a mapping in two directions: from the network to the user it translates the available NS into metaphors for the possible QoS options, and from the user to the network it translates the end-user option choice into a QoS request (QoS requirements and traffic specification) towards the network.

4   Traffic Classes – Engineering the IP Quality of Service

This chapter focuses on selected technical QoS prerequisites at network level. To achieve this goal, the key issues are appropriate router configurations beside traffic engineering tasks, e.g. network topology or link dimensioning. The proposed solution aims to produce reliable differentiated network QoS, known as *Traffic Classes (TC)*.

4.1   Router Capabilities

QoS sensitive routing entities have a wide range of settings and configuration capabilities to optimise the store-and-forward processes, which form the basis for advanced network design [4]. Even some vendors prefer fixed settings for key features, like queue configuration. IP packets are stored in large memory arrays with multiple access. Traditional FIFO-queuing is replaced by a flexible pointer-handling scheme.

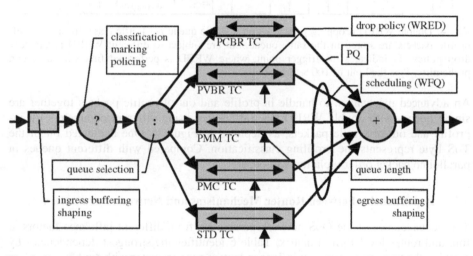

Fig. 3. Parameter setting locations within a QoS sensitive router entity: After checking various selectors (ʔ the queue selection decision (:) is made. Packets of parallel queues have to be merged (+) before sending them onto the outgoing link

At the router ingress *classification*, *marking/colouring* and *policing/profiling* are performed. *Interface selection* and *queue selection* lead to a realisation of the handling defined by the TC, where *queue dimensioning* and *drop policies* influence the packet handling. AQUILA uses five TCs, mirroring a face to face mapping of the five NSs. While the PCBR TC is tail dropped, PVBR, PMM, PMC and STD make use of Weighted Random Early Detection (WRED). *Scheduling* among multiple queues influences the traffic merging. The TC for PCBR is prioritised, Priority Queuing (PQ) against the other four, which are handled with Weighted Fair Queuing (WFQ) with adjustable weights. *Buffers* are located at several places and support *shaping,* but are kept at the minimum level to avoid additional delays. Figure 3 illustrates the packet flow through a routing entity. The decision made for the handling of selected packets is indicated by a field of the packet header. For AQUILA it is stored in the precedence bits of the Type of Sevice (ToS) byte.

4.2   Traffic Classes and Profiling

Packets, that exceed the SLS limit are the first to be marked as *out-of-profile* already at the access router ingress. If traffic jams occur at any routing entity of the network, they are the first to be dropped.

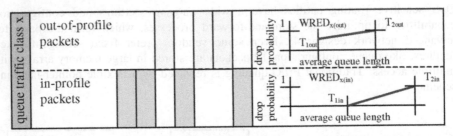

Fig. 4. Double WRED dropping policy within a single queue per traffic class. In- and out-of-profile packets are stored in the same queue, but are subject to different WRED parameters' drop policy. T_1 indicates the trigger point, where WRED is performed first with a certain probability. T_2 is the limit of 100 % dropping

An advanced mechanism to handle in-profile and out-of-profile packets together are single queues with double WRED per traffic class using different parameters for in-profile and out-of-profile packets, as depicted in Figure 4. One dedicated bit of the ToS byte represents the profiling classification. Compared with different queues in parallel no packet order violation will occur.

4.3   Dependencies between Router Mechanisms and Network Parameters

The dependencies of the QoS network parameters from different influence factors at link and router level form a matrix. Table 6 identifies the strongest dependencies by marking the two most important influence factors per parameter with *and .*

Table 6. Abstraction of QoS parameters and their main (*) and additional (*) influence factors. Real relations are much more complex

Influence factor	Bandwidth	Packet loss	Packet delay	Packet delay variation	Packet order violation
Link/path capacity	*				
Link utilisation	*	*			
Buffer/queue length		*	*		
Scheduling			*	*	
Multiple paths/queues				*	*

A TC definitely does not need optimisation for all parameters simultaneously. At network level it is useful to optimise only one or a subset of parameters for a certain

TC to maximise the overall throughput benefiting from statistic gains. Thus no quality relation order of TCs exists.

5   Measurements – The Proof Technique at Network Level

Any agreements concerning QoS make only sense, if they can be monitored, proven and thus also priced [9]. Therefore the following two goals can be identified:

- Network operator: monitoring of the network performance and initiating counter-measures, if necessary (before severe problems arise).
- Customer: request of a proof that the QoS guarantees are kept.

These goals have to be fulfilled by an adequate measurement system. Following, some issues and techniques concerning the measurement of the network performance are highlighted. The chapter closes with an overview of the *Distributed Measurement Architecture* (DMA), which was developed within the AQUILA project and currently deployed during the recent trial phase.

5.1   Round-Trip- vs. One-Way-Measurements

There are two ways to perform measurements on the QoS delay parameters:

- Round-trip-measurements include the way both to a destination and back (A-B-A), thus making it impossible to distinguish performance differences between the two directions.
- One-way-measurements give separate results for the directions (A-B and B-A).

Measurements on *round-trip-delay (RTD)* compared to the *one-way-delay (OWD)* do not take into account the asymmetric nature of the demands of many applications, of upcoming access lines, e.g. ADSL, and of hotspots within the network itself, e.g. international peering points. Thus, it is meanwhile widely accepted, that it is necessary to perform not only round-trip-measurements but also one-way-measurements.

Concerning one-way-measurements an adequate time synchronisation of all measurement points in the network is required in order to get precise measurement results at the selected time scale. There are two major methods to synchronise the nodes in the network:

- Synchronisation via the *Network Time Protocol (NTP)*:
  The achievable synchronisation accuracy is between 1 to 10 ms.
- Synchronisation via the *Global Positioning System (GPS)*:
  The achievable synchronisation accuracy is about 1 µs.

The NTP synchronisation accuracy of some milliseconds leads to a measurement accuracy in the range of 10 to 20 ms. Considering the QoS requirements of some applications (real time online games e.g., 50 to 100 ms delay) GPS synchronised equipment, resulting in a measurement accuracy well better than 1 ms, is necessary and therefore mainly used within the AQUILA project.

5.2   Passive and Active Measurements

With *passive measurements* no specific traffic is generated. Either the deployment of statistics recorded by network elements (like information in router Management Information Bases) or measurement results derived from real user traffic are possible. With *active measurements* specific measurement traffic is generated. It is assumed that this traffic experiences to a sufficient degree the same network performance as the user traffic per TC. Within AQUILA both passive and active measurements are used.

5.3   Measurement Techniques within the AQUILA Trial Platform

Figure 5 illustrates three measurement techniques used in the AQUILA trial platform.

Traffic generators that produce application-like flows (MAa) allow reproducible experiments as opposed to real applications. The results show the achievable QoS for certain services.

Active network probing (MAp, here connected to an edge router) allows a constant monitoring of the whole network concerning the network QoS parameters OWD and delay variation. All NS (traffic classes) are monitored in parallel.

Router QoS monitoring (MIC) supplies additional information about queue lengths, packet drop counters and others of the network elements along the transmission path by reading the according management information bases (MIBs).

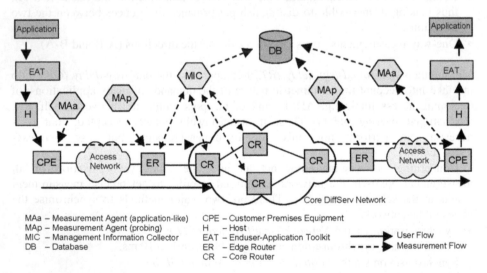

MAa – Measurement Agent (application-like)   CPE – Customer Premises Equipment
MAp – Measurement Agent (probing)   H   – Host
MIC – Management Information Collector   EAT – Enduser-Application Toolkit   ——▶ User Flow
DB – Database   ER – Edge Router   ----▶ Measurement Flow
                                                CR – Core Router

Fig. 5. Measurement techniques used within AQUILA trial platform combined in a Distributed Measurement Architecture

In order to handle all information that is produced by the DMA the results are collected and stored in a single centralised database (DB) for easy post-processing.

All three parts of the DMA in AQUILA are under control of the same web-based Graphical User Interface for configuration, visualisation and statistical evaluation of the measurement results [13].

The tests in the first trial phase that were carried out with the AQUILA DMA and commercially available test equipment proved the basic concept of AQUILA concerning NSs. The different TCs worked successfully together [16]. Identified issues for improvement will be taken into account for the second trial phase by the end of 2002.

6   Summary and Outlook – The Next Steps in the AQUILA Project

In this contribution an end-to-end QoS provisioning from the end-user perception via application requirements and towards network engineering and routers is described. The solution takes into account customer-operator-relationship (SLS), application's needs and their mapping down to network parameters (AP, NS and TC) as summarised in Figure 6. The concepts have been defined towards efficiency and applicability for network operators and ISPs. Advanced measurements are invoked to support the resource management by admission control.

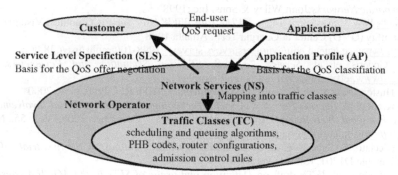

Fig. 6. Network Services as intermediate between application/end-user's request and Traffic Classes

A first implementation of the solution has been evaluated. A more common definition of NSs, called Globally Well-Known Services, will be proposed to the IETF, taking into account the results of the first AQUILA trial. Default parameters for the TCs will be adjusted to optimise the QoS aware router throughput, which results in a higher network performance.

In addition to SLSs between customer and ISP or network operator, SLSs among multiple ISP or network operators become more and more important to deliver reliable end-to-end QoS to the customers. The specification of the second trial focuses on Multi-ISP scenarios.

The measurement results derived with the techniques described, will be used to influence the admission control performed by the AQUILA resource control layer, which is based on a modular and hierarchical architecture. As an extension to the current implementation it is planned to investigate the possibilities, advantages and disadvantages of a feedback from the performance measurements to the resource control layer, entitled as measurement based control loops. This will be an important step towards the final goal of an adaptive resource control software architecture, which will be scalable to very large networks like the current Internet.

References

1. AQUILA consortium. *Adaptive Resource Control for QoS Using an IP-based Layered Architecture.* AQUILA homepage, URL: http://www.ist-aquila.org/.
2. N. Bhatti, A. Bouch, Kuchinsky: *Integrating User-Perceived Quality into Web Server Design*, In Proceedings of the 9th International World-Wide Web Conference, pages 1-16. Elsevier, May 2000, URL: http://www9.org/w9cdrom/92/92.html.
3. CADENUS consortium. *Creation and Deployment of End-User Services in Premium IP Networks.* CADENUS homepage, URL: http://www.cadenus.org/.
4. CISCO White Paper. *Technical Benefits of Using a Service Provider with a Cisco Powered Network.* URL: http://www.tradespeak.com/htmldocs/1245.html.
5. European Commission. *Information Society Technologies Programme (IST).* IST homepage, URL: http://www.cordis.lu/ist/.
6. P. Ferguson, G. Huston. *Quality of Service, Delivering QoS on the Internet and in Corporate Networks*;John Wiley & Sons, Inc.;1998
7. GVU's WWW Surveying Team. *GVU's 10th WWW User Survey.* Graphics, Visualization & Usability (GVU) Center at Georgia Tech, Atlanta 1998 http://www.cc.gatech.edu/gvu/usersurveys/survey- 1998-10/graphs/use/q38.htm.
8. D. Goderis et al. *Service Level Specification Semantics and Parameters.* URL: http://www.ietf.org/internet-drafts/draft-tequila-sls-00.txt.
9. G. Huston; *Next Steps for the IP QoS Architecture.* IETF RFC2990, Nov. 2000
10. R. Kraut et al. *Internet Paradox; A Social Technology that reduces Social Involvement and Psychological Well-Being?* American Psychologist, December 2000, Vol. 55, No. 12. http://www.apa.org/journals/amp/amp5391017.html.
11. F. Ricciato, S. Salsano et al. *Specification of traffic handling for the first trial.* AQUILA deliverable D1301, Rome, June 2000.
12. S. Salsano et al. IETF draft on *Definition and usage of SLSs in the AQUILA consortium.* URL: http://www.ietf.org/internet-drafts/draft-salsano-aquila-sls-00.txt, November 2000.
13. F. Strohmeier et al. *Report on the development of measurement utilities for the first trial.* AQUILA deliverable D2301, Salzburg, September 2000.
14. TEQUILA consortium. *Traffic Engineering for Quality of Service in the Internet, at Large Scale.* TEQUILA homepage, URL: http://www.ist-tequila.org/.
15. M. Winter et al. *System architecture and specification for the first trial.* AQUILA deliverable D1201, Munich, June 2000.
16. ZKopertowski et al. *First Trial Report.* AQUILA deliverable D3201, Warsaw, July 2001.

Mobility Support for Replicated
Real-Time Applications

Jörg Roth

University of Hagen
Department for Computer Science
58084 Hagen, Germany
Joerg.Roth@Fernuni-hagen.de

Abstract. Replicated real-time applications such as co-operative document editors have to continuously update a shared state, thus require low network delays. If we use such applications in mobile and weakly connected environments, state information often cannot be broadcasted immediately, and thus it is difficult to maintain consistency. We discuss this problem with the help of *DreamTeam*, our framework for distributed applications, which we extend to the mobile version *Pocket DreamTeam*. The DreamTeam environment allows the developer to generate replicated applications (e.g., collaborative diagram tools, multi-user text editors, shared web browsers) in the same way as single user applications, without struggling with network details or replication algorithms. For our mobile extension, we suggest an architectural decomposition according to the *remote proxy pattern*. This architecture has a number of benefits: it tolerates weakly connected devices and allows a developer to heavily re-use existing stationary applications.

1 Introduction

Replicated real-time applications play a major role for e.g. shared document editors, co-operative software development environments or shared workspaces. Replicated states are a basis for collaborative multi-user applications, which allow geographically distributed teams to collaborate without significant time delays. Replicated real-time applications store their state information on each participating site without the need for a central server. They have, compared to applications with centralised architectures, a lower response time, since state information is available locally. The network and processing load is distributed among all sites, thus performance bottlenecks are avoided.

To support developers of replicated real-time applications or synchronous groupware we developed the *DreamTeam* platform [6, 10]. We successfully used Dream-Team for practical software courses and diploma theses at the University of Hagen. There exists a huge variety of about 20 DreamTeam applications such as a distributed sketch tool, a diagram tool, text editor, a collaborative slide presentation program, a brainstorming tool and a group web browser.

Currently, there exists a growing market for mobile devices such as PDAs, mobile phones, electronic pens etc. Upcoming communication technologies like UMTS and

H.Unger, T.Böhme, and A.Mikler (Eds.): I²CS 2002, LNCS 2346, pp. 181-192, 2002.
© Springer-Verlag Berlin Heidelberg 2002

Bluetooth promise new services for mobile communication. We strongly believe that mobile computing combined with distributed applications provides a great potential, thus we want to extend the DreamTeam architecture to support mobile users. The corresponding DreamTeam extension called *Pocket DreamTeam* should support weakly connected devices with reduced computational power and limited input/output capabilities. The Pocket version and the stationary version of DreamTeam should run inside the same network. To save development costs, existing shared applications based on the old DreamTeam platform should run without any modification.

The problems to create a mobile platform extension are manifold. In this paper we focus on two major problem areas:

- Replication strategies based on low network delays and high network reliability are not suitable for wireless networks, which still suffer from temporary disconnections and high latency. Thus, we adapted the existing DreamTeam replication mechanism [10] to support mobile devices.
- A developer of mobile replicated applications has to develop for stationary as well as for mobile computers with completely different characteristics. To reduce development costs, we introduce an approach, which allows the developer to re-use code of the functional core for both platforms.

Before we present our approach in more detail, we discuss related work.

2   Related Work

Several toolkits have been developed so far to address consistency problems in mobile environments. *Coda* [4] provides a distributed file system similar to NFS, but allows disconnected operations. Applications based on Coda are fully mobility transparent, i.e. run inside a mobile environment without any modification. Disconnected mobile nodes have access to remote files via a cache. Operations on files are logged and automatically applied to the server when the client re-connects. Coda applications can either define themselves mechanisms for detecting and resolving conflicts or ask the user in case of conflicts. A follow-on platform, *Odyssey* [9], extends data distribution to multimedia data such as video or audio data. To support real-time data, bandwidths and available resources have to be monitored. Odyssey applications are mobility aware.

Rover [3] supports mobility transparent as well as mobility aware applications. To run without modification, network-based applications such as web browsers and news readers can use network proxies. The development of mobility aware applications is supported by two mechanisms: *relocated dynamic objects (RDOs)* and *queued remote procedure calls (QRPC)*. RDOs contain mobile code and data and can reside on a server as well as on a mobile node. During disconnection, QRPCs are applied to cached RDOs. As in Coda, operations are logged and applied to server data after re-connecting.

Bayou [19] provides data distribution with the help of a number of servers, thus segmented networks can be handled. In contrast to Coda, replicated records are still accessible, even when conflicts were detected but not resolved. Bayou applications have to provide a conflict detection and resolution mechanism, thus user intervention is not necessary. Bayou is not designed to support real-time applications.

Sync [7] allows asynchronous collaboration between mobile users. Sync provides collaboration based on shared objects, which can be derived from a Java library. As in Bayou, data conflicts are handled by the application. Sync applications have to provide a *merge matrix*, which contains a resulting operation for each pair of possible conflicting operations. With the help of the merge matrix, conflicts can be resolved automatically.

Lotus Notes [5] has not primarily been designed for mobile computers, but allows replicated data management in heterogeneous networks. Nodes can be disconnected and merge their data after re-connection. Data in Lotus Notes have a record structure. Fields may contain arbitrary data, which are transparent to Notes. Records can be read or changed on different nodes simultaneously. When re-connecting, users resolve conflicting updates.

A completely different approach to support mobile users introduces *Pebbles* [8]. It allows users to remotely control applications running on a server. It follows a collaboration and mobility transparent concept. Instead of using the mouse and keyboard directly, input is taken from the touch screen and handwriting area. It is possible to remotely control off-the-shelve applications (e.g. MS Word) with handheld devices.

As a last example, we want to mention our own mobile platform *QuickStep* [11, 14]. The replication mechanism based on the *database* abstraction integrated into most handheld operating systems [1]. The consistency strategy relies on a strong connection between data rows and involved users. Although QuickStep was primarily designed to exchange well-structured record-oriented data among a group of mobile handheld users, it highly influenced our second platform Pocket DreamTeam.

3   Pocket DreamTeam

The original DreamTeam environment mainly consists of a huge hierarchical class library with approx. 200 classes and 125000 lines of code. The stationary part is entirely written in Java, which can be run on many operating systems, e.g. Windows, Linux or Solaris. The mobile part is written in C++. A *runtime environment* establishes the underlying task structure and provides a front-end for configuring and controlling the system. It is divided into eight so-called *managers*. Each manager runs independently in the background and performs a specific task. E.g., the *Session Manager* handles session profiles, starts and stops sessions and supports joining and leaving sessions. The *Connection Manager* is active during a session and handles the communication between shared applications. It provides multicast mechanisms for information distribution between participating sites. The *Rendezvous Manager* offers services for activities before a session begins, including, e.g., session announcement to other team members.

Fig. 1 shows the stationary DreamTeam runtime stack with two sites. In reality, we often have sessions with more sites. To simplify this figure, we only show one groupware application. Usually, more than one application runs in a collaborative session simultaneously. We distinguish three levels of communication:

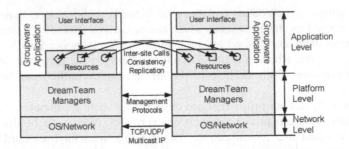

Fig. 1. The DreamTeam runtime and communication stack (stationary version)

- On *network level*, DreamTeam uses the Internet protocols TCP, UDP and, if available, native multicast with Multicast IP. The latter provides better scalability if a session contains a large number of communicating sites. Since Multicast IP does not provide reliable data transport, we integrated a reliable multicast layer into the platform.
- On *platform level,* each manager runs its own protocol. The most important protocols are the rendezvous protocol, the session management protocol, the protocol for member registration and the resource management protocol.
- The *application level* is the only level, an application developer perceives. On this level, we find state replication and consistency management as described in the next section.

3.1   Replication in a Stationary Environment

DreamTeam is based on a fully replicated communication infrastructure. Each site involved in a collaborative session is logically connected to each other site and runs an own instance of the shared application.

Distributed applications are built up of so-called *resources*. Resources are the shared building blocks of an application, e.g. shared texts, shared diagram elements, shared web pages or shared slides in a slide presentation tool. Resources can communicate with their corresponding peer resources by so-called *inter-site calls* – method calls which are synchronously executed on all participating sites. E.g. an inter-site call

```
anyResource.anyMethod(param₁, ..., paramₙ);
```

executes the method `anyMethod` on all replicated resource instances of `anyResource` in the session. To distinguish inter-site calls from local calls, the developer has to enter a specific keyword in the program code. Inter-site calls can roughly be compared to the *remote method invocation* (RMI) concept of Java. As a major difference, inter-site calls are sent to more than one site. In addition, the developer has not to manually load remote instances, since the runtime system builds up the identical resource structure on all sites automatically. The replicated structure makes all resources available locally. Inside a site, standard programming mechanism can be used without the need for an additional communication layer. This leads to efficient and straightforward application structures.

We first discuss the simple replication with only stationary users. To ensure consistency of concurrent updates, the runtime system requests pessimistic locks for each inter-site call without any developer's intervention. DreamTeam uses distributed locks as introduced by Suzuki and Kasami [18]. If an application changes a resource R by means of an inter-site call I(R), the runtime system performs the following operations:

```
request(L(R))
apply I(R) to resource R
multicast I(R) to other sites
release(L(R))
```

Here, L(R) denotes the lock associated to R. The request statement blocks, when the lock is currently in use. This is acceptable in the stationary DreamTeam environment, where connections are reliable and fast. Thus, delays caused by locks are usually very short. The developer can override this generic scheme to increase parallel execution capabilities if consistency can be relaxed.

3.2   Replication in a Mobile Environment

Finding an appropriate architecture for the mobile extension is of central importance. To have real-time applications and weakly connected devices at the same time results in conflicting requirements: on one hand, updates of resource states should be distributed to all participants in real-time. On the other hand, disconnections are unavoidable in wireless networks. Often, handheld devices are simply disconnected because of auto-power-off services carried out by the operating system to safe battery power.

We resolve this conflict with the help of a design pattern called the *remote proxy pattern* [12]: the mobile device does not connect directly to other sites, but asks another computer, called the *proxy*, to act as a placeholder. The proxy performs heavy-duty tasks and stores data when the mobile device goes off-line. The idea of proxy pattern in general is not new. The first proxy pattern designed to describe networked applications was introduced by Shapiro [15]. His concept contains a *client*, a *service*, which the client wants to use across a network, and a *proxy*, which mediates between client and service. A similar idea was presented by Silva et al. [16]. Their proxy, called the *distributed proxy*, has a very fine-grained definition, which divides a system into *client, server, client proxy, server proxy, client communicator* and *server communicator*. This fine-grained definition is too specific for our intended domain, since only few systems meet this architecture in reality.

Shapiro's and Silva's proxies conceptually differ from the remote proxy pattern. As a major difference, the remote proxy pattern assigns the client and proxy processes to different computers. This offers the required flexibility to solve our problem.

Fig. 2 shows the resulting architecture. Components on the right side, i.e. existing DreamTeam installations, remain unmodified. The protocols on network, platform and application levels of stationary sites are identical to proxy protocols. Thus, DreamTeam systems can, from the viewpoint of communication, not distinguish mobile from stationary users. This saves implementation costs, since the proxy can use most of the DreamTeam managers without modification.

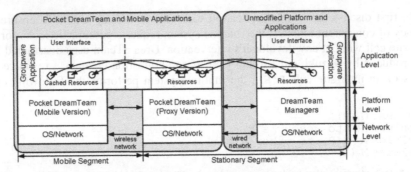

Fig. 2. The extended DreamTeam architecture with mobility support

The network is divided into a *mobile* and a *stationary segment*. A mobile groupware application has parts running on both segments. This seems to be a high burden, as parts of one application instance have to communicate across the network. We will see in a later section that the runtime system carries out most of the required communication services automatically.

Handheld users request low response time, for e.g. screen updates, even if the underlying wireless network causes high latencies. As a rule, handheld applications have to process user events in less than one second [1]. Thus, the mobile device stores for each resource a corresponding *cached resource*. The runtime system automatically updates cached resources when the original resources change their state.

3.3 Joining a Session

When a mobile user wants to join a session, the system has to perform three steps:
1. In the first step, a mobile device has to look up a proxy. A groupware infrastructure may have an arbitrary number of proxies running in stand-by mode. The proxy discovery protocol uses broadcast to ask all computers in a network whether they offer the proxy service. If the network supports DHCP (Dynamic Host Configuration Protocol), we can add the proxy address to the DHCP service record, which is passed to a mobile device when it enters a new subnet.
2. The proxy performs a *group rendezvous* [13], i.e. it looks up other DreamTeam sites that are currently on-line. Note, that there is no central server where DreamTeam sites are registered, thus the rendezvous protocol has to run completely decentralised.
3. The Session Manager on the proxy performs a *join* operation [10]. This operation copies the current resource structure from another participant and loads the current state information. Since other members change resources concurrently during the join operation, a complex protocol has to avoid race conditions.

3.4   The Role of the Proxy

In this architecture, a proxy computer has an important role, thus we have to discuss problems related to disabled or disconnected proxies. There exist three variations of this problem:

The proxy disconnects from other session members, but still has contact to the mobile device: In this case, the stationary network is partitioned into two or more segments. The proxy automatically performs a *leave* operation. The mobile user cannot collaborate with other session members, but can rejoin as soon as the interruption ends (steps 2 and 3 in section 3.3).

The proxy disconnects from the mobile user, but still has contact to the stationary segment: This case is more likely, since the mobile segment is much more prone for disconnections than the stationary segment. Other session members can continue without interruption. The proxy keeps track of all shared state changes, thus the mobile user can continue immediately after re-connection. During disconnection, a user can continue her or his work on the cached resources. Inter-site calls cannot be performed directly, as a network connection is a prerequisite for modifying a shared state. They have to either return an error or have to be queued up. In principle, it is possible to pass an arbitrary number of queued inter-site calls to the proxy after re-connection. Too large queues however may confuse users, thus the application developer can limit the size of the inter-site queue. Note that during disconnection other users may modify the shared state. Nevertheless, the consistency concept (see next section) preserves consistency of the shared state.

If a mobile user is disconnected longer than a certain time (e.g. some minutes), a *leave* operation is performed. In this case, the mobile user can look up another proxy inside the network and rejoin (steps 1 to 3 in section 3.3)

The proxy disconnects from both segments or breaks down: This is a combination of the cases above. Since application states stored inside the resources are replicated, no information gets lost.

3.5   Consistency

Obtaining consistency of shared data is a crucial point in weakly connected systems. Having loosely connected devices, we cannot solely use pessimistic locks any longer. A mobile device holding a lock could be disconnected for a certain time, thus other members would be blocked for a long time.

Pocket DreamTeam provides a hybrid approach for concurrency control: we use pessimistic locks for the stationary segment and optimistic conflict detection and resolution [4, 19] for the mobile segment. For this, the proxy contains two threads, which wait for incoming messages. The first thread waits for inter-site calls from other participants (i.e. all session members apart from the associated mobile member). We outline the thread as follows:

```
do {
    receive inter-site call I(R) from other site
    // note: other site already requested the lock
    apply I(R) to local resource R
    increase T(R)
    if (mobile device is on-line)
```

```
         send state of R and T(R) to mobile device
    else
         store state and T(R) and send when device re-connects
} until (session stops)
```

This thread updates the local resource state continuously. In addition, it copies new states to the mobile device, which stores them in its cache. $T(R)$ denotes a logical timestamp used in the second thread for conflict detection. The second thread waits for messages from the mobile device:

```
do {
    receive inter-site call I(R) and T'(R) from mob. device
    request(L(R))
    if (T'(R)<>T(R))   // i.e. conflict!
        solve conflict
        // i.e. generate new I(R) without conflicts
    apply I(R) to resource R
    increase T(R)
    send state of R and T(R) to mobile device
    multicast inter-site call I(R) to other sites
    release(L(R))
} until (session stops)
```

To detect conflicts, the mobile device sends in addition to $I(R)$ the logical time-stamp $T'(R)$ of the last cache copy of R. This allows the proxy to detect easily, whether $I(R)$ is associated to an older copy of R. In this case, the proxy has to perform a conflict resolution. Two generic conflict resolution strategies are:

- $I_{new}(R):=I(R)$, i.e. the mobile device has priority,
- $I_{new}(R):=null$ operation, i.e. other members have priority. This is the generic way for Pocket DreamTeam to resolve conflicts.

Sometimes, a more fine-grained resolution strategy suits better. An optimal strategy takes into account the state of R, which the mobile device has perceived *before* it applied $I(R)$. We can get this state in two ways:

- The mobile device sends in addition to $I(R)$ and $T'(R)$ the old state of R. This however increases network traffic.
- The proxy stores old states in a hash table and uses $T(R)$ as key. Whenever it receives a new timestamp $T'(R)$, it can remove older entries.

With this extension, we could implement even complex consistency algorithms based on *operational transformation* [2]. Note that the consistency mechanism realised inside the platform ensures data consistency on a basic level. An application developer however is free to implement high-level strategies based on e.g. social protocols. A shared text editor can, e.g., offer functions to reserve text paragraphs for exclusive editing. Such strategies are highly application-dependent and not part of the platform. Nevertheless, they require low-level consistency of data as provided by our consistency mechanism.

3.6   Implementation Issues

Realising software for handheld devices is hard work, since developers have to deal with small memories, slow processors and restricted operating system capabilities. Pocket DreamTeam requires portions of code on the handheld under C++ as well as portions under Java. One design goal of Pocket DreamTeam was to heavily re-use stationary portions in mobile applications. In order to create a Pocket DreamTeam application, we have to perform four steps:

1. For the proxy portion, we can copy resources from the stationary version. We have to add code for marshalling/unmarshalling the state, since state information is transferred across language borders (Java to C++).
2. We have to add code for conflict resolution, if the generic strategy is not suitable.
3. For the mobile portion, we have to transfer parts of the resource code to the target platform (i.e. C++). As a minimum we have to code all data fields. The runtime system automatically passes inter-site calls to the proxy. The proxy in turn performs the appropriate state change and sends the new resource state back. This can cause long turn-around times. As a solution, we can transfer time-critical inter-site calls to the mobile device, which then modify cached state directly.
4. We implement the rest of the mobile portion, especially the user interface, like a single user application without considering communication or replication issues.

3.7   Testing Environment and Sample Applications

We completely implemented and tested Pocket DreamTeam. As a technical platform for mobile end-user devices we use handhelds as shown in fig. 3. We in particular decided not to use notebooks. Due to their size, weight and battery life, mobile working capabilities with notebooks are limited.

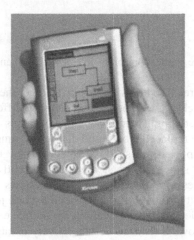

Fig. 3. End-user device with Pocket DreamTeam running a collaborative diagram application

Our development and testing system consists of
- two handheld devices (Palm m505 with PalmOS 4.0) equipped with wireless LAN (IEEE 802.11b) adapters,
- a number of stationary workstations (Windows PCs, Solaris workstations),
- a wireless LAN infrastructure connected with the campus Internet.

Although our testing environment primarily bases on wireless LAN, we strictly paid attention to be as independent as possible of the network. In principle, Pocket Dream-

Team could run on other wireless networks such as IrDA (Infrared), Bluetooth or GSM. Since not all networks support the Internet Protocol (IP) sufficiently, we isolated network related functions in a component we call *Network Kernel Framework* (*NKF*). NKF can roughly be compared to a network driver and offers a uniform interface to higher communication layers.

As mentioned above, software for the end-user devices were coded in C++. Even though Java would fit much better into the overall system architecture, the handheld version (*Java Micro Edition*) was not capable enough for our project. We decided to use the well-established development environment *CodeWarrior* for PalmOS.

To test the concept, we implemented the DreamTeam core applications as well as two groupware applications on top of Pocket DreamTeam.

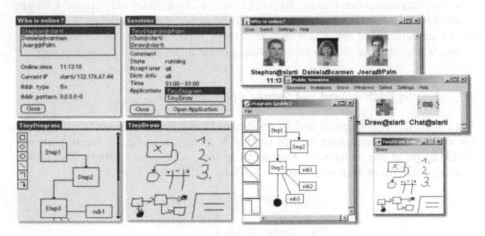

Fig. 4. Groupware applications on mobile device (left) and desktop (right)

Fig. 4 shows Pocket DreamTeam windows (left) and the corresponding desktop DreamTeam windows (right). Corresponding screens on different platforms may look completely different. Overlapping windows, context menus and icons are not useful on small screens. E.g., we replaced icon-based dialogs by simple textual lists.

The users use the upper frames to view contextual information and control sessions. The *On-line list* shows all users, which are currently on-line, i.e. can participate in a collaborative session. The *Sessions* frame shows all running and planned sessions. A user can select a running session from a list and join. From the 20 Dream-Team applications, we selected two applications for mobile extension:

- The *Diagram* tool allows a team to collaboratively create diagrams such as flow charts, entity relation ship or class diagrams.
- With the *Draw* tool, a group can draw and share simple free-hand sketches.

To realise these applications, we performed the steps as described in section 3.5:

1. For e.g. a diagram resource (i.e. a rectangle or a circle) we had to enter code to marshall the co-ordinates, size, colour etc.
2. *Draw* as a very simple application uses the generic resolution method. *Diagram* is more complex. Conflicts occur, when two users modify the same resource simultaneously. Our conflict resolution method first investigates, whether the modification

affects the same data fields. If not, we apply both modifications, since no real conflict occurs. Otherwise, we branch to the generic conflict resolution.

3. To increase performance of the *Draw* application, we transferred the method, which adds a line to the sketch to the mobile device. This significantly improves response time during free-hand drawing.

4. We implemented all dialog frames, menus, buttons etc. inside the target environment.

Table 1. Comparison of DreamTeam implementations

	Stationary	Proxy	Re-used	Mobile
Core platform binary	2.3 MB	2.0 MB	-	72 KB
Core platform source	125000 lines	110000 lines	98 %	9500 lines
Diagram source	6900 lines	5200 lines	92 %	600 lines
Draw source	930 lines	520 lines	90 %	410 lines

Table 1 summarises our implementation efforts. This table compares the implementation efforts for stationary DreamTeam and Pocket DreamTeam (proxy and mobile portions). The column *Re-used* indicates how much source code of the stationary version could be re-used in the proxy. We can see a high degree of re-usable source code for the proxy implementation. In addition, the required source codes for mobile portions are considerable small. Especially the platform core binary of 72 KB demonstrates that Pocket DreamTeam is suitable for devices with small memories.

4   Conclusion and Future Work

Pocket DreamTeam demonstrates how we could effectively extend a distributed application platform for mobile usage. We used the remote proxy pattern as a guideline for our architecture. Mobile users can access high-demanding applications through devices with low computational power. The software architecture based on resources dramatically simplifies the implementation, since the runtime system is able to carry out most of the required communication and replication services automatically. Drawbacks related to the remote proxy pattern (e.g., problems with disabled proxies) are addressed by higher-level mechanisms. For replication and consistency, the system offers generic mechanisms, which a developer can adapt. Especially the combination of pessimistic concurrency control for the stationary segment and optimistic concurrency control on the mobile segment is unique and combines the advantages of two concurrency control concepts.

In the future, we want to reduce the implementation efforts for mobile applications even more. For this, we plan to develop a program, which generates source code for proxy resources and mobile cached resources automatically from stationary resources. This however requires some syntax extensions, e.g. new keywords, but would significantly reduce development costs.

References

1   Bey C., Freeman E., Hillerson G., Ostrem J., Rodriguez R., Wilson G., Dugger M.: Palm OS Programmer's Companion, Volume I, Palm Inc, July 2001
2. Cormack G. V.: A Calculus for Concurrent Update, Department of Computer Science, University of Waterloo, Waterloo, Canada, 1995
3. Joseph A. D., Tauber J. A., Kaashoek M. F.: Mobile Computing with the Rover Toolkit, IEEE Transactions on Computers, Vol. 46, No. 3, March 1997, 337-352
4. Kistler J. J., Satyanarayana M.: Disconnected Operation in the Coda File System, ACM Transaction on Computer Systems, Vol. 10, No. 1, Feb. 1992, 3-25
5. Lotus Development Corporation: Lotus Notes, http://www.lotus.com/home.nsf/welcome/developernetwork
6. Lukosch S., Roth J.: Reusing Single-user Applications to Create Multi-user Internet Applications, Innovative Internet Computing Systems (I2CS), Ilmenau, June 21-22, 2001, LNCS 2060, Springer, 79-90
7. Munson J. P., Dewan P.: Sync: A Java Framework for Mobile Collaborative Applications, special issue on Executable Content in Java, IEEE Computer, 1997, 59-66
8. Myers B. A., Stiel H., Gargiulo R.: Collaboration Using Multiple PDAs Connected to a PC, Proceedings of the ACM 1998 conference on Computer supported cooperative work, 1998, 285-294
9. Noble B., Satyanarayanan M., Narayanan D., Tilton J. E., Flinn J., Walker K.: Agile Application-Aware Adaptation for Mobility, Proceedings of the 16th ACM Symposium on Operating System Principles, Oct. 1997, St. Malo, France
10. Roth J.: DreamTeam - A Platform for Synchronous Collaborative Applications, AI & Society (2000), Vol. 14, No. 1, Special Issue on Computer-Supported Cooperative Work, Springer London, March 2000, 98-119
11. Roth J.: Information sharing with handheld appliances, 8th IFIP Working Conference on Engineering for Human-Computer Interaction (EHCI'01), Toronto, Canada, May 11-13, 2001, LNCS 2254, Springer, 263-279
12. Roth J.: Patterns of mobile interaction, Proceedings of Mobile HCI 2001: Third International Workshop on Human Computer Interaction with Mobile Devices, M. D. Dunlop and S. A. Brewster (eds), IHM-HCI 2001 Lille, France, Sept. 10, 2001, 53-58
13. Roth J., Unger C. : Group Rendezvous in a Synchronous, Collaborative Environment, in R. Steinmetz (ed): Kommunikation in Verteilten Systemen (KiVS'99), 11. ITG/VDE Fachtagung, 2.-5. March 1999, Springer, 114-127
14. Roth J., Unger, C.: Using handheld devices in synchronous collaborative scenarios, Personal and Ubiquitous Computing, Vol. 5, Issue 4, Springer London, Dec. 2001, 243-252
15. Shapriro M.: Structure and Encapsulation in Distributed Systems: the Proxy Principle, Proc. of the 6th Internal. Conference on Distributed Computing Systems, Mai 1986, 198-204
16. Silva A. R., Rosa F. A., Gonçalves T., Antunes M.: Distributed Proxy: A Design Pattern for the Incremental Development of Distributed Applications, Proceedings of the 2nd International Workshop on Engineering Distributed Objects (EDO 2000), Davis, November 2000, California, USA, LNCS 1999, Springer, 165-181
18. Suzuki I., Kasami T.: A distributed mutal exclusion algorithm, ACM Transactions on Computer Systems, Vol. 3, No. 4, Nov. 1985, 344-349
19. Terry D. B., Theimer M. M., Petersen K., Demers A. J.: Managing Update Conflict in Bayou, a Weakly Connected Replicated Storage System, Proceedings of the fifteenth ACM symposium on Operating systems principles, Copper Mountain, CO USA, Dec. 3-6, 1995, 172-182

Empirical Study of VBR Traffic Smoothing in Wireless Environment*

Youjip Won and Bowie Shim

Division of Electrical and Computer Engineering
Hanyang University, Seoul, Korea, 133-791
{yjwon,shim77}@ece.hanyang.ac.kr

Abstract. This work presents the result of the empirical study on the effect of VBR smoothing in broadband wireless network. Traffic smoothing of VBR stream has been the subjects of intense research during past several years. While preceding algorithms successfully remove burstiness in the underlying process, these works do not address how the respective smoothing algorithm can effectively improve the QoS in practical environment. We developed MPEG-4 streaming system and instrument the client terminal which is handheld mobile device. We examine the effect of smoothing over the packet loss behavior and empirical QoS under various different system settings. We use the rate variability as optimization criterion in generating the packet transmission schedule. We find that smoothing with small size buffer(10 Kbyte) brings a significant improvement on packet loss ratio and greatly enhances the QoS perceived by the end user. Via adopting smoothing technique in transporting multimedia traffic, we are able to increase the *acceptable quality* frame rate by 50%.

1 Introduction

1.1 Motivation

Due to the rapid advancement of CPU computing capability as well as the network transmission speed, we can enjoy the real-time remote playback of video stream without much difficulty these days. Further, the deployment of third generation wireless technology[4] makes it possible to access to streaming service without geographic limitation. Rapid proliferation of usage of mobile device accompanied by the availability of wireless network connection makes efficient support of video streaming service in mobile terminal emphasized more and more.

Unlike the general-purpose desk-top computer, which has abundant computing resources and storage capacity, mobile device in consumer electronics domain have stringent resource constraints due to its restriction on power consumption, pricing, reliability, etc. Thus, in this type of devices, special care needs to be taken in allocating resources to application and over-provisioning of resources should be strictly avoided.

* This work is funded by KOSEF through Statistical Research Center for Complex System at Seoul National University.

H. Unger, T. Böhme, and A. Mikler (Eds.): I²CS 2002, LNCS 2346, pp. 193–204, 2002.
© Springer-Verlag Berlin Heidelberg 2002

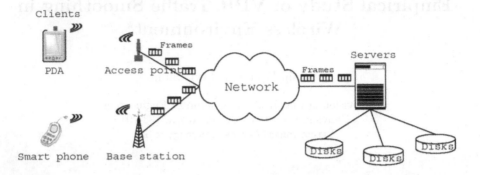

Fig. 1. Streaming Service in Wireless Internet Environment

Due to the inter frame coded nature of constant quality compression scheme, the resulting compressed video stream exhibits order of magnitude difference in successive frame sizes. This large variance in frame sizes raises burstiness in transmitting the compressed video for the real-time playback. Seamless delivery of multimedia data mandates that a certain amount of resources involved in transporting the VBR data from the server to the client needs to be dedicated. Although the mobile terminals can allocate resources, e.g. CPU cycles, memory buffers, based on peak-bit rate of the source stream, such over-provisioning is extremely wasteful and undermines the benefits of VBR encoding technique. Bandwidth smoothing techniques can reduce the burstiness of traffic and subsequently can facilitate more efficient resource usage.

The objective of *smoothing* is to provide better quality streaming service with minimum amount of resources by reducing the *burstiness of the traffic*. A number of elaborate smoothing algorithms have been published in various forums and literatures, each of which uses different performance metrics to compute the packet transmission schedule, e.g. rate variations, number of rate changes, client buffer utilization, to list a few. These techniques successfully removes the burstiness of the original packet traffic. However, we yet do not know how these smoothing techniques actually contribute to improving the *Quality of Service* perceived by the end user. Indeed, none of preceding works address how their smoothing algorithms can improve the *packet loss* and *jitter* behavior in actual system.

In the context of smoothing of VBR stream, there are two important issues which deserve more attention. The first issue is to identify *relationship between smoothing criteria and packet loss*(and jitter) behavior. The second issue is to identify the *relationship between packet loss(and jitter) and Quality of Service* perceived by the user. Packet loss and jitter is two widely accepted metric for quality of service. However, these two metrics does not deliver sufficient clue about the quality of service perceived by the user. Same number of packet losses can affect the quality of service in many different ways. We carefully believe that even with the same number of packet losses, burstiness of packet losses and/or the type of frame which the lost packets belong to can significantly alter the way that the lost packet affects the QoS of the stream. In this work, we like to present the result of our empirical study on VBR traffic smoothing in broadband wireless Internet. Particularly, the client application runs on the mobile handheld device which may exhibit unique characteristics different from general purpose desk-top PC. We instrument the effect of smoothing on packet loss behavior in mobile terminal under various different system settings. Our experimental results reveal that smoothing enables the end system to effectively handle the incoming stream. We are able to increase the frame rate by 50% with the adoption of smoothing algorithm.

1.2 Related Works

A number of smoothing algorithms have been proposed, each of which uses different performance metrics and each of which generates different schedules. The performance metrics include the number of rate changes[6], the variability of the bandwidth requirement[17], the number of on-off segments in an on-off transmission model[21], the client buffer utilization[5], and general cost metrics through dynamic programming[14]. Feng and Rexford provide in depth survey of these techniques[7]. Boudec and Verscheure developed smoothing technique for guaranteed service network, e.g. RSVP[2]. Chang et al[3] proposes an window based smoothing algorithm which can be used for online smoothing. There have been a number of efforts to quantify the quality of service[1,9,18] in realtime multimedia delivery. Apteker et al[1] investigated the relationship between the number of streaming sessions and the quality of service of individual streams. Ghinea et al[9] investigated not only the degree of satisfaction but also the degree of understanding as a parameter to QoS.

The rest of the paper is organized as follows. Section 2 describes VBR traffic used in this experiment. Section 3 presents the smoothing technique used in this work. Section 4 presents the results of the experiments. Section 5 concludes the paper.

2 Empirical VBR Process

2.1 Characteristics of Compressed Stream

MPEG coding scheme exploits the temporal and spatial difference between successive frames. Stochastic characteristics of VBR bandwidth process may vary depending on the nature of the original video clip. It is worth noting that frame sequence we are dealing with is the one which is actually transmitted and is different from the order in which the frames are displayed. The B type frame has bidirectional dependency. It depends on the preceding I or P frame as well as the following I or P frame. To resolve the forward referencing problem, encoder reorders the frames such that the frame does not have to wait for the arrival of another frame for decompression.

From the original video scene, we generated 4 streams with frame rates 4, 5, 6, and 10 frames/sec, respectively. Table 1 summarizes the traffic characteristics.

Each clip is encoded with MPEG 4(DIVX) codec. It is worth noting that DIVX codec does not have fixed GOP pattern. User only specifies the maximum distance between successive I frames and thus, the frame sequence yields irregular pattern.

Proper characterization of VBR traffic plays critical role in designing various components of the system: server, router, client, network transport, etc. and importance of which cannot be emphasized any further. There have been a number of efforts which rigorously examine the stochastic characteristics of empirical VBR process[12,16,8,20,13]. Most of these works focus their effort on properly identifying the inter GOP and intra GOP correlation structure of the frame size sequence. While the results of various traffic characterization studies have their own assumptions, the common findings are that the VBR traffic exhibits very bursty behavior.

Figures in Fig. 2 illustrates the frame size sequence of compressed frames. It plots the size sequence of the first 500 frames. Simply from eyeball test, we can observe that the traffic exhibits very bursty characteristics. It is worth noting that our VBR bandwidth process is not linearly proportional to frame rate. For example, increasing the frame rate by 50% from 4 frames/sec to 6 frames/sec entails the increase in the playback rate by 18% from 4.0 Kbyte/sec to 4.7 Kbyte/sec. This is because the encoder exploits the inter frame dependency in compressing the original scene. The relationship between the frame rate and playback rate and their respective impact of QoS is subject to further investigation.

2.2   Creation of Stream File

From technical point of view, streaming of video file should be distinguished from the playback of multimedia data from local storage. In local playback, the unit of data transfer is disk block which is usually 4 KByte(or multiples thereof). The components which constitutes the route from the local storage to the display in multimedia playback, e.g. disk interface, I/O bus, memory, system bus, decoder, CPU, video card, etc. has sufficient data rate and capacity. Thus, violation of timing constraints for a single frame can easily be identified and can be recovered. Further this process occur in single address domain. However, transporting the multimedia data over the network requires more elaborate mechanism. I/O unit size is much smaller. Maximum packet size is determined by MAC layer and usually is 1500 Byte(Ethernet MAC). This value includes the size of header and trailer and data payload. Further, the end systems(server and client) does have any control on jitter, delay, loss which occurs somewhere in the middle of transportation. In an effort to partly compensate this uncertainty, each packet is enhanced with information about the packet sequence number, arrival deadline, type of information, size of data payload, etc[15]. Adding this information to individual packets on the fly requires excessive CPU cycles. The MPEG-4 standard file format(*.mp4) suggests that the file contains the array of elements called *hint track* where each element contains the size of packet, deadline, decoding deadline, etc.

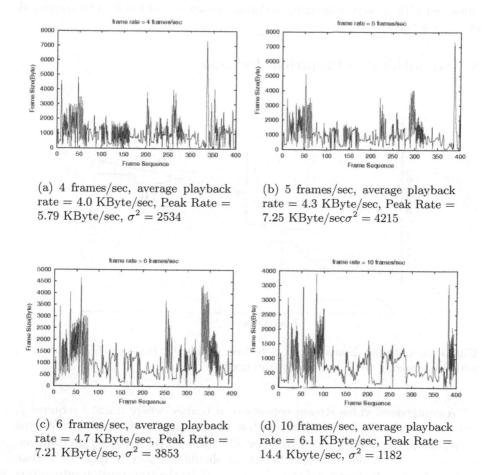

(a) 4 frames/sec, average playback rate = 4.0 KByte/sec, Peak Rate = 5.79 KByte/sec, $\sigma^2 = 2534$

(b) 5 frames/sec, average playback rate = 4.3 KByte/sec, Peak Rate = 7.25 KByte/sec$\sigma^2 = 4215$

(c) 6 frames/sec, average playback rate = 4.7 KByte/sec, Peak Rate = 7.21 KByte/sec, $\sigma^2 = 3853$

(d) 10 frames/sec, average playback rate = 6.1 KByte/sec, Peak Rate = 14.4 Kbyte/sec, $\sigma^2 = 1182$

Fig. 2. Basic Statistics of Compressed Streams

Creating the *streamable* MPEG-4 file involves a series of conversion. This is not elaborate nor state of art technology at all. However, we like to present the process briefly mainly to help the understandings. Original video clip contains audio and video information. Each information is compressed by the respective encoder, i.e. audio codec and video codec. In case of video, original YUV signals are compressed with divx codec and *.cmp file is created as a result. In case of audio file, it is compressed using audio codec, e.g. G.723 and the respective *.cmp file is created. *.cmp files for video and audio are then multiplexed into single file *.mp4 file. MP4 file format is rooted at Quicktime file format[10]. MP4 file format introduces additional data structures(atom) which further faciliates the manipulation of MPEG-4 compressed data. They include the atom for copyright information, object descriptor, track information, etc. In the last step, mp4 file is enhanced with packetization information as known as *hint track* and is converted into mov format file.

3   Smoothing of Empirical Process

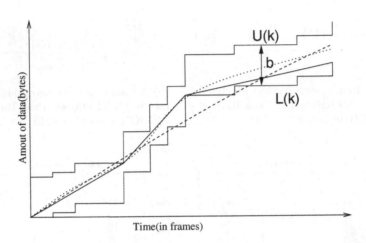

Fig. 3. Smoothing: Transmission schedule should lie between $L(k)$ and $U(k)$ while minimizing the burstiness of the traffic

A compressed video stream consists of n frames, where frame i requires f_i byte of storage. To avoid the underflow of the data in the client buffer, the server alway transmit enough data by k^{th} frame, $L(k) = \sum_{i=1}^{k} f_i$. However, since the client buffer size is b, the client should not receive more data than $U(k) = L(k) + b$ by frame k. Let $c_i, i = 1, \ldots, N$ be the transmission rate during frame slot i of the smoothed video stream. Then, any valid transmission plan should satisfy that $L(k) \leq \sum_{i=1}^{k} c_i \leq U(k)$. The objective of smoothing is to find c_i which minimizes burstiness of the traffic while satisfying the continuity requirement. Fig. 3 illustrates the various schedule and upper and lower bound of the schedule. Any valid transmission plan should lie between $L(k)$ and $U(k)$.

The smoothing algorithm generates different schedule depending on the optimization criteria and thus appropriate smoothing algorithm needs to be carefully chosen depending on the characteristics of the system. For example, when the client has small size buffer, the optimization should focus on minimizing the client buffer utilization. In the current version of our streaming system, we find that the packet loss mostly occurs at the client's end. In our system, the typical situation of packet loss is that buffer space for UDP socket is full and decoding process is not fast enough to decode the frames and to make the room for newly arriving packets in the decoding buffer. This situation is more likely to happen when the packets arrive at bursty manner. In an effort to minimize the packet losses, we generate the schedule which minimizes the variability of the packet arrival rate, $\sum_{i=1}^{N}(c_i - \bar{c})^2$, $\bar{c} = \frac{\sum_{i=1}^{N} c_i}{N}$, with the given buffer size. This algorithm is originally developed by Salehi et al[17]. The objective of our work is to perform empirical study on the effectiveness of VBR smoothing in real testbed and thus we like to omit the detailed description of the algorithm itself.

Table 1. Characteristic of Smoothen Traffic

Frame Rate	r_{frame}	4 fps	5fps	6fps	10fps
Original Traffic	μ	4.0	4.3	4.7	6.1
	σ^2	2534	4215	3853	1182
	Peak	5.79	7.25	7.21	14.4
Buffer Size = 10KByte	σ^2	1178	1882	1791	688
	r_{peak}	5.2	7.0	6.8	12.2
Buffer Size = 20KByte	σ^2	842	989	661	412
	r_{peak}	4.6	6.8	5.8	10.1
Buffer Size = 30KByte	σ^2	718	524	459	342
	r_{peak}	4.2	4.9	4.9	7.2

Table 1 illustrates the statistical characteristics of the empirical processes. For each of the original video clips, we generate three different transmission schedules based on different client buffer sizes: 10KByte, 20KByte, and 30KByte, respectively. The buffer size used for smoothing is very small compared to the buffer size used in the preceding works which typically ranges from 64KByte to 32MByte. The smoothing buffer size bears direct relationship to service startup latency. In this work, we assume that longer than 5 sec's startup latency is not acceptable and we select the appropriate smoothing buffer size given this maximum startup latency constraint. To be described in detail in section 4, benefits of smoothing with these small size buffers are quite phenomenal. r_{frame} and r_{peak} in Table 1 denotes frame rate(frames/sec) and peak data rate(Byte/sec), respectively. As can be seen, adoption of smoothing algorithm reduces the variance(σ^2) of the VBR sequence. Variance decreases with respect to increase in the size of smoothing buffer. Fig. 4 visualizes the VBR traffic sequences under various smoothing conditions.

4   Experiment

4.1   Environment Setup

Development of comprehensive streaming system is itself rather challenging task, which took us two years of effort. Our MPEG-4 streaming system, *SMART* is developed on Linux environment and runs on Linux box with dual pentium II(550MHz) processors. The client application(MPEG-4 player) is developed on WinCE platform(iPAQ with 64 MByte of main memory)[11]. The client connects to the server via 10 Mbits/sec wireless LAN connection. Control informa-

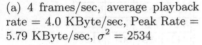

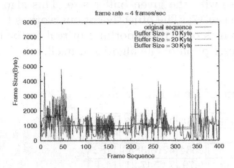

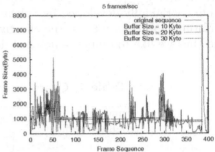

(a) 4 frames/sec, average playback rate = 4.0 KByte/sec, Peak Rate = 5.79 KByte/sec, $\sigma^2 = 2534$

(b) 5 frames/sec, average playback rate = 4.3 KByte/sec, Peak Rate = 7.25 KByte/sec$\sigma^2 = 4215$

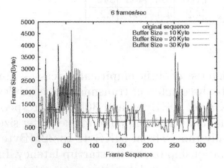

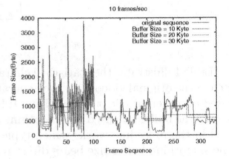

(c) 6 frames/sec, average playback rate = 4.7 KByte/sec, Peak Rate = 7.21 KByte/sec, $\sigma^2 = 3853$

(d) 10 frames/sec, average playback rate = 6.1 KByte/sec, Peak Rate = 14.4 Kbyte/sec, $\sigma^2 = 1182$

Fig. 4. Original VBR sequence and the smoothen traffic

tions, e.g. `open`, `play`, `pause`, `stop`, `close`, are transferred over RTSP protocol. Streaming data is transported using RTP protocol implemented over UDP. Original video clip is 6 min long. Basic statistics on the underlying processes are shown in Table 1.

When transmitting the MPEG-4 packet over RTP, we can specify the required packet transmission time in RTP packet header. The actual value in this field corresponds to the offset from the original frame display time. If the transmission time fields of all packets are 0, the packets belonging to the same frame are transmitted in bursty manner as if the frame is the unit of transmission. By properly adjusting this value, we can distribute the packet transmission over the time line and can make the resulting packet traffic *smoother*. Packetization information along with the respective packet transmission timing is recorded in the hint track of the file. File format and hint track structure are developed compliant with[19].

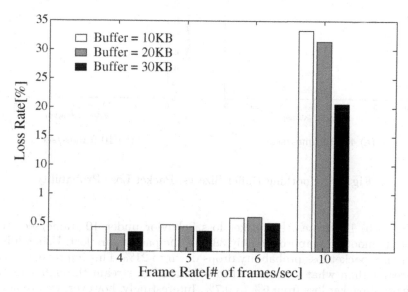

Fig. 5. Frame Rate vs. Packet Loss

Average playback of each file corresponds to 4.0KByte/s, 4.3KByte/s, 4.7KByte/s and 6.1KByte/s, respectively. RTP packetization and the packet transmission time information is attached to this file. For each frame rate, we generate three files each of which has different packet transmission schedule. We use three different buffer sizes: 10 KByte, 20 KByte, and 30 KByte for smoothing.

4.2 Result of Experiment

Fig. 5 illustrates the packet loss behavior of the streaming session. X-axis and Y-axis denote the frame rate and packet loss probability, respectively. When the frame rate is relatively low, i.e. upto 6 frames/sec, smoothing the traffic brings rather significant improvement on packet loss even though the smoothing buffer size is very small, e.g. 10 KByte. However, introducing larger size buffer beyond 10 KByte does not entail profitable improvement in the packet loss behavior. Meanwhile, in the stream with higher playback rate(10 frames/sec), using larger size buffer for smoothing continuously improves the packet behavior.

Fig. 6 illustrates the packet loss behavior under different buffer size. Smoothing the original stream with 10 KByte buffer size dramatically decreases the packet loss behavior. Especially for 6 frame/sec stream, the packet loss probability drops from 7% to 0.5%. This is phenomenal leap from practical point of view. When packet loss probability is 7%, the quality of the scene is *not acceptable* for service. However, when the packet loss is 0.5%, we are actually not able to recognize any frame corruption nor jitter in playback.

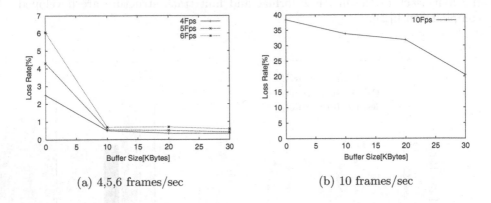

(a) 4,5,6 frames/sec   (b) 10 frames/sec

Fig. 6. Smoothing Buffer Size vs. Packet Loss Probability

Fig. 6(b) illustrates the packet loss behavior under 10 frame/sec stream. Without smoothing, approximately 38% of the packets are lost. Using 30KByte buffer size, packet loss probability drops down to 21%. This improvement seems far greater than what we achieved in 6 frames/sec stream through smoothing: decrease of packet loss from 6% to 0.7%. Interestingly, however, we are not able to recognize any improvement on quality of stream in case of 10 frames/sec stream. With or without smoothing, the quality of the stream is far from what can be accepted with reasonable tolerance. We found that in 10 frames/sec stream, the number of corrupt frames, i.e. the frame one of whose constituents is lost, remains almost the same even with smoothing. Refer to the figures in Fig. 7. They illustrates the fraction of corruption frame with different smoothing buffer size, 10 KByte, 20 KByte, and 30 KByte, respectively. Frame is said to be corrupt if one or more of its packets are missing. With 4 to 6 frames/sec playback, less than 1 % of the frames are corrupt. However, in 10 frames/sec playback, more than 20% of the frames are corrupt even with the smoothing. This may suggest that human perception behavior is actually more vulnerable to the frame corruption than to the packet loss.

5   Conclusion

This work presents the result of our study on VBR smoothing in broadband wireless network. A number of elaborate smoothing techniques have been proposed in various public forums and literatures. Each of these techniques has different assumption and smoothing criteria. These algorithms successfully removed burstiness in the original empirical process. However, their works leave much to be desired to obtain practical implications of smoothing on the user perceivable QoS. There are two important points which need further attention in the area of traffic smoothing. The first one is the impact of smoothing on packet loss and jitter behavior. This work requires sophisticated modeling the

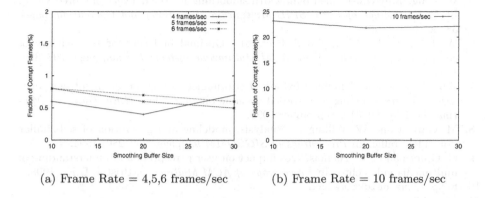

(a) Frame Rate = 4,5,6 frames/sec   (b) Frame Rate = 10 frames/sec

Fig. 7. Frame Corruption Behavior in %

actual system. The second one is the relationship between the packet loss and jitter and QoS perceived by the end user. Even though we discard the fact the human perception is by nature subjective, same packet loss and jitter can affect the QoS in many different ways depending on its distribution as well as the frame type of the respective packet. Thus, it is by no means trivial task to investigate the benefit of smoothing from the perspective of user perceivable QoS. In this work, we like to address both of these issues. We develop MPEG-4 streaming suite and embed the smoothing algorithm in the transport layer. We examine the packet loss behavior with respect to different frame rates and different smoothing buffer sizes. We also examine the quality of each scene with different frame rates and different smoothing buffer size. We use the rate variability as the metric for optimization. With smoothing, we were able to increase the acceptable quality frame rate by 50%(10% in bandwidth). Also, the experimental results suggest that human perception *may* be more vulnerable to frame corruption behavior than the packet loss behavior. Novelty of our work lies in the fact that our work present the benefit of smoothing in actual broadband wireless Internet environment. This study cannot be possible without rigorous system modeling and comprehensive system development and implementation.

References

1. R.T. Apteker, J.A. Kisimov, and H. Neishlos. Video acceptability and frame rate. *IEEE Multimedia*, 2(3):32–40, Fall 1995.
2. Jean-Yves Boudec and Olivier Verscheure. Optimal smoothing for guaranteed service. *IEEE/ACM Trans. on Networking*, 8(6):689–696, 2000.
3. Ray-I Chang. Dynamic window-based traffic-smoothing for optimal delivery of online vbr media streams. pages 127–134, 2000.
4. M Dinis and J. Fernandes. Provision of sufficient transmission capacity for broadband mobile multimedia: A step toward 4g. *IEEE Communications Magazine*, 39(8):46–54, Aug. 2001.

5. W. Feng. Rate-constrained bandwidth smoothing for the delivery of stored video. In *In Proceedings of IS&T/SPIE Multimedia Networking and Computing*, pages 58–66, Feb. 1997.

6. W. Feng, F. Jahanian, and S. Sechrest. Optimal buffering for the delivery of compressed prerecorded video. *ACM Multimedia Systems Journal*, pages 297–309, 1997.

7. Wu-Chi Feng and Jennifer Rexford. Performance evaluation of smoothing algorithms for transmitting prerecorded variable-bit-rate video. *IEEE Trans. on Multimedia*, 1(3):302–313, September 1999.

8. M. Garrett and W. Willinger. Analysis, modeling and generation of self-similar vbr video traffic. In *Proceedings of SIGCOMM 94*, pages 269–280, 1994.

9. G. Ghinea and J.P. Thomas. Qos impact on user perceptoin and understanding of multimedia video clips. In *Proceedings of ACM Multimedia*, Bristol, U.K., 1998.

10. http://www.quicktime.com.

11. http://www.reakosys.com.

12. M. Krunz and S. Tripathi. On the characterization of vbr mpeg streams. In *Proceedings of SIGMETRICS '97*, pages 192–202, 1997.

13. P. Manzoni, P Cremonesi, and G. Serazzi. Workload models of vbr video traffic and their use in resource allocation policies. *IEEE Trans. on Networking*, 7(3):387–397, June 1999.

14. J. M. McManus and K. W. Ross. Video on demand over atm: Constant-rate transmission and transport. *Telecommunication Systems*, 9, 1998.

15. A framework for the delivery of mpeg-4 over ip-based protocols. Technical Report draft-singer-mpeg4-ip-03, Audio-Video Transport WG, Internet Draft, July 2001.

16. K. Ryu and A. Elwalid. "the importance of long-range dependence of vbr video traffic in atm traffic engineering: Myths and realities". *ACM Computer Communication Review*, 26:3–14, October 1996.

17. J. Salehi, Z. Zhang, J. Kurose, and D. Towsley. Supporting Stored Video: Reducing Rate Variability and End-to-End Resource Requirements through Optimal Smoothing. In *Proceedings of ACM SIGMETRICS*, Philadelphia, PA, May 1996.

18. R. Steinmetz. Human perception of jitter and media synchronization. *IEEE J. Selected Areas in Communication*, 14:61–72, Jan. 1996.

19. Y. Matsui T. Nomura and H. Kimata. RTP Payload Format for MPEG-4 Audio/Visual Streams. In *ISO/IEC*, November 2000.

20. Youjip Won and Jongwoo Jeon Soohan Ahn. Performance analysis of nonstationary model for empirical vbr process. In *Proceedings of IEEE Globecom '01*, St. Antonion, TX, USA, Nov. 2001.

21. J. Zhang and J. Hui. Traffic characteristics and smoothness criteria in vbr video transmission. In *In Proceedings of IEEE Int. Conf. Multimedia Computing and Systems*, June 1997.

Compiling Rule-Based Agents for Distributed Databases

K.W. Ko[1], I.T. Kim[2], S.B. Yoo[1], K.C. Kim[2],
Y.S. Lee[3], S.D. Kim[2], and J.S. Kim[2]

[1] Dept. of Automation Engineering Inha University, Inchon, Korea
[2] Dept. of Computer Engineering Inha University, Inchon, Korea
[3] Dept. of Electrical and Electronic Engineering, Yonsei University, Korea

Abstract. A set of geologically distributed databases can be connected through the internet and served as a single database to the user. To connect them, we need a global manager that can interface the user and convey user's requests to the local databases, and an agent for each database that can translate the global manager's requests to the local database commands. The per-database agent not only processes the user's database requests, but also performs integrity checking on the requested database operations. Since integrity constraints are expressed as rules and maintained by the global manager too, an efficient way of integrity checking in the local agent is needed. Conventional technique is either introducing another agent in the local database that monitors the behavior of the request-processing agent and handles integrity checking when there is a need, or hard-coding the rules into the local agent. The former suffers a delay in request processing due to the communication overhead between the agent and the global manager, while the latter lacks flexibility on adapting to changing rules and programmability because it is typically very hard for a regular application programmer to understand and code properly the complex integrity rules. This paper proposes a compiler-based solution that does not cause a heavy communication overhead, and is flexible enough to accommodate changing rules, and shifts the burden of rule coding from individual programmers to the compiler. We explain the technique and show its effectiveness using examples from spatial distributed databases.

1   Introduction

Commercial database systems provide only limited supports for data integrity checking because of the high cost. However, integrity maintenance is very important in collaborative engineering environments such as GIS, CAD/CAM, or CIM because the behavior of the whole system is not predictable unless the integrity of the shared data properly is maintained. As the internet grows, these databases are connected to the internet, and there is a growing need to unite the geologically distributed databases and to present them as a single coherent database to the user. Integrity checking becomes a harder problem here because the same set of constraint rules should be applied to each local database, and the rules typically stored and maintained in a central place should be communicated efficiently to the local database systems.

H.Unger, T.Böhme, and A.Mikler (Eds.): IICS 2002, LNCS 2346, pp. 205-215, 2002.
© Springer-Verlag Berlin Heidelberg 2002

For this purpose, we need a global manager that can interface the user and convey user's requests to the local databases, and an agent for each database that can translate the global manager's requests to the local database commands. The per-database agent not only processes the user's database requests, but also performs integrity checking on the requested database operations.

Since integrity constraints are expressed as rules and maintained by a global manager, an efficient way of integrity checking in the local agent is needed. Conventional technique is either introducing another agent in the local database that monitors the behavior of the request-processing agent and handles integrity checking when there is a need, or hard-coding the rules into the local agent. The former suffers a delay in request processing due to the communication overhead between the agent and the global manager, while the latter lacks flexibility on adapting to changing rules and programmability because it is typically very hard for a regular application programmer to understand and code properly the complex integrity rules. This paper proposes a compiler-based solution that does not cause a heavy communication overhead, is flexible enough to accommodate changing rules, and shifts the burden of rule coding from individual programmers to the compiler. We propose to put the constraint-checking code back in the application programs automatically by a compiler and remove the intervention of the integrity constraint managing system during the run time. Since the application program accesses the database directly and checks the integrity constraints by itself without the intervention of the integrity constraint manager, it can run faster. And since the code for checking constraints is inserted by a compiler, the programmers do not have to worry about rule coding. When there is a change in rules, the global manager notifies the agents, and the agents rebuild themselves with the new rules. We show how this can be done and explain using examples taken from spatial databases.

The remainder of this paper is structured as follows. In Section 2, we survey related researches. In Section 3, we overview integrity rules for spatial objects for which our local agents should be compiled. In Section 4, we explain the proposed compilation algorithm, and in Section 5, we show a portion of YACC file that implements the proposed algorithm. Finally in Section 6, we give conclusions.

2   Related Work

Storing rules in the rule base and checking integrity constraints based on it is an approach studied by many researchers in universities and industry [2,5,7,9,10,15]. [5] describes the basic algorithm of this approach as follows.

Algorithm 1: Rule execution algorithm

Input   : data modification event
Output : result of the execution of the action part in the corresponding rule
Method :
    1. Find a corresponding rule (triggered rule) for the input event, and insert it into the triggered rule set.
    2. While the triggered rule set is not empty, repeat following.

2.1. Fetch a triggered rule, R, from the triggered rule set.
2.2. Compute the condition part of R.
2.3. If the condition is true, execute the action part of R.

Researches have been centered around three aspects of above algorithm: optimizing the computation of the condition part (step 2.2 above), defining rule languages (language for rules above), and efficient event monitoring (providing input events above). Studies on rule languages have been published in [1,3,8,9]. [9] describes a rule language with flexible execution modes for active databases. Their language expresses not only simple triggering events but also composite triggering events and supports nested transaction model. [8] extends their previous rule language, O++, to express integrity constraints and triggers. Triggers can be used to monitor complex triggering events and to call appropriate procedures. Efficient event monitoring techniques have been reported in [1,11]. [1] incorporates the monitoring system directly into the kernel of the database system to support a fast event detection. [11] uses Petri-net to detect events efficiently. The optimization techniques for rule conditions are published in [3,4,13,14]. [3] compiles the rules beforehand and links the resulting object codes with the triggering monitor. This improves the rule processing time considerably. However, each time a new rule is added or an existing rule is modified, the rule module has to be re-compiled and re-linked with the triggering monitor. [4,14] suggests techniques based on discrimination networks. A discrimination network accepts a database operation as an input and outputs corresponding rules. [13] suggests incremental evaluation methods. It observes that the same condition tends to repeat in several rules and saves the result of the computation of one condition to reuse it later.

Above systems have a similar structure as shown in Figure 1, where the integrity constraint manager is located between the database system and the application program. The manager intercepts all database operations from the application program, executes the corresponding rule codes, and passes them to the database system if the constraints are satisfied. To find the corresponding rules, it asks the integrity rule manger which is responsible for inserting, updating, and deleting rules in the rule base.

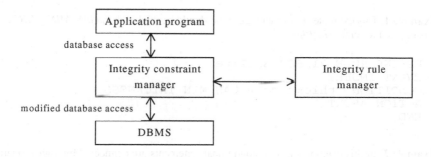

Fig. 1. A structure of general integrity constraint managing system

We propose to take the integrity constraint manager out from the path between the application program and the database system. The application program will be modified by the integrity constraint manager to contain necessary codes for checking proper constraints and be allowed to access directly the database system. Figure 2 shows our approach.

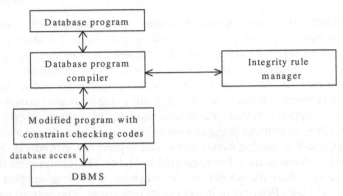

Fig. 2. Overview of the compiler-based integrity checking approach

3   Integrity Rules for Spatial Objects

Before explaining how to insert integrity rules into the local agents, we need to explain about spatial integrity rules and show how the global manager stores and maintains them. The compiler needs this information to communicate appropriately with the global manager. Integrity constraints for spatial objects specify rules that should be satisfied whenever spatial objects and their attributes are inserted, updated, or deleted. In principle, they are similar to those of ordinary databases. However, the coexistence of geometry, topology, attributes, and multiple layers in spatial databases makes the semantics more complicated. Below we show four examples of spatial integrity rules and explain how they are stored and mainted.

Example 1. This example states that a gas pipe should be thicker than *GAS_MIN_THICKNESS*. It is targeted for class *GasPipe*.

```
DEFINE RULE R1 FOR GasPipe
EVENT INSERT
CONDITION  thickness < GAS_MIN_THICKNESS
ACTION ABORT
END;
```

Example 2. In this example, several conditional statements are connected by logical operators. It states that if the type of a sewer pipe is *sending* or the material is *steel* while the diameter is less than 350 in both cases, then the diameter should be increased by 350.

```
DEFINE RULE R2 FOR SewerPipe
EVENT INSERT
```

```
CONDITION ((SewerPipe.type == sending) OR
          (SewerPipe.material == steel)) AND
          (SewerPipe.diameter < 350)
ACTION   SewerPipe.diameter = SewerPipe.diameter + 350
END;
```

Example 3. This example restricts the type and diameter of a new sewer pipe. If the type of pipe is *sending* but the diameter of the pipe is not less that 1800, we should cancel the insertion of this pipe.

```
DEFINE RULE R3 FOR SewerPipe
EVENT INSERT
CONDITION  SewerPipe.type == sending AND
          ( NOT(SewerPipe.diameter < 1800) )
ACTION   cancel()
END;
```

Example 4. This example states that whenever a *sending* type sewer pipe is updated, the material should be *steel*.

```
DEFINE RULE R4 FOR SewerPipe
EVENT UPDATE SewerPipe.material
CONDITION SewerPipe.type == sending AND
SewerPipe.material != steel
ACTION   SewerPipe.material = steel
END;
```

Integrity rules are stored and managed in a rule base. When a user database program is compiled, the rule base is consulted for any related rules with the events defined in the program. Upon receiving an event type, the rule base manager searches for all the candidate rules to be triggered by the event. These candidate rules are sent to the compiler and inserted into the local agent. Once the rules are inserted, checking the conditions and validating integrity are executed during run time.

4   Inserting Integrity Rules into Local Agents

Integrity constraints have to be checked whenever a persistent object[1] is inserted, updated, or deleted. Compiler should be able to say which objects are persistent and what kind of events had happened to them. It maintains three lists to remember them. "pclist" (persistent class list) is used to remember persistent classes. Whenever a persistent class is declared, the compiler puts it in this list. "polist" (persistent object list) remembers persistent objects. Whenever a persistent object is declared, its name, class, and reference type is inserted into this list. "celist" (class-event list) remembers events. Whenever a persistent object is created, updated, or deleted, it is reported in

---

[1] We are considering object-oriented database systems as the target systems. However, the same techniques can be applied to relational database systems.

this list. For each event, the related class name, event type, and rule codes to be checked are inserted into this list. The compiler asks the rule manager of corresponding rules for this event.

The best place to insert the rule code (or constraint-checking code) will be where the event happened. However, inserting rule codes right after each event point is not practical. Creation or deletion of an object is not difficult to detect, but updating of an object usually takes several instructions which may be spread over the code. Some fields might be modified several times and only the last modifications will be effective. It will be too costly if compiler follows all these modifications until it decides an update is completed. We give up detecting the exact completion points of events, and we make a conservative assumption that all events are completed right before the "commit()" statement. Therefore, the compiler inserts rule codes for each event happened during the program right before the "commit()" statement. This means the compiler should remember all events in terms of the involved object's identification (object id), class name, event type, and the corresponding rule code.

However, the information on the object itself can be obtained only during the run time. The compiler can only know which event happened to which class and what rule code should be applied to this event. The remembering of the objects themselves should be done by the application program during the run time. To make this happen, the compiler inserts codes into the program so that whenever an event happens the affected object be pushed into a stack. "molist" (modified object list) is used for this purpose. When an event happens, the compiler inserts codes into the application program so that the program by itself save the object id, class name, and the event type in its local data structure, called "molist". Also, the application program should pop objects from this "molist" right before the "commit()" statement and execute corresponding rule codes. To make this happen, the compiler also inserts appropriate codes into the application program.

We show below an algorithm that the compiler executes.

Algorithm 2   : Rule code insertion

Input   : An database program
Output   : The same program with rule codes inserted
Method :
   The compiler executes following during the parsing.
   1. Whenever a persistent class is declared, its name is inserted into "pclist".
   2. Whenever a persistent object is declared, its name is inserted into "polist".
   3. Whenever an event (creation, update, or deletion) happens to a persistent object, the class name, the event type, and the corresponding rule code are inserted into "celist". At the same time, the application program is modified such that it saves the related object id, class name, and event type into its local data structure, "molist".
   4. When the "commit()" statement is detected, the application program is also modified such that it pops each object in "molist" and executes the corresponding rule code.

Below we show the main data structures used in the above algorithm.

```
list <pc>  pclist;
struct  pc {
        char *name;
 };
list<po>  polist;
struct  po{
        char  * oname;    // object name
        char    vtype;    // object reference type.V_HANDLE
                          // or V_ITERATOR
        char  * cname;    // class name this object
                          // belongs to
}
list<ce>  celist;
struct  ce{
        char  * cname;    // class name
        char    event;    // event type. E_CREATE,
                          // E_DELETE, E_UPDATE
        char  * rule;     // rule code for (cname, event)
}
list<mo>  molist;
struct  mo{
        T_OID    oid;     // object id
        char   * cname;
        char     event;
        char     vtype;
}
```

The following is a program written in Objectivity/C++[16]. We will apply Algorithm 2 to this program. Line numbers are attached for explanation purpose.

```
1   class  Pipe: public  ooObj{
2       public:  int  thickness;
3       ......................
4   }
    ......................
5   main(){
6       ooHandle(ooDBObj)  DBh;
7       ooHandle(Pipe)  Ph;
8       ooItr(Pipe)      Pi;
9       ooTrans          trans;
10      ooInit();
11      trans.start();
        ......................
12      Ph = new(DBh) Pipe;
13      Ph->thickness = 40;
        ......................
14      Pi.scan(DBh, oocUpdate);
15      while (Pi.next()){
16          ......................
17      }
18      trans.commit();
19  }
```

Line 1: In Objectivity/C++, a persistent class is declared as a sub-class of ooObj class. Therefore, "Pipe" is inserted into "pclist" (see Fiure 3 (a)).

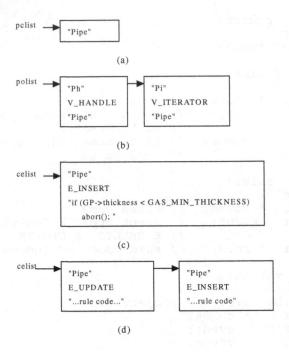

Fig. 3. Data structures for inserting integrity checking code

Line 7,8: In Objectivity/C++, a persistent object is declared through ooHandle, ooRef, or ooItr class. We insert persistent objects into "polist:" (see Figure 3 (b)).

Line 12: A persistent object is created. This event is reported in "celist". The third inserted value is a string that shows the corresponding rule code (see Figure 3 (c)).

Also, after line 12 in the program, the compiler adds two lines to insert the object id, class name, and event type into "molist". The declarations of "molist", "mo", and "build_mo" will be provided through linking with compiler-generated files.

```
12   Ph = new(DBh) Pipe;
mo = build_mo(Ph, "Pipe", E_INSERT, V_HANDLE);
molist.insert(mo);
```

Line 14,15: Updating on a persistent object is detected. This event is inserted into "celist" (see Figure 3 (d)).

Also, the application program is modified to insert this event into "molist".

```
15   while (Pi.next()){
        mo = build_mo(Pi, "Pipe", E_UPDATE, V_ITERATOR);
        molist.insert(mo);
16      . . . . . . . . . . . . . . . . . .
```

Line 18: "commit()" statement is detected. The application program is modified such that each object in the "molist" be popped, and the corresponding rule code be executed. Currently, only two events are reported in "celist" (therefore, two kinds of rule codes), and the compiler let the program select one of these rule codes by examining the class name and event type. After this checking, the original "commit()" statement will be executed.

```
while  (!molist.empty()){
  mo = molist.pop();
  if ( (strcmp(mo->cname, "Pipe")==0) &&
       (mo->event==E_INSERT)){
    if  (mo->oid->thickness < MIN_GAS_THICKNESS)
        abort();
  }
  else if ((strcmp(mo_cname, "Pipe")==0) &&
          (mo->event==E_UPDATE)){
        .......... rule cods for this event .........
  }
}
18  trans.commit();
```

The added code is shown in thick letters above. To show the exact location of adding, the line numbers before or after the added code is also shown.

5   Implementation

Algorithm 2 in the previous section has been implemented by modifying GCC YACC file. Below we explain the construction process for "celist" as an example, which corresponds to the step 3 in the algorithm. The YACC file is tuned for Objectivity/C++, which is one of popular object-oriented database programming languages. In Objectivity/C++, *new()* creates a persistent object, *open(..., oocUpdate, ...), lookupobj(..., oocUpdate, ...)*, and *scan(..., oocUpdate, ...)* modifies it, and *delete_object()* removes it. Therefore the YACC file starts to build "celist" and "molist" when it finds these functions are called for a persistent object.

```
1 expr_no_commas:
2             ..............
3             {found_persistent_oname=found_new=false;}
4             expr_no_commas  '='  expr_no_commas
5             { if (found_persistent_oname && found_new){
6                 cname=find_cname(oname);
7                 vtype = find_vtype(oname);
8             ..........................................
9                 ce = build_ce(cname, E_CREATE);
10                celist.insert(ce);
11                emit_mo_line(lineno, oname, cname,
                  event, vtype);}
12            ......................}
```

Line 1-4 above captures statements such as "Ph = new(dbH) Pipe;" which creates a persistent object. The compiler should have known that "Pipe" is a persistent object from its declaration. In Line 4, when the first "expr_no_commas" is parsed, if it represents a handle (that is, a variable) for a persistent object, we will have the name of the handle in "oname" and "found_persistent_oname" a true value. For the second "expr_no_commas", if it represents a creation of a persistent object, we will have "found_new" a true value, too. Therefore, if both conditions are met, we enter the "if" statement in Line 5. In Line 6 and 7, "find_cname" returns the class name of the object, while "vtype" returns the type of it as explained in the previous section. In Line 9, the compiler builds a "ce" structure for this creation event and inserts it into "celist". Now having finished building its own internal data structures, the compiler inserts appropriate code into the user's program in Line 11 so that the user's code, when run, can build "molist" by itself.

6   Conclusion

Needs for maintaining integrity of shared data have been increased recently as multiple tools work more cooperatively in networked environments. However the overhead involved in runtime monitoring all the changes of database states is too expensive to support general features of integrity maintenance in commercial DBMS products. In this paper, we present a compiler-based approach, in which codes for validating integrity rules are inserted into spatial database programs. This approach eliminates the overhead involved in runtime monitoring of database transactions. According to the type of operations in database programs, candidate rules are searched from the rule base and inserted into the programs. In order to facilitate the searches in the rule base, the rules are stored in a directed acyclic graph and indexed properly.

A prototype implemented on an object-oriented DBMS (i.e., Objectivity/DB) and outline of the implementation is introduced in this paper. There remain several respects that need improvements in further research. Firstly, evaluation of the conditions in rules should be more optimized by classifying the range of related objects. A rule is said local if it concerns only single object instance. Otherwise, it is global. Usually evaluation of global rules is more expensive than that of local rules and there are many rooms that can be optimized in evaluation of global rules. The other thing is that the compilation procedure is system dependent because different DBMS systems provide different DMLs. In order to be a more general solution, it needs to be implemented on standard interface languages such as ODMG [17].

Acknowledgements

The work reported in this paper has been supported by the National Research Laboratory Program of the Korea Institute of S&T Evaluation and Planning Under Grant 2000-N-NL-01-C-246.

References

1. C. Collet, T. Coupaye, and T.Svensen, "NAOS-efficient and modular reactive capabilities in an object-oriented database system," Proceedings of the Twentieth International Conference on Very Large Data Bases, pp132-143, Santiago, Chile, September 1994.
2. E.N.Hanson, "Rule condition testing and action execution in Ariel," Proceedings of the ACM SIGMOD International Conference on Management of Data, pp 49-58, San Diego, California, June 1992.
3. E.Simon, J.Kiernan, and C. de Maindreville, "Implementing high level active rules on top of a relational DBMS," Proceedings of the Eighteenth International Conference on Very Large Data Bases, pp 315-326, Vancouver, British Columbia, August 1992.
4. F. Fabret, M.Regnier, and E.Simon, "An adaptive algorithm for incremental evaluation of production rules in databases," Proceedings of the Nineteenth International Conference on Very Large Data Bases, pp 455-467, Dublin, Ireland, August 1993.
5. L.M.Haas, W.Chang, G.M.Lohman, J.McPherson, P.F.Wilms, G.Lapis, B.Lindsay, H.Pirahesh, M.Carey, and E.Shekita, "Starburst mid-flight: As the dust clears," IEEE Transactions on Knowledge and Data Engineering, 2(1):143-160, March 1990.
6. M.Stonebraker, "The integration of rule systems and database systems," IEEE Transactions on Knowledge and Data Engineering, 4(5):415-423, October 1992.
7. M.Stonebraker, E.N. Hanson, and S.Potamianos, "The POSTGRES rule manager", IEEE Transactions on Software Engineering, 14(7):897-907, July 1988.
8. R.Agrawal and N.Gehani, "Ode(Object database and environment): The language and the data model," Proceedings of the ACM SIGMOD International Conference on Management of Data, pp36-45, Portland, Oregon, May 1989.
9. S.Chakravarthy, B. Blaustein, A.P. Buchmann, M.carey, U.Dayal, D.Goldhirsch, M.Hsu, R.Jauhari, R.Ladin, M.Livny, D.McCarthy, R.McKee, and A.Rosenthal, "HiPAC: A research project in active, time-constrained database management," Technical Report XAIT-89-02, Xerox Advanced Information Technology, Cambridge, Massachusetts, July 1989.
10. S.Chakravarthy, V.Krishnaprasad, E.Anwar, and S.K.Kim, "Composite events for active databases: Semantics, contexts, and detection," Proceedings of the Twentieth International Conference on Very Large Data Bases, pp 606-617, Santiago, Chile, September 1994.
11. S.Gatziu and K.R. Dittrich, "SAMOS:An active object-oriented database system," IEEE Data Engineering Bulletin," Special Issue on Active Databases, 15(4):23-26, December 1992.
12. S.Gatziu and K.R. Dittrich, "Detecting composite events in active database systems using petir nets," Proceedings of the Fourth International Workshop on Research Issues in Data Engineering, pp 2-9, Houston, Texas, February 1994.
13. X.Qian and G.Wiederhold, "Incremental recomputation of active relational expression," IEEE Transactions on Knowledge and Data Engineering, 3(3):337-341, September 1991.
14. Y.W.Wang and E.N.Hanson, "A performance comparison of the Rete and TREAT algorithms for testing database rule conditions," Proceedings of the Eighth International Conference on Data Engineering, pp 88-97, Tempe, Arizona, February 1992.
15. S. Chakravarthy and K. Ono, "ECA Rule Support for Distributed Heterogeneous Environments," Proceedings of the Fourteenth International Conference on Data Engineering, pp 601, Orlando, Florida, February 1998.
16. Objectivity, Inc., Using Objectivity/C++, Version 4, 1996.
17. R. Cattell and D. Barry ed., The Object Database Standard: ODMG 2.0, Morgan Kaufmann Publishers, Inc., 1997.

A Formal Framework for E-Barter Based on Microeconomic Theory and Process Algebras[*]

Natalia López, Manuel Núñez, Ismael Rodríguez, and Fernando Rubio

Dept. Sistemas Informáticos y Programación
Universidad Complutense de Madrid, E-28040 Madrid. Spain
{natalia,mn,ir,fernando}@sip.ucm.es

Abstract. In this paper we presen t a formal framework for the definition of *e-barter* architectures. By e-barter we mean the possibilit y of (electronically) exc hanging goods without reducing transactions to money. Actually, in our setting, money can be considered just as another *good*, so that e-barter generalizes seller/buyer architectures. An advan tage of e-barter systems, in contrast with most current systems, is that multilateral exc hanges can be performed. Customers are first grouped into *local* markets, according mainly to their localities. Next, a higher order construction allows to compose markets, so that a *global market* takes a tree-lik e shape.

In order to methodically build our systems, w e consider a process algebraic notation. This allo ws us to specify all the stages of a system (from customers to markets, markets of markets, etc). We introduce an operational semantics for our language so that exchanges of goods are formally defined. Besides, we use some concepts borrow ed from microeconomic theory. Specifically, we consider utility functions (i.e. functions returning the valuation that customers/markets give to goods), exchange of goods, and equilibria.

We will show that the integration of microeconomic theory and process algebras provides t wo important *gains*. Firstly, it allows to avoid ambiguity in the understanding of the behavior of systems. Secondly, it gives a scheme to appropriately structure, in a bottom-up way, e-barter systems.

1 Introduction

Due to the wide implantation of internet, there has been a great proliferation of systems devoted to the (electronic) commerce of goods. How ev er, most of these systems have very little (or not at all) theoretical foundations. During the last y ears there has been a great effort for setting the basis of e-commerce systems on more solid grounds, in particular, some prototypes (e.g. Kasbah [5]) hav e been developed in academic environments. In order to build these systems, it is important to make a clear structure of the different stages leading to the construction of an electronic marketplace (see e.g. [1]). Moreov er, electronic entities replacing real buyers and sellers can be expressed in terms of (intelligent) agents

---

[*] Researc h supported in part ly the CICYT project TIC2000-0701-C02-01.

H. Unger, T. Böhme, and A. Mikler (Eds.): I²CS 2002, LNCS 2346, pp. 217–228, 2002.
© Springer-V erlag Berlin Heidelberg 2002

([9] presents a survey on the topic). Even though a generalized incorporation of intelligen t agents should produce a big step, current e-commerce systems make a very limited use of them, being their tasks mainly restricted to be so-called *shopping assistants*. That is, their main role consists in helping the client to find the *best de al*once the user has decided which item he wan ts to buy/sell. In some cases, they are also able to guide the user in the search for the corresponding good. So, it is hard to consider that these agents are *representing* the user in a *virtual* market. Ideally ,users should indicate agents about their *preferences*. Then, agents should interact with other agents in order to get the goods that their users desire. Moreov er, they should be real representatives of the users. In particular, they should be able to bargain for a good deal. In order to add these characteristics into agents, a formal framework is needed. Fortunately, *microeco-nomic theory* provides this theoretical basis. In particular, it allows to formally specify markets where customers own their products and they are willing to exchange them according to some preferences. Following this line, several proposals include, into the definition of electronic markets, either a notion of *utility*[1] or a notion of resources allocation (e.g. [13 ,23,8 ,6]). Such notions are very relevant if we want to provide our agents with some *negotiation* capacity [14,10].

In this paper we propose that microeconomic concepts are very profitable for the description of some kind of electronic markets. We will mainly borrow three concepts: Utilit y function, exc hange of resources, and equilibrium.[2] A *utility function* is simply a function $u : \mathbb{R}^n_+ \to \mathbb{R}_+$ assigning a real value to any basket of resources (assuming that there are n different kinds of resources, baskets are represented as tuples belonging to $\mathbb{R}^n_+$). The higher the value returned by u is, the most preferred the basket is. A set of agents will be willing to *exchange* resources if none of them decreases its utility and at least one of them improv es. Besides, we have reached an *equilibrium* (also called *Pareto optimum*) if no exchange is possible. That is, it is not possible to improv e the situation of one agent without deteriorating another one. We apply these concepts to our notion of *e-barter*. In contrast to the usual understanding of e-commerce, e-barter does not necessarily reduces all the transactions to *money*. An exchange is made if both parts are *happy* with their new items. In particular, e-barter allows a richer structure of exc hanges. Suppose a very simple circular situation where for each $1 \leq i \leq n$ w ehav e that agent A_i owns the good a_i and desires the good $a_{(i \bmod n)+1}$. In our environment, this multi-agent transaction can be easily performed. On the contrary , it w ould not be so easy to perform it if these items must be first *converted* in to money. Let us remark that money[3] can be considered just as another possible resource: A may be willing to change its good a by (m units of the good) money.

---

[1] It can be shown that any preference relation preserved under limits can be expressed as a continuous utility function.

[2] An easy introduction to microeconomic theory, covering the concepts appearing in this paper, can be found in [11].

[3] Let us remark that this is not the usual treatment of money in general equilibrium theory. It is not considered as a resource and it is simply used to set *relative* prices.

In order to create a *global market*, customers will be associated with *local markets*. These local markets will be also grouped into markets and so on. This structure will generate a *tree* of markets. Once the global market is created, the behavior will be as follows. Customers (more exactly, their corresponding agents) will be located at the leaves of the tree. They will exchange items within their local market until no more exchanges are possible. When such a situation is reached, their local market will try to negotiate within the next level market. That is, there will be a second order market making transactions in the name of their representatives. Again, exchanges will be made until no more exchanges are possible. Then, transactions will be performed at a third order market and so on until the root of the tree is reached. By doing so, we get that exchanges are made between agents that are as close as possible between them.

We have decided to use a formal tool to define our markets structure. They will be specified by using a process algebraic notation (see [4] for a good overview on the subject). Our language is inspired in PAMR [12]. This formalism was specially developed to deal with the specification and analysis of concurrent and distributed systems where resources play a fundamental role. Unfortunately, PAMR does not provide a *higher order* constructor as the one needed in e-barter systems, so we need to extend the language. That is, an easy modification of pure PAMR would allow us to define local markets, but there is no mechanism to combine markets. This fact complicates the formal definition of the language presented in this paper. Nevertheless, the addition of these features adds enough expressive power. Thus, our markets can be easily specified. In addition to a syntax, we define an operational semantics for our language. By doing so, every stage of the creation of an e-barter system may be formally specified, avoiding ambiguities and providing a clear structure of the system. Moreover, a designer of e-barter systems does not need to go through all the semantic machinery. It is enough to understand how the syntax of our language works.

The rest of the paper is structured as follows. In Section 2 we introduce some auxiliary notation. Section 3 gives an informal description of the behavior of e-barter systems. In Section 4 we present a formalization of all the concepts appearing in Section 3. Finally, in Section 5 we present our conclusions and some lines for future work.

2   Preliminaries

In this section we introduce some concepts that we will use during the rest of this paper. Specifically, we present the notions of utility function and we explain how our operational rules work. First we present some mathematical notation.

Definition 1. We consider $\mathrm{I\!R} = \{x \in \mathrm{I\!R} \,|\, x \geq 0\}$. We will usually denote *vectors* in $\mathrm{I\!R}^n$ (for $n \geq 2$) by $\bar{x}, \bar{y}, \ldots$. Given $\bar{x} \in \mathrm{I\!R}^n$, x_i denotes its *i-th* component. We extend to vectors some usual arithmetic operations. Let $\bar{x}, \bar{y} \in \mathrm{I\!R}^m$. We define $\bar{x} + \bar{y} = (x_1 + y_1, \ldots, x_n + y_n)$, and $\bar{x} \leq \bar{y}$, if for any $1 \leq i \leq n$ we have $x_i \leq y_i$.

We will usually denote *matrices* in $A^{n \times m}$ (for $n, m \geq 2$, and a set A) by calligraphic letters $\mathcal{E}, \mathcal{E}_1 \ldots$.   □

The relevant characteristics of the customers of an e-barter system will be their *baskets of resour ces*(indicating the items that they own) and their *utility functions* (indicating preference among different baskets of resources).

Definition 2. Let us suppose that there are $m > 0$ different kinds of resources. *Baskets of resour es* are defined as v ectors $\bar{x} \in \mathbb{R}_+^m$. A *utility function* is any function $u : \mathbb{R}_+^m \longrightarrow \mathbb{R}$. □

In microeconomic theory, there are some restrictions that are usually imposed on utility functions (mainly strict monotonicity, conv exit y and continuity). In-tuitively, giv en a utilit y function u, w e have that $u(\bar{x}) < u(\bar{y})$ means that the basket $\bar{y}$ is preferred to $\bar{x}$.

Finally, our operational rules will be defined as usual deduction rules. A rule

$$\frac{\text{Premise}_1 \wedge \text{Premise}_2 \wedge \ldots \wedge \text{Premise}_n}{\text{Conclusion}}$$

indicates that if all of the premises hold, then w e can deduce the conclusion. Premises indicate individual behavior of components of a system, while conclu-sions indicate how the system behav es according to individual performances.

3   An Informal Presentation of E-Barter Systems

In this section we present how e-barter systems are organized (in the next sec-tion w e show how they can be constructed b y using our methodology). First, customers are *represente d* by (electronic) agents.[4] Agents are provided with tw o data: The *basket of resour es* that the customer is willing to exc hange and a *utility function*. The utility function relates the preference that a customer has for the o wned items with respect to the corresponding preference for desired items. Let us remark that, in most cases, utility functions will take a very simple form. For example, indicating that a customer C is willing to exchange the item a b y the items b and c. Nevertheless, there exists several proposals showing how agents can be trained on the user preferences (see e.g. [14,6]). Finally, let us remark that a customer has always the possibility of changing both his utilit y function and his basket of resources. Once the agent is notified of these changes, it will change its negotiation strategy. Besides, once an agent has reached a (pos-sibly multilateral) deal, it must be notified to the customer. If all the customers give their approv al, the deal will be effectively performed.

F rom now on we concentrate on the behavior of the different electronic enti-ties. The behavior of an e-barter system works according to the following algo-rithm:

1. Each agent generates the barters that its customer would be willing to per-form (according to the corresponding basket of resources and utility func-tions).

---

[4] In terms of [15], our agents present as information attitude belief (vs. knowledge), while as pro-attitudes, commitment and c hoice (vs. intention and obligation).

2. Agents exchange goods inside their local market. A multilateral exchange will be made if (at least) one of the involved agents improves its utility and none of them decreases its utility. This is repeated until no more exchanges are possible. In this case, we say that the local market is *saturated* In microeconomic terms, this situation is usually called equilibrium.
3. Once a market is saturated, their agents are combined to create a new agent. The new agent will have as basket of resources the addition of the corresponding to each agent. Its utility function will encode the utilities of the combined agents. Let us remark that this new agent behaves as a representative of the combined agents. *First order* agents will be combined again into markets, according to *proximity* reasons.
4. Higher order agents trade between them until their market is saturated.
5. Once a (higher order) market is saturated, the agents start to allocate the resources in a top-down way through the tree of markets until the resources arrive to the leaves of the tree (i.e. the *original* agents). Then, they create a new agent (as indicated in step 3).
6. Once their markets are saturated, new markets are created by combining agents until there exists a unique market. Once this market is saturated, and the resources are conveniently allocated, the whole tree of agents is removed, and we start again at the first step.

The previous algorithm ensures some good properties:

- Exchanges are made between agents located as near as possible. That is, we try to minimize possible shipping costs.
- Partial equilibria are reached in each market. That is, once a market is saturated we may assure that one (of the possible) Pareto optimum distribution of resources has been found. In other words, agents belonging to a saturated market cannot improve their utility within that market without decreasing the corresponding to another agent.
- Once the last (unique) market is saturated we may assure that one (of the possible) global equilibrium has been reached. That is, no more exchanges can be performed (according to the current utility functions and available resources).

Finally, let us comment on the advantages of using partial equilibria versus global equilibria. If we would pretend to reach a global equilibrium, we should perform exchanges until no more exchanges are possible. Once all this (possibly) enormous amount of exchanges has been performed, the resources can be sent to their new owners. This would strongly delay some *trivial* transactions between not very distant agents (and their corresponding customers).

4   Formalizing Agents and Markets

In this section we provide a formal syntax and semantics for the definition of e-barter systems. Even though we use a process algebraic notation (mainly when defining the operational rules) we do not need most of the usual operators for this kind of languages (choice, restriction, etc). In fact, our constructions remind a parallel operator (although we use a different syntax).

Definition 3. A *market system* is giv en b y the follwing EBNF:

$$MS ::= ms(M)$$
$$M \;\; ::= A \mid \mathtt{unsat}(M, \ldots, M) \mid \sigma(M)$$
$$A \;\;\; ::= (S, u, \bar{x})$$
$$S \;\;\; ::= [\,] \mid [A, \ldots, A]$$

$\square$

First, we annotate market systems with the non-terminal symbol ms to av oid ambiguity of the grammar. Intuitiv ely $M = (S, u, \bar{x})$ (that is, $M = A$) represents a saturated market. There are tw o possible situations. Either S is an empty list or not. In the first case, we have that M represents an *original* agent, that is, a direct representative of a customer (note that a single agent is trivially saturated). In the second case, if $S = [A_1, \ldots, A_n]$ we have that M represents an agent associated with the (possible higher order) agents $A_1, \ldots, A_n$ belonging to a saturated market. In both cases, $\bar{x}$ represents the total amount of resources that M is responsible for, while u is its utility function. $M = \mathtt{unsat}(M_1, \ldots, M_n)$ represents an *unsaturated* market consisting of the markets $M_1, \ldots, M_n$. Let us remark that in this case, some of the submarkets may be saturated and some of them unsaturated. Once all the markets of the system are saturated, the whole system is turned again into unsaturated. The term $\sigma(M)$ will represent that such operation must be performed on M. Before we introduce the operational semantics, we present an example showing how an e-barter system may be constructed. In this example we will also (informally) introduce operational transitions.

Example 1. Let us consider a total of six agents $A_i = ([\,], \overline{x_i}, u_i)$, for $1 \leq i \leq 6$. We suppose that these agents are grouped into three different markets (see Figure 1). Initially , these markts are unsaturated (unsaturated markets are represen ted b y a single square in the figure), so w make the following definitions:

$$M_1 = \mathtt{unsat}(A_1, A_2) \qquad M_2 = \mathtt{unsat}(A_3, A_4) \qquad M_3 = \mathtt{unsat}(A_5, A_6)$$

Suppose that the first tw o markets are linked, and the resulting market is also link ed with the remaining M_3. We should add the following definitions:

$$M_4 = \mathtt{unsat}(M_1, M_2) \qquad M_5 = \mathtt{unsat}(M_4, M_3)$$

Finally, the global market is defined as $M = ms(M_5)$.

Following the philosophy explained in the previous section, transactions will be made within a market only betw een saturated submarkets (saturated markets are represented b y doble squares in the figure). So, only M_1, M_2, and M_3 are allow ed to perform transactions (note that original agets are trivially saturated).

We will denote exc hange of resources b y $\leadsto$. Suppose that after some exchanges, M_1 becomes saturated. That is, there exists a sequence of exchanges

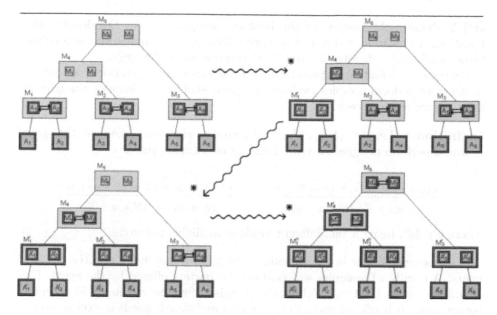

Fig. 1. Example of the evolution of a market system

$M_1 \rightsquigarrow M_1^1 \rightsquigarrow M_1^2 \cdots \rightsquigarrow M_1^n = M_1'$ such that $M_1' \nrightarrow$. In this case, the market grouping the first two agents should be labeled as saturated. So, the agents effectively perform all the achieved transactions becoming A_1' and A_2'. Note that agents will (possibly) change their initial distributions, but the total amount of resources belonging to the local market remains constant. Then, the first market will be turned into $([A_1', A_2'], f(u_1, u_2), \overline{x_1} + \overline{x_2})$, where f is a function combining utility functions (such a function will be formally defined). In parallel, M_2 will have a similar behavior.

Once both M_1 and M_2 are saturated, the transactions between them will be allowed. Note that these transactions (inside the market M_4) will be performed according to the new utility functions, $f(u_1, u_2)$ and $f(u_3, u_4)$ respectively, and to the new baskets of resources, $\overline{x_1} + \overline{x_2}$ and $\overline{x_3} + \overline{x_4}$ respectively.

The process will iterate after M_5 gets saturated. Finally, we will have a market as $\sigma(M_5')$. Then, the global market is structurally *reset*.   □

In order to simplify forthcoming operational rules we introduce the following notation to deal with utility functions. Utility functions associated with original agents (that is, $A = ([\ ], u, \overline{x})$) will behave as explained in Definition 2, that is $u(\overline{z})$ indicates the relative preference shown by A towards the basket of resources $\overline{z}$. Nevertheless, if $A = ([A_1, \ldots, A_n], u, \overline{x})$ then we will consider that in addition to its usual meaning, the utility function also keeps track of how a basket of resources is distributed among the (possible higher order) agents $A_1, \ldots, A_n$. That is, $u(\overline{z}) = (r, \overline{z_1}, \ldots, \overline{z_n})$, where r still represents the utility, while $\sum \overline{z_i} = \overline{z}$

and $\bar{z_i}$ denotes the portion of the bask et $\bar{z}$ assigned to A_i. Overloading the notation, if we simply write $u(\bar{z})$ w e are referring to the first componert of the tuple, while $u(\bar{z}).i$ denotes the $(i+1)$-*th* component of the tuple.

In the next definition we present the *anchor case* of our operational semantics. In order to perform complex exchanges, agents should first indicate the barters they are willing to accept.

Definition 4. Let $A = (S, u, \bar{x})$ be a saturated market. The *exchanges* the agent A would perform are given b y the follewing operational rules:

$$\frac{u(\bar{x}+\bar{y}) \geq u(\bar{x}) \ \wedge \ (\bar{x}+\bar{y}) \geq \bar{0}}{(S,u,\bar{x}) \xrightarrow{\bar{y}} (S,u,\bar{x}+\bar{y})} \qquad \frac{u(\bar{x}+\bar{y}) > u(\bar{x}) \ \wedge \ (\bar{x}+\bar{y}) \geq \bar{0}}{(S,u,\bar{x}) \xmapsto{\bar{y}} (S,u,\bar{x}+\bar{y})}$$

where $\bar{y} \in \mathbb{R}^n$, being n the different kinds of av ailable resources.   □

Let us remark that in the previous definition, $\bar{y}$ may hav e negative components. A ctually , thesetuples will contain the barters offered by the agent. For example, if $\bar{y} = (1, -1, 0, 1)$ fulfills the premise, then the agent would accept a barter where it is offered one unit of the first and fourth goods in exchange of a unit of the second good. Regarding the rules, the first premise simply indicates that the agent would not decrease (resp. would increase) its utility. The second premise indicates that the agent does not run into *red numbers*, that is, an agent cannot offer a quantity of an item if it does not own enough. For example, if we consider the previous situation, we would hav e a transition as $A \xrightarrow{\bar{y}} A'$. More-o ver, if we consider $\bar{y} = (1, -1, 0, 2)$ then we would have both[5] the transitions as $A \xrightarrow{\bar{y}} A'$ and $A \xmapsto{\bar{y}} A'$. Let us note that $\longrightarrow$ denotes that the market does not w orsen, mearwhile transition $\longmapsto$ denotes that the market does improve. Next we sho w how these proposals are combined.

Definition 5. Let $M = \texttt{unsat}(M_1, \ldots, M_n)$. Let $I = \{s_1, \ldots, s_r\} \subseteq \{1, \ldots, n\}$ be a set of indexes denoting the saturated markets belonging to M (that is, for any $i \in I$ we have $M_i = (S_i, u_i, \overline{x_i})$). We say that the matrix $\mathcal{E} \in (\mathbb{R}_+^m)^{n \times n}$ is a *valid exchange matrix for* M, denoted by $\texttt{valid}(M, \mathcal{E})$, if for any $1 \leq i \leq n$ we have $\sum_j \mathcal{E}_{ij} \leq \overline{x_i}$, $\mathcal{E}_{ii} = \bar{0}$, and $\forall 1 \leq k \leq n$ such that $k \notin I$, $\mathcal{E}_{ki} = \bar{0}$ and $\mathcal{E}_{ik} = \bar{0}$.   □

First, let us remark that the notion of *valid* matrix is considered only in the context of unsaturated markets: If a market is saturated then no more exchanges can be performed. Second, only saturated markets belonging to an unsaturated market may perform exchanges among them. This restriction is imposed in order to give priority to transactions performed by *closer* agents belonging to unsaturated submarkets. Regarding the definition of *valid* matrix, let us note that

---

[5] We are assuming that all the items are *goods* Nevertheless, agents could also trade *bads*. For example, a customer would be willing to giv e an apple pie if he *receives* minus s bro wn leaves in his garden. Ho w everbads are usually not considered in microeconomic theory, as they can be easily turned into goods: Instead of considering the amount of leaves, one may consider the absence of them.

matrixes $\mathcal{E}$ have as components baskets of resources (that is, elements belonging to $\mathbb{R}_+^m$). $\mathcal{E}_{ij}$ represents the basket of resources that the market M_i would give to M_j. So, the condition $\sum_j \mathcal{E}_{ij} \leq \overline{x_i}$ indicates that the total amount of resources given by market M_i must be less than or equal to the basket of resources owned by that market. Finally, let us comment that an exchange does not need to include all of the saturated markets. For example, if we have an exchange where only r' markets participate, then the rows and columns corresponding to the remaining $r - r'$ saturated markets will be filled with $\bar{0}$, as they are for the unsaturated markets.

Next we introduce the rules defining the exchange of resources. Intuitively, if we have a valid exchange matrix, where (at least) one of the involved agents improves and no one worsens, then the corresponding exchange will be performed.

Definition 6. Let $M = \mathtt{unsat}(M_1, \ldots, M_n)$. Let $I = \{s_1, \ldots, s_r\} \subseteq \{1, \ldots, n\}$ be a set of indexes denoting the saturated markets belonging to M (that is, for any $i \in I$ we have $M_i = (S_i, u_i, \overline{x_i})$). The operational transitions denoting exchange of resources that M may perform are given by the rule:

$$\frac{\exists\, k \in I : M_k \xmapsto{\overline{y_k}} M_k' \wedge \forall\, i \in I, M_i \xrightarrow{\overline{y_i}} M_i' \wedge \mathtt{valid}(M, \mathcal{E})}{M \xrightarrow{\mathcal{E}} \mathtt{unsat}(M_1', \ldots, M_n')} \quad \left[M_i' = \begin{cases} M_i & i \notin I \\ (S_i, u_i, \overline{x_i} + \overline{y_i}) & \text{otherwise} \end{cases} \right]$$

where $\overline{y_i} = \sum_j \mathcal{E}_{ji} - \sum_j \mathcal{E}_{ij}$ and $\mathcal{E} \in (\mathbb{R}_+^m)^{n \times n}$. We say that M is a *local equilibrium*, denoted by $M \nrightarrow$, if there do not exist $M', \mathcal{E}$ such that $M \xrightarrow{\mathcal{E}} M'$.   □

The previous operational rule is applied under the same conditions appearing in the definition of a valid exchange matrix: It is applied to unsaturated markets and the exchange is made among a subset of the saturated submarkets. The premises indicate that, at least, an unsaturated market will improve after the exchange and that no one deteriorates. Let us remind that, in general, a market may generate both $M_i \xrightarrow{\bar{y}} M_i'$ and $M_i \xmapsto{\bar{y}} M_i'$. So, the previous rule also considers situations where more than a market improves (we only require that, at least, one improves). Besides, let us remark that $M_i \xrightarrow{\bar{0}} M_i'$ always holds. So, a market not involved in the current exchange does not disallow the exchange. Regarding the conclusion, submarkets belonging to M are modified according to the corresponding exchange matrix, while unsaturated submarkets do not change. We need to consider two more exchanging rules.

$$\frac{M_k \xrightarrow{\mathcal{E}} M_k'}{\mathtt{unsat}(M_1, \ldots, M_k, \ldots, M_n) \xrightarrow{\mathcal{E}} \mathtt{unsat}(M_1, \ldots, M_k', \ldots, M_n)} \qquad \frac{M \xrightarrow{\mathcal{E}} M'}{ms(M) \xrightarrow{\mathcal{E}} ms(M')}$$

The first one indicates that if an unsaturated submarket produces an exchange, then the market must take that situation into account. The second rule reflects modifications in the environment of the constructor ms.

If a market reaches an equilibrium, we have that it has become saturated. In this case, we need to modify the attribute of the market, replacing a term unsat$(M_1, \ldots, M_n)$ by an adequate term as $(S, u, \bar{x})$. In addition, resources are recursiv ely mo ed from the corresponding agents to the leav es of the tree (indicating original agents). Let us remark that a necessary condition for a market to be saturated is that all its submarkets are also saturated. The following rule uses tw o auxiliary notions that will be formally presented in the forthcoming Definition 8.

Definition 7. Let $M = \text{unsat}(M_1, \ldots, M_n)$ be a market, where we have that $M_i = (S_i, u_i, \bar{x}_i)$ for an y $1 \leq i \leq n$. The following rule modifies the market from unsaturated to saturated:

$$\frac{M \not\leadsto}{M \leadsto ([M_1', \ldots, M_n'], u, \sum \overline{x_i})}$$

where $u = \text{CreateUtility}(u_1, \ldots, u_n, \overline{x_1}, \ldots, \overline{x_n})$ and for any $1 \leq i \leq n$ we hav e that $M_i' = (S_i', u_i, \overline{x_i})$ and $S_i' = \text{Deliver}(S_i, u_i, \overline{x_i})$. □

Let us remark that in this rule we do not label the transition $\leadsto$. These transitions play a role similar to internal transitions in classical process algebras. We need to add tw o more rules, as in the previous case, to record this transformation in the context of different constructors:

$$\frac{M_k \leadsto M_k'}{\text{unsat}(M_1, \ldots, M_k, \ldots, M_n) \leadsto \text{unsat}(M_1, \ldots, M_k', \ldots, M_n)} \qquad \frac{M \leadsto M'}{ms(M) \leadsto ms(M')}$$

Next w e present the pending auxiliary functions. In tuitively, the function $\text{Deliver}(S, u, \bar{x})$ distributes the basket of resources $\bar{x}$ among the original agents appearing in the leav es of the tree S. This distribution takes into account utilit y functions of the agents, as w ell as the quantities of resources con tributed b y each agent. On the other hand, $\text{CreateUtility}(u_1, \ldots, u_n, \overline{x_1}, \ldots, \overline{x_n})$ computes a combined utility function from the ones provided as arguments, so that it is possible to negotiate for maximizing the o v erall profit of the represented agents. Let us remind that, in this section, utility functions associated with higher order agents do not only reveal preference. In addition, they also tak e in to account how resources will be distributed among agents. Thus, if w e are considering an agent representing n agents, a new utilit y function returning a tuple with $n + 1$ components will be created. The first component (the value of the utility function) will return the worst utility (0) if any of the represented agents worsens. In this wa y, it is guaranteed that the market does not make any exchange which deteriorates any of its clients.

Definition 8. Let $A = (S, u, \bar{x})$ be an agent. The *allocation* of the basket of resources $\bar{x}$ among the agents belonging to S, with respect to the utility function u, denoted by $\text{Deliver}(S, u, \bar{x})$, is recursively defined as:

$$\text{Deliver}(S, u, \bar{x}) = \begin{cases} [\,] & \text{if } S = [\,] \\ [M_1', \ldots, M_n'] & \text{if } S = [M_1, \ldots, M_n] \end{cases}$$

where for any $1 \leq i \leq n$ w e have that $M_i = (S_i, u_i, \overline{x_i})$, $M_i' = (S_i', u_i, u(\bar{x}).i)$, and $S_i' = \text{Deliver}(S_i, u_i, u(\bar{x}).i)$.

Given n pairs $(u_i, \overline{x_i})$ w e define the *utility function* defined from the utility functions $u_1, \ldots, u_n$ with respect to the *initial* bask ets of resources $\overline{x_1}, \ldots, \overline{x_n}$, denoted by $\texttt{CreateUtility}(u_1, \ldots, u_n, \overline{x_1}, \ldots, \overline{x_n})$, as:

$$\texttt{CreateUtility}(u_1, \ldots, u_n, \overline{x_1}, \ldots, \overline{x_n}) = u_{market}$$

where $u_{market}(\overline{x}) = max(\{(r, \overline{x_1'}, \ldots, \overline{x_n'}) | r = \sum_{1 \leq i \leq n} u_i(\overline{x_i'}) \wedge \sum_{1 \leq i \leq n} \overline{x_i'} = \overline{x} \wedge \bigwedge_{1 \leq i \leq n} u(\overline{x_i'}) \geq u(\overline{x_i})\})$, maximizing o ver the first argument (representing the *utility*), and supposing $max(\emptyset) = (0, \overline{0}, \ldots, \overline{0})$. □

Next, to define how a market evolv es, w e compose sequences of transitions.

Definition 9. We say that a market M *evolves into* a market M', and we write $M \rightsquigarrow^* M'$, if there exist markets $M_1, \ldots, M_{n-1}$ such that

$$M \overset{a_1}{\rightsquigarrow} M_1 \overset{a_2}{\rightsquigarrow} M_2 \overset{a_3}{\rightsquigarrow} \cdots M_{n-1} \overset{a_n}{\rightsquigarrow} M'$$

where for any $1 \leq i \leq n$ we hav e a_i is an empty label or an exchange matrix. □

Finally, w e prøvide a mechanism to reset a global market. If the root of the tree becomes a saturated market, then the whole tree of markets is created again. This is done by considering the following five rules:

$$\frac{}{ms((S, u, \bar{x})) \hookrightarrow ms(\sigma((S, u, \bar{x})))} \qquad \frac{}{\sigma(([\,], u, \bar{x})) \hookrightarrow ([\,], u, \bar{x})}$$

$$\frac{S = [A_1, \ldots, A_n]}{\sigma((S, u, \bar{x})) \hookrightarrow \texttt{unsat}(\sigma(A_1), \ldots, \sigma(A_n))}$$

$$\frac{M_k \hookrightarrow M_k'}{\texttt{unsat}(M_1, \ldots, M_k, \ldots, M_n) \hookrightarrow \texttt{unsat}(M_1, \ldots, M_k', \ldots, M_n)} \qquad \frac{M \hookrightarrow M'}{ms(M) \hookrightarrow ms(M')}$$

We finish this section by providing a result showing that the last saturated market represents one of the possible P areto optimums for the whole set of original agents. The proof is immediate.

Theorem 1. Let M, M' be markets and A be an agent such that

$$M \rightsquigarrow^* M' \hookrightarrow ms(\sigma(A))$$

The distribution of resources provided b y $\sigma(A)$ represents a P areto optimum with respect to the original agents belonging to M. ⊔

5   Conclusions and F utureWork

We hav e presented a formal framework for the definition of *e-barter* arc hitectures. In contrast with most current systems, by using e-barter, multilateral exchanges can be performed. The use of a hierarc hical structure of markets allows local markets to evolve in parallel, but preserving the property that the global market still reaches P areto equilibria. By doing so, the efficiency is notably increased, as most of the exchanges are done in (near) local markets. Let us remark that the in tegration of microeconomic and process algebra has provided tw o important advantages. Firstly, it has av oided ambiguity in the understanding the behavior of systems. Secondly, it has allo w edto appropriately structure, in a bottom-up way, e-barter systems. As future work we plan to study the behavior of markets where customers pay commissions when exchanging goods. Thus, it can be modelled how he markets are distorted when intermediates appear. We also plan to study alternative semantics. In particular, based on the w ork presented in [7] for analyzing the termination of processes, we are working on a testing semantics for c haracterizing markets equilibria.

References

1. G. Babin, T.G. Crainic, M. Gendreau, R.K. Keller, P. Kropf, and J. Robert. T ow ards electronic marketplaces: A progress report. In *4th ICECR*, pages 637–648, 2001.
2. M. Barbuceanu and W.K. Lo. Multi-attribute utility theoretic negotiation for electronic commerce. In *AMEC 2000, LNAI 2003*, pages 15–30. Springer, 2001.
3. H. Ben Ameur, B. Chaib-draa, and P . Kropf. Multiagent auctions for m ultiple items. In *A utonomous Agents 2001*, pages 33–40, 2001.
4. J.A. Bergstra, A. Ponse, and S.A. Smolka, editors. *Handbook of Process Algebra*. North Holland, 2001.
5. A. Chavez and P . Maes. Kasbah: An agent marketplace for buying and selling goods. In *P AAM '96* pages 75–90, 1996.
6. M. Dastani, N. Jacobs, C.M. Jonker, and J. Treur. Modelling user preferences and mediating agents in electronic commerce. In *A gent Mediated Electronic Commerce, LNAI 1991*, pages 163–193. Springer, 2001.
7. D. de Frutos, M. Núñez, and J. Quemada. Characterizing termination in LOTOS via testing. In *PSTV XV*, pages 237–250. Chapman & Hall, 1995.
8. T. Eymann. Markets without makers - a framework for decentralized economic coordination in multiagen t systems. In*WELCOM 2001, LNCS 2232*, pages 63–74. Springer, 2001.
9. R. Guttman, A. Moukas, and P. Maes. Agent-mediated electronic commerce: A survey. *Knowledge Engineering Review*, 13(2):147–159, 1998.
10. A.R. Lomuscio, M. Wooldridge, and N.R. Jennings. A classification scheme for negotiation in electronic commerce. In *A gent Mediate d Ele ctronic Commerce, LNAI 1991*, pages 19–33. Springer, 2001.
11. M. Núñez. Including microeconomic theory into FDTs: A first approach. Available at: http://dalila.sip.ucm.es/~manolo/papers/exchange.ps.gz, 2000.
12. M. Núñez and I. Rodríguez. PAMR: A process algebra for the management of resources in concurrent systems. In *F ORTE 2001*, pages 169–185. Kluwer Academic Publishers, 2001. An extended version of this paper is available at: http://dalila.sip.ucm.es/~manolo/papers/pamr.ps.
13. L. Rasmusson and S. Janson. Agents, self-interest and electronic markets. *Knowledge Engineering Review*, 14(2):143–150, 1999.
14. T. Sandholm. Agents in electronic commerce: Component technologies for automated negotiation and coalition formation. In *CIA '98, LNCS 1435*, pages 113–134. Springer, 1998.
15. M. Wooldridge and N.R. Jennings. In telligent agents: Theory and practice. *The Knowledge Engineering Review*, 10(2):115–152, 1995.

Peer-to-Peer beyond File Sharing

Ulrike Lechner

University of Bremen, Dept. for Mathematics and Computer Science
P.O. 330 440, D-28344 Bremen, Germany
lechner@informatik.uni-bremen.de

Abstract. Peer-to-peer architectures gained much attention through their main application domain file sharing. First, we analyze the music industry and the architectural innovations of online services for sharing music files on the business model of the music industry. In the second main part of the paper, we generalize our observations to the design of media for the creation of economic value and the social and economic impact of peer-to-peer architectures. We analyze here virtual communities and other peer-to-peer architectures.

1 Introduction

The architecture of an information system has impact on the economic and social structure in which it is being embedded. Information systems with peer-to-peer architectures have gained much attention in the past years. Napster and Gnutella are early examples for this technology and file sharing in particular of music files is still the killer application for this architecture. The distinguishing property of those peer-to-peer networks is that all members of such a network are both server and client of services and that all the clients connect among each other. In a pure peer-to-peer architecture there are no centralized services and there is no hierarchical control. Currently, the first professional applications are under development and in the early stages of deployment. The main application scenarios for this architecture are ad hoc networks, temporary collaboration platforms beside the file sharing environments.

The online services for sharing music and other kinds of content demonstrate the impact of this architecture on business models. The users obviously liked it, they drove the innovations and they inhabited the architectures quickly. Yet it is unclear whether there are sustainable business models for the existing systems and whether this architecture can be successful in other kinds and professional of application domains. This paper contributes to the discussion on the future and open research questions in this area. We contribute an analysis of existing architectures, the development of those architectures, the social and economic impact.

This paper is organized as follows. First, we present the analysis of the services for sharing files online and their impact on the business models of the media industry (Sect. 2). We consider static and dynamic issues and conclude this part with an analysis of the open questions. In the second main part (Sect. 3), we consider the design of services. We present the media model to guide our discussion and analyze virtual communities and services. We conclude with a brief summary (Sect. 4).

H.Unger, T.Boehme, and A.Mikler (Eds.): I²CS 2002, LNCS 2346, pp. 229-249, 2002.
© Springer-Verlag Berlin Heidelberg 2002

2   Case Study Music Industry

Over the past few years, a variety of new models for content management in the music industry have been implemented on the Internet. MP3.com, Napster.com, and gnutella are early examples for services for online content management. Many more services have followed in the past two years. All those new services have severe impact on the business model of the music industry. Moreover, those services distinguish themselves in the architecture of value creation significantly from the traditional model of the music industry and there are various good reasons of why to analyze those services. First, the music industry and the online service are an example for a technology driven innovation. Second, the impact of the innovation on the business model of a whole industry is profound and any other industry whose business is the processing and distribution of information might eventually be changed by a similar innovation as well. Third, from all the different architectures, it is the peer-to-peer architecture that induces the most dramatic changes in the business model and that benefits the customer most. Fourth, the consumers are driving the development and the architectural innovation in this sector and they inhabit the new architectures quickly. However, static architecture is just one aspect that needs to be considered - the momentum of interaction and dynamics is a phenomenon on its own. This particular dynamics is the fifth reason on why the development should be analyzed carefully - it could give a hint on whether there are sustainable business models for such systems in the long run.

In this section, we describe the development in the music sector in the past two years based on an analysis of four different architectures of services for content management, namely the traditional music industry, mp3.com, Napster and gnutella. First, we consider the architecture of the infrastructure. In a second step we analyze the business model with the value chain for content management and, third, we consider the system dynamics of the interaction in those architectures. We conclude this first part of the paper with a discussion of the findings and open design questions.

2.1   System Architectures

Following (Booch et al. 1998), we consider a (software) architecture to encompass the set of significant decisions about the organization of a software system, i.e., the selection of the structural elements and the interfaces by which a system is composed, the behavior as specified in collaborations among those elements, the composition of these structural and behavioral elements into larger subsystems, and the architectural style that guides this organization.

Let us consider the structure of the composition of components first. We observe that a client-server with bi-directional communication channels accompanies the classic architecture of the traditional music industry with unidirectional communication channels. The consumers and artists communicate with the service - the server MP3.com holds most of the data. MP3.com is an example of implementation of this architecture. Napster.com exemplifies a combined client-server with peer-to-peer architecture. Further on, there are pure peer-to-peer architectures. Gnutella is one example for such a peer-to-peer architecture.

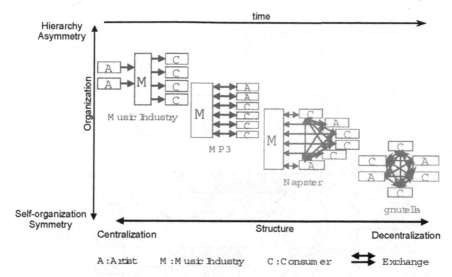

Fig. 1. System architectures for content management in the music industry

The organization of the system for content management goes hand in hand with the structure. The hierarchical model, where the music industry had a strong position is being challenged by novel architectures that follow the peer-to-peer paradigm, i.e., with self-organization and symmetric positions of all actors involved.

These architectures reflect the actors and their roles as well as the infrastructure for content management. The position of the industry or service provider weakens and the consumers or clients strengthen. The impact of those architectural changes however goes deeper. Subsequently, we analyze the business model with the value chain the processes of content management in more detail and again compare the various models and the impact the change has on the architectural innovation.

2.2   Business Model and Value Chain

The architectural changes induce changes in the business model. As Timmers (Timmers, 1998), we consider a business model to be an architecture for the product, services and information flows including a description of the various business actors and their roles and a description of the potential benefits for the various business actors and their roles; and a description of the sources of revenues. The system architecture is part of the business model.

In terms of value creation, we distinguish seven steps in the value chain and a respective communication model (Wössner, 2000). There are also seven steps in the traditional uni-directional value chain of the music industry. The artist is responsible for the creative part, the idea. The contents are established. Artists and music industry work together. Then, the product is packaged, marketed, copied, and distributed. The music industry controls these stages in the creation of economic value. The role of the consumer consists of purchasing the product. This value chain is depicted as the classical value chain of the music industry in Fig. 2 (Music Ind.).

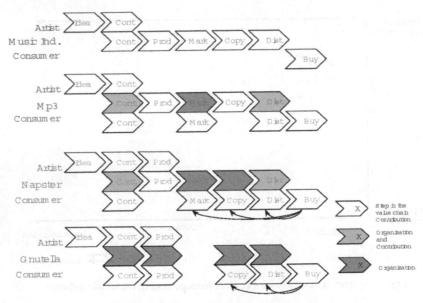

Fig. 1. Value chains in the music industry

The novel services for content management - MP3, Napster and gnutella - implement these steps in the value chain in different ways. Each service is briefly introduced. Then, its value chain, as depicted in Fig. 2, is analyzed.

MP3.com considers itself an online repository of the users' music files to facilitate access to that music from everywhere on the Internet (source: www.mp3.com). Users are allowed to upload pieces of music up to a certain extend and rent further storage capacity if necessary - or identify themselves in the so-called beamer services as owners of a carrier (CD) for some piece of music. Each user has an account that allows access the pieces of music online. Access to music is granted via Internet technology and general browsers of all kind. MP3 gives unknown artists the opportunity to release a CD online and offers to produce, ship, and offer CDs on demand. The artist sets the price and receives up to 50% of the revenues.

MP3 offers a matching or recommendation service that points out artists and music to match an individual's profile. In addition, MP3 offers various services of community interaction, since the architecture is client-server based. The client has files, registry and, because of the community services of recommendations and interaction, all information about the consumers and the artists.

In terms of the value chain, the consumers, service, and artists contribute mp3 files. The service of MP3.com contributes the storage space for content and some means to structure and organize access to content, for example search engines and directories. The consumers are also doing some kind of marketing through reviews and a recommendation service for peer groups (but of course the main parts are still done by the music industry). MP3.com structures and organizes those contributions. They play an essential role for the distribution part of the value chain.

Thus, MP3 implements three steps in the value chain in a different way: the production of contents, the marketing, and the distribution. In all three cases, the consumers assume some role for production for content - Mp3.com provides the means for structuring and organizing and allows for some interrelationship between community and contents. However, only the step of marketing follows community architecture. Only at this step of the value chain, do the community members interact following a peer-to-peer architecture - the implementation of the other "novel" implementation follows patterns that are more similar to the original model.

Napster.com (we refer to the "original Napster of the year 2000) considers itself "the world leading file sharing community" (source napster.com). The server Napster.com offers a directory of lists of files to be shared and software to participate in the community. Each Napster client offers mp3 files in a dedicated folder on the hard disk to be shared with the community and allows registration of those files in the central directory. To search a file, the Napster client accesses the server and its directory of files at napster.com. Swapping of files takes place following a peer-to-peer architecture. Napster.com offers interaction and a recommendation service.

Napster.com has all the information necessary for community management. Every member of the community contributes content, storage facilities for files, and digitized profiles. The Napster clients are, in turn, servers for the swapping of files.

In terms of the value chain depicted in Fig. 2 the service itself is involved in the marketing, copying, and distribution of the titles. The decision of a consumer to download (buy) an mp3 file influences the marketing implemented in a recommendation service. This dependency is represented as backwards arrows in Fig. 2. Note that consumers themselves provide the resources for multiplication and distribution and trigger multiplication and distribution. This is also depicted as backwards arrows. When compared to the traditional model, Napster implements four steps of the value chain in a novel way: production of content, marketing, distribution, and copying. More steps of the value chain follow a peer-to-peer model - it is the community of consumers that contributes as peers to marketing, multiplication, distribution, and content and each step follows community architecture. Moreover, Napster has features such as buddy lists and allows for blocking of certain users - such that the social aspects of a community and the content management within this community are more interrelated. Thus, the architecture of the value chain of Napster is more peer-to-peer and the social function of community spills over to content management.

Gnutella is a file-sharing application without any central structure. It is widely used to swap any kind of file. Gnutella clients form a self-organizing net of peers. To join the net, a client has to know at least one single gnutella client. Searching for files and swapping of files are exercised in a peer-to-peer architecture. A gnutella client is client and server for files. It offers all files in a dedicated directory to be shared on the net; and each client-server swaps files, searches for files, and requests files. There is no central service.

Gnutella clients do not offer any community building services, as e.g., communication or recommendation services, i.e. there is no marketing step in gnutella's value chain. The value chain of gnutella shows that - apart from marketing - all steps in the value chain of the music industry have been taken over by the consumers. They contribute the content, replication and distribution (by their decisions to upload and download music). The service just facilitates all these interactions by the consumers.

Let us briefly mention the revenues for the artists to illustrate how they can profit from these new implementations. The business models are quite different from the traditional one of the music industry. In the business model of the music industry, the artist receives approx. 10-15% of the revenues. At mp3 the artist receives up to 50% of the revenues of the CD being sold. This ratio is even more attractive when mp3 files are sold. At riffage.com the artist receives up to 85% of the revenues. (Haertsch, 2000).

Let us briefly discuss the value chains. First, for all the services providers it is difficult to generate revenues. The position of MP3 seems to be perfect. The server has to be accessed to get files and the service provider has a nearly perfect control over information flows from which revenues might be generated. However, the service provider can hardly generate revenues from the storing and downloading of files and this holds for all service providers independent of architecture. There need to be other sources for revenues – apart from providing access to files. One revenue model is "community organizer", i.e., the service provider structures and organizes the communication and information flows.

Here the architecture of Napster appears to be much more efficient. The system architecture ensures that Napster receives all relevant information about the user and their preferences (at least when files are swapped). Community services encourage interaction via Napster (e.g., on the chat). However, gnutella ensures that files can be swapped without having a single point where all information is gathered. Neither the software nor information of the community can generate revenues - the protocols make gnutella a self-organizing system (similar to Usenet). Therefore, there is hardly any ground left for generating revenues.

In the development of the value chains, we see that various steps are implemented in a peer-to-peer architecture and that the number of steps implemented in a peer-to-peer architecture increases along the architectural changes. The content in the systems such as Napster or gnutella is hereby inseparable from the architecture of the infrastructure: it is the community that contributes content, marketing, duplication, and distribution. Note that it is not the pure content that distinguishes the services - it is the social environment and its organization and the way the environment that is linked with the content.

The developments in this sector are technology driven, but the consumer has an important role. Clear incentives motivate consumers to adopt these novel technologies and services. A static view on the architecture does not suffice any here. While in the traditional model the channel and the interaction are controlled by one player, the system of peers and the content that they share evolves through interaction and the network structures develop a powerful momentum. This momentum of system dynamics is being investigated in the next section.

2.3   System Dynamics

An architect designs architecture for people to interact in some desired way. As architecture of buildings has an impact on the people inhabiting it system architecture has impact on the behavior of its users. This hold in particular for interactive systems and systems that need users and contributions of users. Peer-to-peer networks only exist through the contributions and the interaction of users. Software system architecture designs structures over space and time - in contrast to the architectures of building that typically do not change over time. Moreover, the architecture of information systems may be designed for change. Change and non-persistence are particular features of peer-to-peer networks. A building in which components and connections between components change seems awkward. Even on Internet we expect servers and sites to persist. Change and contents that change over time are (still) considered a feature in peer-to-peer networks. Thus, the dynamics of peer-to-peer networks is expected to be stronger than of other interactive system.

To analyze the dynamic effects we employ the theory of network externalities and feedback effects. Note that the definitions are taken from (Shapiro and Varian, 1999). According to Metcalfe's Law, the value of a network corresponds to $n*(n-1)$ where n is the number of nodes. When the value of a product to a user depends on how many other users are using it, economists' say that this product exhibits network externalities, or network effects. Positive network effects describe that the value of a network increases with the number of nodes - negative network effects occur when the value decreases with an increase of nodes. Feedback effects describe the impact of an action on the actor later in time. Positive feedback effects denote a positive impact and, conversely, negative a negative impact. Positive feedback effects result in the big getting bigger and the small get smaller while negative feedback effects result in the big getting smaller and the small get bigger. Positive feedback effects polarize while negative feedback effects stabilize a network. We also utilize system theory. A system is represented as a graph with the nodes representing the factors that contribute to an effect. The interdependencies or correlation between factors are depicted as the directed edges of the graph and they are adorned with "+" for a positive and with "-" for a negative correlation.

The relation between contribution of the single member to the creation of economic value and the perceived value is a crucial issue. Let us discuss the system describing the relation between value, number of members, contributed and available resources as given below.

Let us explain this system. The kernel of this system is the network effect of communication networks with a positive correlation between value and members. The more members a network has the more valuable it is - since there are more potential communication partners and potentially more contents to be contributed.

The right side captures the "global perspective". The more members the more storage capacity, bandwidth and computing power is available in the network to the disposal of the community members; the number of members and quantity of resources correlate with the value.

The left side describes the "individual perspective" with feedback on content contributions. An increase in content contributions increases the contributions storage capacity, computing power and bandwidth - a download costs the one, who contributed content, bandwidth and processing power in the download. Those contributions of bandwidth, processing power diminish the network value for the contributing user. Worse, this decrease of value is related to the number of users - the more users the higher the contribution gets: more users eventually increase downloads.

This model coincides with empirical studies of peer-to-peer networks (Adar and Huberman, 2000). Adar and Huberman observe that the overwhelming majority of users do hardly contribute content and that only few contribute the majority of content and serve the majority of downloads. The majority of messages focus on very few pieces of content.

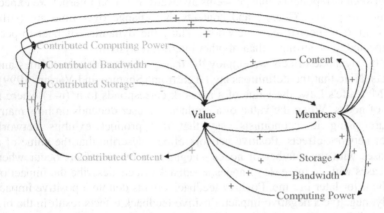

Fig. 3. System dynamics in Peer-to-Peer

It seems that the peer-to-peer infrastructures have an inherent severe drawback. The structures that seem to emerge on peer-to-peer networks in terms of content and messages are not "peer-to-peer". Instead, they resemble more the traditional client-server paradigm. A few servers provide most of the content and few pieces of content are heavily sought after. Moreover, individual contributions are being punished and the larger the network and the better the contributions the more negative the feedback on individual contributions get. This makes contributions unattractive for users and particular unattractive in large networks. In fact many people just log into those networks for downloads and few serve without download.

Note that this seems to be inherent to peer-to-peer and applies both the peer-to-peer and hybrid systems of the Napster architecture. Note furthermore that at least the early systems have hardly any services that can compensate for the negative feedback effects in file sharing. This leaves the question whether a peer-to-peer system for file sharing is a sustainable valid business model at all.

2.4   Peer-to-Peer as a New Architecture for Collaboration – A Brief Discussion

The peer-to-peer architectures have gained much attention in the past few years and there are in fact a number of reasons why one needs to have a closer look on those systems. The users like it, they inhabit such systems, contribute the contents and resources and popular systems develop very soon a powerful momentum. The first professional applications are under development or in the early stages of deployment. However, the success of file sharing applications is declining. The intellectual property right issues still need to be resolved. A peer-to-peer architecture with minimal centralized services however seems to be one way to provide access to music at relatively low-cost - a centralized server is most likely much too costly for the music industry and its consumers. However, MP3 seems to be far from being commercially successful; Napster still needs to turn into a professional service and the gnutella network or other pure peer-to-peer networks are still haunted by network failures, network overload and lack basic services one is accustomed from Internet. To us it seems remarkable that the content and message structure that emerges on such a peer-to-peer network resembles the traditional client-server architecture much closer than the peer-to-peer architecture. The negative feedback effects prevent however contributions from users - only very few users are willing to contribute to such a network. To us it is unclear whether a large peer-to-peer network is really a sustainable business model for file sharing since there are little incentives to contribute. This leaves two research questions open: How to design a sustainable business model for file sharing on a peer-to-peer basis? How to design peer-to-peer infrastructures for professional applications? Subsequently we analyze the design of services in a structured way.

3   Design of Peer-to-Peer Services

Currently the peer-to-peer architectures are mainly constrained to the file sharing application domain and the peer-to-peer model in itself has its particular system dynamics with the inherently negative feedback effects. In this section we analyze media to implement them in a peer-to-peer architecture. The characteristics of peer-to-peer are multi-lateral communication channels with interaction partners that both offer and provide services. This is the feature that we look for in designs.

In our analysis we proceed as follows, first we present the media model to guide our discussion. Then we analyze virtual communities as social networks of peers and finally service design following a peer-to-peer architecture.

3.1   Media

Media used to be mere carriers of information. The platforms provided by information and communication technology are interactive and proactive as they process the information presented to them. As such the distinction between the carrier and the social system in which it is embedded blurs. Those new media mediate more and more interaction and the medium itself is a picture of the social structure it is embedded. Consider workflow management systems compared to traditional media. A workflow management system disposes of a representation of the individual users, of the organization and all the processes of which it used. Moreover, it has a proactive role in controlling a project team and its progress, say in behalf of the management or a human controller. Similar, electronic marketplaces or electronic auctions are electronic representations of economic processes. Workflow systems, electronic marketplaces and electronic auctions are examples of how a medium changes social and economic reality and that media redefine interaction through its mediation. To structure the discussion we utilize the model of media (Schmid, 1997). We follow hereby the notion of a medium as developed in sociology. Societies can be defined as 'system of places', where every agent has a place with rights and obligations. Those societies are called media and they bind the agent at a place (Schmid, 1997).

A medium, i.e. the sphere fore communities of agents is characterized in terms of
- A logical sphere with syntax, semantics and pragmatics of the information that may be communicated via its channels. Note that this includes information about some domain (worlds), and information about the medium itself, i.e., its organization, the channel system and the agents.
- An organizational sphere to describe with roles the places for the agents in terms of rights and obligations and with protocols the interactions of agents.
- A channel system to distribute and exchange information over space and time.

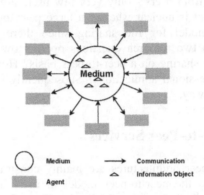

Fig. 4. Medium as Sphere for Communities of Agents (Schmid, 1997)

A community is a collection of agents together with a medium, i.e., Community = Agents + Medium. A community is characterized by a common language and world, by common values and interests. Clans, firms, nations, marketplaces are examples for communities. Agents may be humans, software agents, organizational units - any entity that plays a role in the exchange of information and communication (Lechner and Schmid, 1999). We refer to the physical part of a medium as the platform.

Note that the informal relations among humans within a clan as well as, e.g., the formal interaction processes implemented, e.g., in a workflow or groupware system both have this binding function of a medium. In a clan, the members act according to those rules to avoid getting expelled. Users of stringent workflow systems have to follow implemented sequences of processing steps and the enterprise of which the workflow system is part of enforces the agents to adhere to the rules implemented in the workflow system.

The Media Reference Model (Schmid, 1999), depicted below, details generic components of a medium.
The layers represent the views on a medium:
- The Infrastructure represents the physical components of a medium.
- The transaction view captures the services. One distinguishes - according to the phases the services to exchange information, services for determining and exchanging supply and demand, contracting services to determine and exchange binding obligations and the services for settlement of those obligations.
- The process view represents the organization with interaction processes that combine the services according to community view.

- The community view captures common language, values and interests that characterize the community and the protocols for interaction a community has agreed upon.

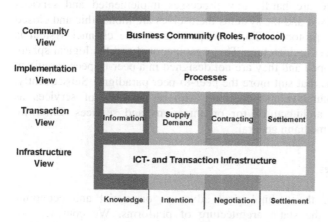

Fig. 5. Media Reference Model (Schmid, 1999)

The four phases distinguish the different kinds of communication acts and the protocols, languages, processes and services that constitute a medium:
- In the knowledge phase, agents exchange information and they establish their knowledge or belief. Processing and exchanging of assertional information is done in that view.
- The intention phase captures messages and services necessary to develop and exchange non-binding intentions in signaling.
- In the contracting phase, agents negotiate contracts. The messages in this phase are binding, in the sense that they oblige agents to act as indicated. Interactions add obligations and rights. This phase ends - in the case of success - with a binding contract.
- In the settlement phase, agents act according to the negotiated contracts, using services offered for this purpose by the service layer. In commerce, this means, e.g., shipping of goods and transaction of money. The interaction reduces obligations and rights.

Note that the media model and the media reference model capture a medium with its carriers, the language with syntax, semantics and pragmatics Note furthermore that both models capture the physical part of the medium, i.e. those structures that are implemented on a platform and those issues that are part of the society but that influence the transmission and understanding of messages.

Let us review peer-to-peer systems with the media and the media reference model. Many peer-to-peer systems are crude in the sense that the common logical sphere, i.e., the language that is spoken within the communities and the system for representation of information are not well developed and there is only one language spoken by those systems. E.g., files are distinguished by their names and this file name represents the content. Also, the organization of the society is not very well developed. Rights and obligations of the single users or intellectual property rights as a common value are not implemented in the medium. The messages that are conveyed through the systems are assertive – messages that carry rights or obligations are not distinguished from assertional messages. There are hardly any processes implemented and services within such a network are fixed and the systems themselves are monolithic and closed through mainly proprietary protocols. To sum up - mainly the channel system is implemented in a peer-to-peer architecture. The organizational and the logical sphere are typically not well developed and they are not designed in a peer-to-peer paradigm. Are there alternative designs that suit more the peer-to-peer paradigm? Subsequently, we consider virtual communities and continue with an analysis of services as examples for peer-to-peer architectures for organizations and services. First, we analyze the architectures of media in general.

3.2   Media Architectures

To analyze the impact of the technological advances on social and economic structures, we begin with the static architecture of platforms. We consider two dimensions (1) the structure on which we distinguish centralized and decentralized architectures and (2) the organizational dimension in which we distinguish centralized hierarchical control and decentralized self-organization. Three basic architectures for interaction can be differentiated.

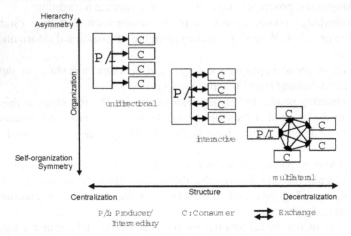

Fig. 6. Interaction Architectures

Uni-directional channels are the basis for the traditional mass communication. Information is transported mainly from the producer/intermediary to the consumer. The Internet as an interaction channel has changed this transactional model profoundly. The new channels are bi-directional or interactive - content can be exchanged between consumer and producer or intermediary rather than transmitted from producers to consumers. Still there is only communication between the producer/intermediary and consumers. On multi-lateral communication channels producers and consumers can communicate among each other.

Uni-directional, interactive and multi-lateral communication channels induce new architectures for the distribution and organization of information. Characteristic of uni-directional communication channel is a client-server architecture with a powerful server that manages information, its flow, coupled with weak clients. In the interactive communication channel, the position of the clients is strengthened relative to the position of the server. The community model of computing induces a way of transaction and computation where all participants interact on an equal basis with respect to communication and computation.

The architecture of the communication channels goes hand in hand with organization of information (or content). On uni-directional channels it is the upstream distributor of information that controls hierarchically the information and that typically disposes of more information than the consumer. The model is asymmetric concerning both information distribution and control. On interactive communication channels, information and control are more symmetrically distributed. The consumers dispose of some information that the intermediary/producer needs in the interaction. Still, the model is asymmetric since the producer/intermediary is in control on each channel to the individual consumer and the contributor maintains most of the relevant information. On multi-lateral channels every participant has the potential to contribute and share the same amount of content and every participant disposes potentially of the same information and the same control over information and its flows.

The architecture of channels is only one aspect in the design of media. The organization and the logical space and their design are another issue that needs to be considered in the architecture (cf. Media Model). The proceeding digitalization captures more aspects of a community to be represented on an electronic medium. Indeed one observes that the decentralized multi-lateral structures get semantically.

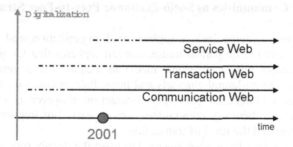

Fig. 7. Digitalization of decentralized structures

Let us consider the development depicted in Fig. 7. The Internet and the Web started as a peer-to-peer architecture for (human) communication. HTML and other communication standards mainly aimed at exchanging information to be consumed not for further processing. Transactions typically need a better support through the infrastructure. The representation on physical infrastructure is richer and the kind of communications is better discriminated according to the organizational connotation that they have (cf. Media Reference Model). File sharing can be seen as a (rather primitive) peer-to-peer infrastructure of transaction. A next and third degree in digitalization are services. Clients within a network offer those services and those services may even interact autonomously to fulfill some task that has been sent to one of them. Currently, those services are in the early stages of development and deployment. One example is Xmethods.com, a directory server and its web of online services. What we observe is that the communication peer-to-peer network is being transformed to a peer-to-peer infrastructure for transactions and, eventually, to a peer-to-peer architecture for services.

Obviously, there are limitations to what kinds of tasks can be handled within such a peer-to-peer architecture. There are not too many tasks that can be split up into a high number subtasks that can be computed rather independently by small peer members with limited processing power and by services in an organization without centralized control, i.e., in an organization with limited reliability and trustworthiness.

Technology-wise this development is driven by the Semantic Web movement (cf. w3c.org). The extensible markup language (XML) family and its sets of standards constitutes such a web of "logical spheres". There is or will be an appropriate logical sphere for such systems.

Note that the organizational component of the peer-to-peer systems is not as well developed. Common values and interest make the people join. It seems however unclear on how to design sophisticated organization for transactions or services for the peer-to-peer paradigm. Such transaction atmospheres are essential for any transactions. Virtual communities are social networks that are based on multi-lateral channels and that rely on member contributions. Interaction is mainly limited to communication and hence those virtual communities can be considered to be one form of peer-to-peer networks. From the communication peer-to-peer networks of virtual communities one can learn on how to design a social atmosphere and a society on such a peer-to-peer infrastructure.

3.3   Virtual Communities as Socio-Economic Peer-to-Peer Structures

Most peer-to-peer systems lack a sophisticated organization and social networks. Those are considered to be part of transaction atmospheres that facilitate transactions. Virtual communities utilize electronic media to mediate the communication and as such they rely on multi-lateral channels and immediate interaction. Thus, they follow the peer-to-peer architectural paradigm. Interaction however is limited mostly to communication and therefore communities are an early but important development, which has not reached the level of transaction.

Virtual communities have been emerged to meet the deeply routed human need for communication, entertainment and social relations. Virtual communities are a model of the social implications of this technology and the potential for forthcoming business models. In this section, we describe virtual communities, their functions, and their social and economic roles.

The term "virtual community" has established itself for communities in which electronic media facilitates communication, in particular, for communities where interaction takes place on the Internet. (Rheingold, 1993). Over time, various aspects of virtual or online communities have been discussed in literature: social, political, and economic aspects. As this discussion has taken place, the perception of virtual communities has changed from a social phenomenon to a valid business model (Hummel and Lechner, 2000) and further on to a socio-economic business model.

Virtual can be viewed through a sociological, economic, or technological prism (Hummel and Lechner, 2001; Hummel, 2002). The first sociological definitions came from Taylor and Licklider who saw the community potential of electronic networks in 1968. They described their vision of a virtual community as "...in most fields they will consist of geographically separated members, sometimes grouped in small clusters and sometimes working individually. They will be communities not of common location but of common interest..." (Licklider and Taylor, 1968).

Probably the definition of Howard Rheingold (Rheingold, 1993) is best known. He defines virtual communities as purely related to the Internet. From his point of view, virtual communities are "...social aggregations that emerge from the Net when enough people carry on those public discussions long enough, with sufficient human feeling, to form webs of personal relationships in cyberspace" (Rheingold, 1993).

Godwin and Jones construct their argument in a similar manner. Godwin is of the opinion "...but in cyberspace, increasingly, the dream is not just 'owning a house' - it's living in the right neighborhood (Godwin, 1994)". Jones even speaks of "virtual settlement (Jones, 1997)". Figallo later stresses the meaning of common values writing "...according to that definition, members of a community feel a part of it. They form relationships and bonds of trust with other members and with you, the community host. Those relationships lead to exchanges and interactions that bring value to members" (Figallo, 1998).

From the view of computer-mediated-communication, the most important elements of a virtual community are shared resources, common values, and reciprocal behavior. Whittaker et al. write in their definition "...members have a shared goal, interest, need,...engage in repeated, active participation,...have access to shared resources,...reciprocity of information,...shared context of social conventions..." (Whittaker et al. 1997). Preece extends this view to include the necessity of common rules "...an online community consists of: People, who want to interact socially..., a shared purpose...that provides a reason for the community, policies ...that guide people's interactions (and) computer systems, to support and mediate social interaction..." (Nonnecke and Preece, 2000; Preece, 2000).

Hagel and Armstrong were the ones who emphasized the notion of virtual communities as sociological phenomenon (Hagel III and Armstrong, 1997). They see in virtual communities a business model, which uses the possibilities of communication on the Internet to create electronic marketplaces and to increase customer loyalty. Referring to Rheingold they define virtual communities "...but virtual communities are more than just a sociological phenomenon. What starts off as a group drawn together by common interests ends up as group with a critical mass of purchasing power, partly thanks to the fact that communities allow members to exchange information on such things as a product's price and quality" (Hagel III and Armstrong, 1997).

The creation of economic value in the business model "virtual community" results from the content and knowledge, the participants bring into the community (Timmers, 1998). Timmers considers "Virtual Community" to be a business model in electronic markets and he characterizes this model in the following manner, "The ultimate value of virtual communities [comes] from the members (customers or partners) who add their information ... ". The members of a community may contribute to the creation of economic value with various kinds of contributions: information, product reviews, recommendations, and pieces of music, files to be shared. Virtual communities, however, provide the social and economic environment that meets human needs and the content that these communities produce and the contributions of the members can hardly be separated from this context. The needs of those communities for information and transaction are common to all those communities and those communities are being supported by a number of services. The service design for each of those five different kinds of communities distinguishes the platform.

Despite the success of a few in particular business fields it seems that virtual communities however, were only partly able to meet the highflying expectations. (Hagel and Bughin, 2001). Therefore many virtual communities have failed and their organizers went out of business in the past couple of years. Often the reason was that the contributions of the community were not valuable enough. Among the successful communities are "The Well" or "The International Chess Club" (Ginsburg and Weisband, 2002).

For many other online organizers, the contributions of users or customers are invaluable. It is just that those contributions are done automatically and with consent. At Amazon, the customers contribute a lot of knowledge on which books are adequate for which customers. They do that automatically through the transactions. The individual transaction data are being collected and fed back to the system in form of recommendations and various bestseller lists. What we observe here is a proceeding digitalization of communities. What started as a communication structure can be implemented through a transaction infrastructure to support transactions.

However, the combination of transaction and communication is problematic. The cluetrain manifesto (Levine et al. 1999) demands in for a radical approach. One of their theses is "Markets are conversations" and they say that the architecture of conversation is the one to which transactions have to adapt to. "Hyperlinks subvert hierarchy," describes that the traditional hierarchical models of value creation will have disadvantages to the market model or community model and that the architectures have profound impact on the business model. They suggest that in the end the architecture of any information flow needs to adapt to the social needs and to the conversation of people and not vice versa. This is a strong argument for peer-to-peer transaction and service infrastructure. The architecture is already successful in communication models and enrichment to transaction and service peer-to-peer networks seems sensible. Conversely, the existing virtual communities provide the organization that current peer-to-peer networks lack and literature suggests that successful communities typically serve needs for communication and transaction (Hummel and Becker, 2001; Hummel and Lechner, 2002) and that they provide the atmosphere that facilitates complex transactions.

Communities and peer-to-peer systems have in common that they suffer from a lack of contributions and from a non-contributing silent consuming majority. Both models need human interaction and contribution to evolve and to develop a momentum. One remedy to overcome this disparity of contributions and consumptions virtual communities are automatic digitalized contributions. A second remedy is a sensible balance of positive and negative feedback effects that communities and also virtual communities have developed.

Various authors have studied the dynamics of communities. Preece (Preece, 2000) explores the social networks within communities and the design of services to support a desired behavior, (Jones, 2000) the dynamics of growth within virtual communities, (Hagel III and Armstrong, 1997; Hagel and Bughin, 2001) the financial benefit from community organizing. In commercially relevant communities the value of communities is expected to increase with the number of members and the number of contributions. Hagel and Armstrong state that Metcalfe's law and positive feedback effects apply to revenues of virtual communities (Hagel III and Armstrong, 1997). The literature in sociology states that social relations are typically limited to communities of small size. However, a critical mass of members it necessary to keep the interaction alive, interesting and hereby valuable for the members.

The model of purely positive feedback effects is however rather euphemistic and seems to hold only to some extent - from a certain size on the positive network effect can turn into a negative one (Noam, 1992). Successful communities rely on a balance of positive and negative feedback effects to balance the social dynamics of virtual communities. In Fig. 8 the social network is depicted. We identify four systems of network effects, which we label Content, Loyalty, Profiles and Focus. Those feedback effects are between four factors that characterize any community: The "Clearly defined group" describes the profile of the collection of agents, the "Interaction" dimension the kind and quality of interaction, "Bonding" the relations among the community members and "Common place" the relation between the members and the community home (Hummel and Lechner, 2002; Hummel, 2002).

The content that is exchanged within a community is defined by the community and its interest and in terms of language and values on the one hand and the actual interaction on the other hand. Interaction increases the available content and the available content increases the group being interested in them or the common knowledge of a groups. The common knowledge may also work as a boundary against newcomers - and these are the negative network effects that balance the positive ones that originate from size and content.

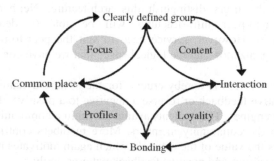

Fig. 8. Social network (Hummel and Lechner, 2002)

The loyalty of a group can be defined in terms of the social relations within a group and to the place. Such social relations increase the interaction within a group as well as the bonding of a community to the platform or its community organizer. Increasing the bonding increases the quantity and often also the quality of interactions and the social relations and bonding to a place draws the interaction of a community to a place. The lock-in of a community to the platform is part of this factor. Loyalty however constitutes also as a boundary that makes it difficult for outsiders to join a community. Again there is a possibly strong negative network effect here.

The profile of a community member and the system of profiles of a community distinguish a member of the community resp. the community as a whole. Profiles and systems of profiles capture the information that is available within the community and the digital representation of community members. The better those are, the more likely they bond the community to the place with its representation. The better the systems of such profiles - the more likely the community members interact and develop a social network. A good profile system again works as a boundary to the outside world. Newcomers do not have good profiles and it takes time to integrate them into a structure.

The focus of a community is determined by the common language, common values, common interest and motivation to contribute. Any group has such a focus and the focus determines the place with the available content, the services and the motivation to shape this place according to the needs of a community to "feel at home" while being at this place. A place designed to meet the needs of a group distinguishes a group and helps it to perceive and maintain the focus. A clear focus and the feeling at home at a common place shapes the community - but again, a well defined group is not open to newcomers to join.

Those four dimensions show that there are both negative and positive feedback effects. Both need to be considered in the design of a social network and a peer-to-peer infrastructure with a social atmosphere. Virtual communities show what is possible for the organization of a peer-to-peer network. What about the services and their design? This is what we discuss in the subsequent section.

3.4   Service Design

A pure peer-to-peer network should contain no centralized service and the contributions of the users distinguish this architecture. Neither file sharing nor professional peer-to-peer infrastructures will be able to deal totally without centralized services. However, service need to suit the peer-to-peer architectures - much alike the organization and the logical space that we have considered in previous subsections.

The design of services is hereby crucial for the system dynamics. A service may neutralize a negative feedback or reverse a negative to a positive effect. One example for this is search engines. The contents available within a community -to some extent-contributed from the community members. More members contribute more content and this increases the value of the network, which again motivates more users to join - the network externalities and positive feedback patterns apply.

But, when one considers location of information and the transaction costs for locating as part of the network the system dynamics changes. There is a positive correlation between quantity of content and the transaction costs for locating information via browsing. An increase of those transaction costs decreases the network value and results in a negative correlation between content and value.

For a search engine this is different. The transaction costs of using a standard search engine can be assumed to be independent of the quantity of content, i.e., they are constant. Some search engines however feature a smart design with positive correlation between quantity of content and frequency of interaction to value. This positive feedback effect is based on a correlation of the quality of search results and the number of searches performed, the number of users and quantity of content.

The ranking of the search results has turned out to be the crucial factor for the users - and not the mere quantity of available information (cf. searchenginewatch.com). Search engines as directhit.com or google.com are designed such that the quality of the ranking has a positive correlation with the number of users and the number of contents. The more users direct hit has, the better the ranking gets, the ranking of google improves with the quantity of content and links.

Similar to search engines several other services (cf. the phases of the Media Reference Model) can be implemented both in more traditional or more peer-to-peer like styles. Consider the knowledge phase. Content can be provided or it can be contributed. In the intention phase, the information needed for determining and signaling intentions can be provided or contributed from pees in a network. Examples are the various opinion sites. Also, signals can be available for a single server or for the whole community. Here, various architectures can be implemented. Also in contracting or coordination various architectures can be chosen.

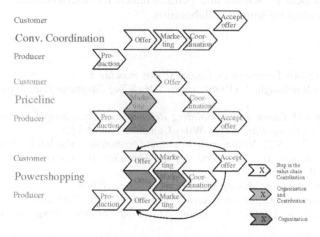

Fig. 9. Models and value chains of coordination

Let us explain the coordination mechanisms of Fig. 9. In conventional architectures most of the product and information is being provided. The consumer has only the choice to accept an offer to buy a good or service. Priceline admits more contributions of the consumer. It is the consumer who plays the active role of making an offer - the intermediary service priceline just makes the producers accept this offer. In powershopping the consumer used to have the most active role. The consumers interact on a peer-to-peer basis, organize and influence the offer. The consumers take hereby roles in marketing the product and service.

Also in settlement various peer-to-peer implementations exist. Virtual teams or organization form to settle a task or to produce a good or service.

Those brief examples show that in all the four phases services can be implemented following at least to some extent the peer-to-peer architecture. Design of services such that they display positive feedback effects and network effects is still a challenge for all the services needed in media for the creation of economic value.

4   Concluding Remarks

Currently peer-to-peer is popular for sharing files. When we look at other application scenarios and other research directions we note that the basic idea of peer-to-peer namely multi-lateral interaction of partners with symmetric positions exists for all the services needed to design any medium and that channel system, logical system and organization can be designed according to the peer-to-peer architecture. Still, it is unclear what a good design would be and whether users would like such a structure and inhabit it.

Acknowledgements

The author is indebted to Beat F. Schmid and Petra Schubert for discussions and in particular to Johannes Hummel for fruitful collaboration.

References

Adar, E. and Huberman, B. (2000) Freeriding on Gnutella. *Firstmonday* **5**,

Booch, G., Jacobson, I. and Rumbaugh, J. (1998) *Unified Modeling Language User Guide*, Addison-Wesley.

Figallo, C. (1998) *Hosting Web Communities: Building Relationships, Increasing Customer Loyality, and Maintaining a Competitive Edge*, Wiley Computer Publishing.

Ginsburg, M. and Weisband, S. (2002) Voluntarism in virtual communities: The International Chess Club (ICC). In: Sprague, E., (Ed.) *Proc. of the Hawaiian Int. Conf. on System Sciences (HICSS 2002)*, IEEE Press]

Godwin, M. (1994) Nine Principles for Making Virtual Communities. *Wired*

Haertsch, P. (2000) *Wettbewerbsstrategien für Electronic Commerce*, Josef Eul Verlag .

Hagel III, J. and Armstrong, A. (1997) *Net Gain: Expanding markets through virtual communities*,

Hagel, J. and Bughin (2001) The operational performance of virtual communities. *EM - Electronic Markets. The International Journal of Electronic Markets and Business Media* **10**,

Hummel, J. (2002) *Virtuelle Gemeinschaften*, To appear 2002.

Hummel, J. and Becker, K. (2001) Profile virtueller Gemeinschaften. University St.Gallen, mcminstitute.

Hummel, J. and Lechner, U. (2001) The Community Model of Content Management - A case study of the music industry. *International Journal of Media Management(JMM)* **2**.

Hummel, J. and Lechner, U. (2000) Communities - The role of technology. In. Proceedings of the European Conference on Information System (ECIS 2000).

Hummel, J. and Lechner, U. (2002) Social profiles of Virtual Communities. In: Sprague, E., (Ed.) *Proc. of the Int. Hawaiian Conf. on System Sciences (HICSS 2002)*, IEEE Press]

Jones, Q. (1997) Virtual Communities, Virtual Settlement & Cyber-Archaelogy: A Theoretical Outline. *JCMC* **3**,

Jones, Q. (2000) Time to Split Virtually: An Analysis of Virtual Community Expandability. In: Sprague, E., (Ed.) *Proc. of the 33th Int. Hawaii Conference on System Sciences (HICSS 2000)*, IEEE]

Lechner, U. and Schmid, B.F. (1999) Logic for Media - The Computational Media Metaphor. In: Sprague, E., (Ed.) *Proc. of the 32th Int. Hawaii Conference on System Sciences (HICSS'99)*, IEEE Press]

Levine, R., Locke, C., Searls, D., and Weinberger, D. (1999) *The cluetrain manifesto. The end of business as usual*, Perseus Books.

Licklider, J.C.R. and Taylor, W. (1968) The Computer as a Communication Device. *Science and Technology* 21-40.

Noam, E. (1992) Innovation, Networks and Organizational Learning. In: Antonelli, C., (Ed.) *The Economics of Information Networks*, pp. 91-102.

Nonnecke, B. and Preece, J. (2000) Lurker demographics: Counting the silent. In: *Proc. of CHI 2000*, ACM Press]

Preece, J. (2000) *Online Communities*, 1 edn. New York:

Rheingold, H. (1993) *The virtual community: Homesteading on the electronic frontier* , Addison-Wesley.

Schmid, B.F. (1997) The Concept of Media. In: Bons, R.W.H., (Ed.) *Workshop on Electronic Markets*,

Schmid, B.F. (1999) Elektronische Märkte - Merkmale, Organisation und Potentiale. In: Hermanns, A. and Sauter, M., (Eds.) *Handbuch Electronic Commerce*, Vahlen Verlag]

Shapiro, C. and Varian, H. (1999) *Information Rules: A Strategic Guide to the Network Economy*, Harvard Business School.

Timmers, P. (1998) Business Models for Electronic Markets. *EM - Electronic Markets. The International Journal of Electronic Markets and Business Media* **3**,

Whittaker, Issacs and O'Day (1997) Widening the web. Workshop report on the theory and practice of physical and Network communities. Report from ACM CHI (Computer Human Interaction),

Wössner, M. (2000) Lecture Notes in Medienwirtschaft Winter Term 1999/2000, Universität St.Gallen.

Author Index

Lecture Notes in Computer Science

For information about Vols. 1–2279
please contact your bookseller or Springer-Verlag

Vol. 2316: J. Domingo-Ferrer (Ed.), Inference Control in Statistical Databases. VIII, 231 pages. 2002.

Vol. 2317: M. Hegarty, B. Meyer, N. Hari Narayanan (Eds.), Diagrammatic Representation and Inference. Proceedings, 2002. XIV, 362 pages. 2002. (Subseries LNAI).

Vol. 2318: D. Bošnački, S. Leue (Eds.), Model Checking Software. Proceedings, 2002. X, 259 pages. 2002.

Vol. 2319: C. Gacek (Ed.), Software Reuse: Methods, Techniques, and Tools. Proceedings, 2002. XI, 353 pages. 2002.

Vol.2320: T. Sander (Ed.), Security and Privacy in Digital Rights Management. Proceedings, 2001. X, 245 pages. 2002.

Vol. 2321: P.L. Lanzi, W. Stolzmann, S.W. Wilson (Eds.), Advances in Learning Classifier Systems. Proceedings, 2002. VIII, 231 pages. 2002. (Subseries LNAI).

Vol. 2322: V. Mařík, O. Štěpánková, H. Krautwurmová, M. Luck (Eds.), Multi-Agent Systems and Applications II. Proceedings, 2001. XII, 377 pages. 2002. (Subseries LNAI).

Vol. 2323: À. Frohner (Ed.), Object-Oriented Technology. Proceedings, 2001. IX, 225 pages. 2002.

Vol. 2324: T. Field, P.G. Harrison, J. Bradley, U. Harder (Eds.), Computer Performance Evaluation. Proceedings, 2002. XI, 349 pages. 2002.

Vol 2326: D. Grigoras, A. Nicolau, B. Toursel, B. Folliot (Eds.), Advanced Environments, Tools, and Applications for Cluster Computing. Proceedings, 2001. XIII, 321 pages. 2002.

Vol. 2327: H.P. Zima, K. Joe, M. Sato, Y. Seo, M. Shimasaki (Eds.), High Performance Computing. Proceedings, 2002. XV, 564 pages. 2002.

Vol. 2328: R. Wyrzykowski, J. Dongarra, M. Paprzycki, J. Waśniewski (Eds.), Parallel Processing and Applied Mathematics. Proceedings, 2001. XIX, 915 pages. 2002.

Vol. 2329: P.M.A. Sloot, C.J.K. Tan, J.J. Dongarra, A.G. Hoekstra (Eds.), Computational Science – ICCS 2002. Proceedings, Part I. XLI, 1095 pages. 2002.

Vol. 2330: P.M.A. Sloot, C.J.K. Tan, J.J. Dongarra, A.G. Hoekstra (Eds.), Computational Science – ICCS 2002. Proceedings, Part II. XLI, 1115 pages. 2002.

Vol. 2331: P.M.A. Sloot, C.J.K. Tan, J.J. Dongarra, A.G. Hoekstra (Eds.), Computational Science – ICCS 2002. Proceedings, Part III. XLI, 1227 pages. 2002.

Vol. 2332: L. Knudsen (Ed.), Advances in Cryptology – EUROCRYPT 2002. Proceedings, 2002. XII, 547 pages. 2002.

Vol. 2334: G. Carle, M. Zitterbart (Eds.), Protocols for High Speed Networks. Proceedings, 2002. X, 267 pages. 2002.

Vol. 2335: M. Butler, L. Petre, K. Sere (Eds.), Integrated Formal Methods. Proceedings, 2002. X, 401 pages. 2002.

Vol. 2336: M.-S. Chen, P.S. Yu, B. Liu (Eds.), Advances in Knowledge Discovery and Data Mining. Proceedings, 2002. XIII, 568 pages. 2002. (Subseries LNAI).

Vol. 2337: W.J. Cook, A.S. Schulz (Eds.), Integer Programming and Combinatorial Optimization. Proceedings, 2002. XI, 487 pages. 2002.

Vol. 2338: R. Cohen, B. Spencer (Eds.), Advances in Artificial Intelligence. Proceedings, 2002. X, 197 pages. 2002. (Subseries LNAI).

Vol. 2340: N. Jonoska, N.C. Seeman (Eds.), DNA Computing. Proceedings, 2001. XI, 392 pages. 2002.

Vol. 2342: I. Horrocks, J. Hendler (Eds.), The Semantic Web – ISCW 2002. Proceedings, 2002. XVI, 476 pages. 2002.

Vol. 2345: E. Gregori, M. Conti, A.T. Campbell, G. Omidyar, M. Zukerman (Eds.), NETWORKING 2002. Proceedings, 2002. XXVI, 1256 pages. 2002.

Vol. 2346: H. Unger, T. Böhme, A. Mikler (Eds.), Innovative Internet Computing Systems. Proceedings, 2002. VIII, 251 pages. 2002.

Vol. 2347: P. De Bra, P. Brusilovsky, R. Conejo (Eds.), Adaptive Hypermedia and Adaptive Web-Based Systems. Proceedings, 2002. XV, 615 pages. 2002.

Vol. 2348: A. Banks Pidduck, J. Mylopoulos, C.C. Woo, M. Tamer Ozsu (Eds.), Advanced Information Systems Engineering. Proceedings, 2002. XIV, 799 pages. 2002.

Vol. 2349: J. Kontio, R. Conradi (Eds.), Software Quality – ECSQ 2002. Proceedings, 2002. XIV, 363 pages. 2002.

Vol. 2350: A. Heyden, G. Sparr, M. Nielsen, P. Johansen (Eds.), Computer Vision – ECCV 2002. Proceedings, Part I. XXVIII, 817 pages. 2002.

Vol. 2351: A. Heyden, G. Sparr, M. Nielsen, P. Johansen (Eds.), Computer Vision – ECCV 2002. Proceedings, Part II. XXVIII, 903 pages. 2002.

Vol. 2352: A. Heyden, G. Sparr, M. Nielsen, P. Johansen (Eds.), Computer Vision – ECCV 2002. Proceedings, Part III. XXVIII, 919 pages. 2002.

Vol. 2353: A. Heyden, G. Sparr, M. Nielsen, P. Johansen (Eds.), Computer Vision – ECCV 2002. Proceedings, Part IV. XXVIII, 841 pages. 2002.

Vol. 2358: T. Hendtlass, M. Ali (Eds.), Developments in Applied Artificial Intelligence. Proceedings, 2002 XIII, 833 pages. 2002. (Subseries LNAI).

Vol. 2359: M. Tistarelli, J. Bigun, A.K. Jain (Eds.), Biometric Authentication. Proceedings, 2002. XII, 373 pages. 2002.

Vol. 2360: J. Esparza, C. Lakos (Eds.), Application and Theory of Petri Nets 2002. Proceedings, 2002. X, 445 pages. 2002.

Vol. 2361: J. Blieberger, A. Strohmeier (Eds.), Reliable Software Technologies – Ada-Europe 2002. Proceedings, 2002 XIII, 367 pages. 2002.

Vol. 2363: S.A. Cerri, G. Gouardères, F. Paraguaçu (Eds.), Intelligent Tutoring Systems. Proceedings, 2002. XXVIII, 1016 pages. 2002.

Vol. 2366: M.-S. Hacid, Z.W. Raś, D.A. Zighed, Y. Kodratoff (Eds.), Foundations of Intelligent Systems. Proceedings, 2002. XII, 614 pages. 2002. (Subseries LNAI).

Vol. 2367: J. Fagerholm, J. Haataja, J. Järvinen, M. Lyly. P. Råback, V. Savolainen (Eds.), Applied Parallel Computing. Proceedings, 2002. XIV, 612 pages. 2002.

Vol. 2374: B. Magnusson (Ed.), ECOOP 2002 – Object-Oriented Programming. XI, 637 pages. 2002.